Maureen Emerson lived in Provence for 20 years, where she worked as a local co-ordinator for CBS and NBC at media festivals in Cannes. During her years in Provence, Maureen became enthralled with the stories of those expatriates who lived on the Riviera in the 1920s and 1930s and how World War II affected their lives. Her first book on the Riviera, *Escape to Provence*, was published in 2008.

D1356547

'A compelling account of life on the French Riviera from 1920 onwards, *Riviera Dreaming* charts the work of renowned architect of the Art Deco era, Barry Dierks. This well-written book is packed with history and glamorous insider stories of the rich and famous, contrasted with the hardships of local residents living under German occupation during World War II. Meticulously researched by long-term resident Maureen Emerson it makes a riveting read; perfect summer holiday reading. Bet you won't be able to put it down.'

Mary S. Lovell, author of *The Mitford Girls*

'Through the work of Barry Dierks and Eric Sawyer, as architect and gardener, Maureen Emerson has created a fascinating account of the South of France in times of glorious peace and hideous war, telling the stories of those who made their homes there. She evokes a particular generation in this wonderful book.'

Hugo Vickers

RIVIERA DREAMING

Love and War on the Côte d'Azur

MAUREEN EMERSON

I.B. TAURIS

LONDON · NEW YORK

Published in 2018 by
I.B.Tauris & Co. Ltd
London • New York
www.ibtauris.com

ISBN: 978 1 78831 162 5
eISBN: 978 1 78672 338 3
ePDF: 978 1 78673 338 2

A full CIP record for this book is available from the British Library
A full CIP record is available from the Library of Congress

Library of Congress Catalog Card Number: available

Typeset by Free Range Book Design & Production Limited
Printed and bound by CPI Group (UK) Ltd, Croydon, CR0 4YY

To Andrew Merton,
without whom this book would not have seen the light of day

Contents

List of Plates

1 Le Trident, with the trident shaped rocks below. © Martin Scott.

2 Elegant Barry. Courtesy of the archives of Andrew Merton.

3 Barry and Eric in their study. Courtesy of the archives of Andrew Merton.

4 Barry and friends relaxing. Courtesy of the archives of Andrew Merton.

5 The upstairs corridor at Le Trident, with its succession of arches. Courtesy of the archives of Andrew Merton.

6 Somerset Maugham in a rooftop folly, built by the previous owner of La Mauresque. Courtesy of the Edward Quinn Archive AG.

7 Maugham and Alan Searle dining in the Moorish patio at La Mauresque. Courtesy of the Lebrecht Music and Arts Photo Library.

8 Maugham on the staircase at La Mauresque. Courtesy of the Edward Quinn Archive AG.

9 Freddy McEvoy, Beatrice's fourth and racy husband. Public domain.

Acknowledgements

I am indebted to Andrew Merton, great-nephew of Eric and godson of both Eric and Barry, without whom this book would not have seen the light of day; Hugo Vickers, for suggesting I write the story of Barry Dierks, and who has stayed in three of his houses. Also for his encouragement and generosity; Peter Riley, brilliant webmaster, whose expertise and friendship I treasure; my daughter Christina Emerson who has guided me so patiently from start to finish, and particularly on architectural detail; Jill Shepperd, who undertook valuable research, which included photography, delving into archives and scrambling over rocks and up hillsides; Malcolm Dunstan, great-nephew of Eric Dunstan, who gave me carte blanche for drawing on the latter's private diaries; Suzanne and Philip Kenny, who shared the dramatic story of Emmanuel Martinez and his hotel; Sebastian and Olivier Dérobert, who knew both Barry and Eric, and their research beyond the call of friendship; François de Guiringaud, who knows all about Melpomene; John Halsey, for his valued reminiscences of life on the Riviera and tales of his friendship with the two Erics; and Patience Marriott, who knew so many over the years.

Sincere appreciation goes to the following for so much help in so many ways: Richard Chapman; Mary S. Lovell; James Buchanan-Jardine; Victor Werny of Puget Théniers;

Yves Pourcher; Jahnene Green; Benjamin Lafore; Keith Jane; Eve Pell; Fredrik Lilloe of Knight Frank; Joanna Millar; Linda Hackett; Ajay Kamalakaran; Dr Robin Darwall-Smith of Magdalen College, Oxford; Wolfgang Frei, Edward Quinn Archive; Daria Wallace, Lebrecht Photo Library; Desiree Butterfield-Nagy, University of Maine.

If I have omitted to include others to whom I am indebted, please forgive me.

PART ONE

Lights and Music

The English Visitor calls the entire coast from Marseilles to Genoa the Riviera; but the French distinguish their portion as the Côte d'Azur, and the Italians distinguish theirs as The Riviera di Ponente.

S. Baring-Gould, *A Book of the Riviera*

Le Trident – 1925
Barry and Eric

How This Coast Smells of Riches!

Laurence Binyon, *For Dauntless France*

So wrote the American Jane de Glehn, wife of the English artist Wilfred de Glehn, when she first set foot on the Riviera after the 1918 Armistice of World War I.[1] A member of the Red Cross Committee, who had worked in the devastated areas of the Haute Marne and was now in the south to report on the medical conditions, she felt the train from the north had deposited her in paradise: 'To eyes fresh from the ruined homes of Eastern France, from the ghastly desolations and sublime endurances of the Front, this previous world of moneyed idleness, these innumerable villas perched on the hills and clouded with flowers, these glowing white walls and basking blue bays' filled her with bemused delight.[2]

Europe had been ablaze and the fires had gone out. Now the Riviera began slowly to return to a semblance of its former self. During the war the area had become a vast hospital for the wounded, but gradually the old life of catering to privileged visitors returned, although in an increasingly different form. Suddenly everything seemed possible. Moving pictures, wonderfully designed automobiles, new music, liberating fashions were all exhilarating. By the early twenties the towns along the coast were alive with a fevered post-war excitement. Among the palm trees, oleander and bougainvillea the belle époque, with its ornate architecture and amply dressed winter visitors, was over. The owners of the great villas of Victorian times were getting older and entering a new era which would transform their way of life in resorts where they had held sway for so long. As a result of the Bolshevik revolution the Russian nobility had either disappeared from the coast, leaving their beautiful onion-domed churches as proof of passage or, now being poor, become taxi drivers, hotel managers and servants. Their sumptuous villas were converted into hotels or taken over by other, richer expatriates. As the trauma of the war faded, crowds of international socialites, both old and new, came to luxuriate in the beauty of the coast.

To this awakening Riviera full of promise, two young men of very different backgrounds arrived to seek their fortunes and begin a new life. Barry Dierks, an American from Pennsylvania, was 26 years old. Slim and handsome, with blond wavy hair, he treated life with insouciance and good humour. Eric Sawyer, 10 years older, was an Englishman from Buckinghamshire. Dark-haired and stockier than the elegant Barry, he possessed a gravitas that was in contrast to the latter's puckish sense of fun. The difference between the two was appealing and as a couple they would become much sought after, being described by their close friend the author and composer Beverley Nichols as 'those two charmers'.[3]

Born in Butte, Montana, in 1899, at 12 years old Barry Dierks moved with his family to the suburb of Edgewood in Pittsburgh, Pennsylvania. Here, with his sister Elizabeth, they settled at 335 Locust Street to what seems to have been a pleasant suburban life. Barry's father, W. C. Dierks, was the respected general manager of the firm of C. C. Mellor, representatives of Steinway pianos. They were a musical family, his mother being an active member of the Edgewood 'Tuesday Music Club', still in existence today. Little is known of Barry's parents. Neither he nor his sister would have children, causing the family trail to go cold. Elizabeth Dierks married a Princeton engineering graduate and became Elizabeth Anderson. And although she and her husband visited Barry occasionally over the years, the sibling bond does not seem to have been strong. This was in contrast to Barry's relationship with his mother to whom, as late as age 44, he would sign his letters 'your own boy'.[4]

A sub-lieutenant in the American Army during the war, but without seeing active service, in 1921 Barry graduated as an architect from the Carnegie Institute of Technology. An entry in the alumnae yearbook of 1921 states that he is deemed 'the Petronius of the school' (Petronius having been a Roman courtier during the time of Nero, a voluptuary; a no-holds-barred satirist and an arbiter of taste). The entry continues: 'He is very imaginative' but has 'never made an 8.30 in his life because that time is devoted to matching his necktie with his socks. Women bore him. However Barry is a real "medalist" and we predict a great future ahead for him.'[5] The writer had foresight.

Like so many cultivated Americans of the time, Barry was drawn to the Old World and the year of his graduation found him enrolling at the École des Beaux Arts in Paris. One of the most famous of the Beaux Arts studios was run by the architect Léon Jaussely and Barry was lucky enough to be accepted as his pupil. He found Paris with all its dignified beauty to be extremely agreeable, even more so when he was awarded one gold and three silver medals for his work at the Beaux Arts. To help fund his studies, he took a cashier's job at a merchant bank where Eric Sawyer happened to be the general manager.

While Barry's background was firmly middle-class provincial American, Eric's was firmly British. Born in Aldershot, Surrey, in 1889, he was the third of five children. His father, William Harcourt Sawyer, was a distinguished career soldier who won the Sword of Honour at the Royal Military Academy at Sandhurst. His mother was born Edith Mary Hanbury, always known as Mary, whose family home was Blythewood House (now Hitcham House) near Burnham in Buckinghamshire. Mary Sawyer was a distant relative of Sir Thomas Hanbury who, in 1867 with his brother Daniel, created the famous Hanbury Gardens at La Mortola near Ventimiglia on the Italian Riviera. The gardens became known for their dramatic planting on a calcareous clay hillside which sweeps steeply down to the Mediterranean. Through the estate runs the Via Julia Augusta of 241 BC which linked Rome to Gaulle, running through Genoa to Menton, above Monaco and on through Cannes, then over the Esterel Mountains to Frejus, Marseilles and finally to Arles. A total of around 800 kilometres. At La Mortola this ancient route is now sunk below ground level but still evocatively visible. Thomas Hanbury would later buy land at Wisley in England in order to donate it to the Royal Horticultural Society so the latter could move from Chiswick in London to bigger premises. The Hanbury family connection, remote though it was, would do no harm to Barry and Eric's future social standing.

Educated at Cheltenham College in Gloucestershire, Eric did not follow his father into the army but graduated as an engineer from the Royal School of Mines in London. Military service did not elude him and as an officer during the 1914–18 war he acquitted himself well. Serving with the ill-fated British Expeditionary Force in both France and Belgium, followed by a post in the Claims Commission in the Intelligence Corps, he was mentioned in dispatches and awarded the Légion d'Honneur and Croix de Guerre by the French government. By the time he was demobbed in 1919 he had achieved the rank of lieutenant-colonel and, although he would wear a soldier's uniform once again, now his way of life changed irrevocably. However, he would always refer to himself as Colonel Sawyer. Having served in France he stayed on perhaps, like so many others, appreciating the aura of tolerance and lack of interference. With an apartment in 15

Boulevard des Italiens in Paris, he was comfortably part of the cosmopolitan set of the city.

Almost every evening Barry and Eric would repair to the bars of the Ritz Hotel on the Place Vendôme. In the frenetic gaiety of post-war Paris the Ritz bars were the place to see and be seen. They became the melting pot of the demi-monde and, as the playwright Noel Coward saw it, the semi-monde of the capital. The hotel itself had begun life in the seventeenth century as an aristocratic town house. In 1897 the architect Charles Mewès transformed the building for the hôtelier Cesar Ritz and, among other luxuries, it became the first in the world to have a bathroom for every bedroom. Over the years kings, sultans and aristocrats of society and the arts flocked to its all-embracing luxury.

Now those who jostled into Le Café Parisien through the side entrance on the rue Cambon were joined by a vibrant new clientele. After the armistice of 1918 Paris was awash with soldier students who had served with the American Expeditionary Force. It was felt by their superior officers that to follow training in the arts, in that most artistic of cities, was to be encouraged and, after all, they were on the spot. The journalist O.O. McIntyre wrote in the *Rochester Evening Journal* of 1928 of the cocktail hour when Americans headed for the Ritz bars where, using a baseball term, 'everything is as American as the seventh inning stretch'. Among the cosmopolitan crowd, English was the common language. They came to drink champagne cocktails or dry martinis, some with more than a touch of absinthe, and socialise with other expatriate Americans. Although the hotel housed several bars, accounts of the time seem to mention only the Petit Bar and the small panelled Ladies Bar, the *salon de correspondence* – for women weren't yet allowed in the other bars in spite of the sterling work many had accomplished during the war.

At this point in history the United States had firm links with France. In 1914, in a programme of aid unprecedented in history, socialites, bankers, merchants and young graduates of American Ivy League universities had come together, turned their thoughts towards Europe, formed committees and began to pour money, equipment and themselves into the Allied cause. The country felt indebted to France for the support the latter had provided during the American War of Independence. However, as Alfred Allan Lewis stated in *Ladies and Not-So-Gentle Women*, the American impresario Elisabeth Marbury would later remark dryly: 'The French did not ask for charity. France's friends did the asking while she was worshipped for her grace in receiving.'[6] But the links were strong and, for many, the social attitudes of the French appealing. As far as the private lives of individuals were concerned, France did not judge. Both men and women found a haven in which they could liberate inclinations unacceptable in their homeland, for while homosexuality was simply illegal in Britain, in the United States it was classed as a 'clinical mental disorder'. Napoleon had decriminalised homosexuality and France did not condemn those who, although they did not usually break the ties with their own countries, found here a refuge for their particular proclivities.

In 1926 Noel Coward wrote a play which he called *Ritz Bar* – the title being later changed to *Semi-Monde*. It is hard to understand now why it was considered so scandalous, for although the sexual preferences of the characters are fairly clear, they are subtly drawn. Only the theme of adultery is obvious, but in England the Lord Chamberlain, Rowland Baring, censored it, declaring the play immoral. Philip Hoare in his biography of Noel Coward wrote of the frustration of Coward, over lunch, vented to the author Beverley Nichols: 'I cannot agree', remarked Coward, 'that it is within the province of the Lord Chamberlain, or of anybody else, to concern himself with what I happen to do with my thighs.'[7] In fact *Semi-Monde* wasn't staged until 1977, probably due to the perceived value of the work and its need for a large cast, rather than its immorality.

But Coward knew his Ritz and its habitués well, and those who float through its lobbies and bars in *Semi-Monde* are surely true to life. 'You haven't', queries Marion to an acquaintance in the play, 'seen a dark little American girl with a sort of wood-violet face loitering, have you?'[8]

From his book *Twilight: First and Probably Last Poems*, Beverley Nichols in 'Ladies of the Ritz' would describe a group of elderly women 'half dead and half alive' sinking into chairs in the grand salon until:

> Now from the shadows creep the stallions
> magnificently muscled and equipped
> dark-suited, double-breasted, heavy-lipped.[9]

For the clientele of the Ritz would always provide and receive diverse services.

Both Barry and Eric, so different in background and character, felt very much at home among the cocktails, repartee and *flâneurs* of the Ritz Bar. Here they would meet useful acquaintances, make loyal friends and pick up certain information that would change the course of their lives. Already lovers, they would become life-long partners, their relationship surviving the attention of many admirers and the vagaries of war.

Who did they see, greet and converse with as they relaxed over their cocktails in those early years of the 1920s? They would have rubbed shoulders with the musician and song writer Cole Porter and his wife Linda, arriving from their sumptuous apartment on the rue Monsieur. With Scott Fitzgerald, a still impecunious Ernest Hemingway, perhaps even with Rudolph Valentino and Charlie Chaplin, for the Ritz was their preferred hotel in Paris. Coco Chanel, who made it one of her homes for 30 years, would have walked the corridors as her own – and the voice of the outrageous American actress Tallulah Bankhead may have rung out from the Ladies Bar. Some habitués became

close friends, such as Nichols and Coward, the latter having
in common with Barry that they were both the sons of piano
salesmen. It was here they first met another regular visitor,
Somerset Maugham, who would soon play an important part
in their lives.

At this time the couple were undecided what course their
future would take, but an event at the Ritz helped make the
decision for them. Much credit must be paid to Georges, the
barman, for creating an opportunity which would facilitate
the aspirations Barry and Eric had for the future. The short-
lived Dawes Plan had recently been launched, proposed
by Charles G. Dawes, an irascible vice-president of the
United States. The plan was set up in 1924 to manage the
reparation payments demanded from Germany after the war.
The scheme involved a large loan from the US government
to allow for foreign investment in Germany and stayed
in effect until replaced by the Young Plan in 1929. One
evening Georges, seeing Barry alone in the bar, discreetly
suggested he sit near two men, who were obviously enjoying
their cocktails, and one of whom was talking loudly to the
other. The discourse of the voluble gentleman was on the
imminent investments which the Dawes Plan anticipated
and the companies which were set to profit from these. This
was an opportunity not to be missed, and Barry called Eric
immediately. On being asked by him, 'How good is your
information?' Barry's reply was, 'Straight from the horse's
mouth'.[10] They took advantage of this knowledge rapidly,
placing their funds in some of those companies whose
names had been so freely declaimed. Their investments did
well, allowing them to plan their future together and begin
to seek their fortune.

The south of France, the Midi, stretches down to the
coast from the Alps in the north, from the Atlantic Ocean
in the west to the Italian border in the east. Although on
the same land mass, in weather, atmosphere and lifestyle

it is very different to the rest of France – virtually another country. Barry and Eric went south, to the Riviera. Having now decided they would spend their lives together, they began the search for land on which to build a house which would also act as a showcase for Barry's architectural practice. There seem to have been three prerequisites for the plot – the price of land; privacy so they could enjoy a lifestyle which would not, perhaps, be always acceptable to neighbours; and, above all, desire to be on the sea. So it was under the flame-red peaks of the Esterel Mountains, above the indigo Mediterranean and 11 kilometres to the west of Cannes, that they built their future home.

They chose a piece of coast at Miramar near the village of Theoule, between La Napoule to the east and St Raphael to the west. The plot they purchased in 1925 was isolated and no more than a rock face at l'Esquillon, a steep jagged cliff which swept from the hills above to the sea below. The land was situated below the coast road, the Corniche d'Or.

The small towns along this stretch of coast have much history. At St Raphael, Napoleon Bonaparte landed in August 1799 after his Egyptian campaign and marched towards Paris and his eventual election as first consul four months later. Towards the end of the nineteenth century the town became a popular coastal resort, particularly for artists and writers. It was in 1924 at the Villa Marie at Valescure on the outskirts of St Raphael that Scott Fitzgerald wrote much of *The Great Gatsby*. Nearer Miramar itself is the village of Agay, with its deeply curved sandy bay, beloved of the author Guy de Maupassant and the author/aviator Antoine de St Exupery.

The Corniche d'Or road begins at the old Roman settlement of Fréjus, west of St Raphael and famous for its Roman arenas. It then continues on to Mandelieu, six kilometres before Cannes. This spectacular road, almost always in sight of the sea, runs parallel to the railway line which runs from Marseilles to Italy, sometimes travelling under and sometimes over the road, using two imposing viaducts. The railway reached this stretch of the Riviera in 1863, but the corniche road was not built until 40 years later, sponsored by the Touring Club de France and officially opened in 1903. Until that time access along the coast was by narrow, dusty, sometimes tortuous paths. The completion of the Corniche d'Or created a continuous stretch of road along the Riviera. Those who now speed along this road to the coastal towns drive between the beauty of the jagged red rocks rising on one side and the steep incline to the sea sparkling far below while, high above, the scrubland rises away into the hills.

At Theoule, the district of the Var is left behind and the Alpes Maritimes begin. The small stretch of coast which is Miramar comes under the auspices of Theoule. The latter has a natural harbour which was, in the fifth century, one of the most important ports on the coast. When trading there ceased, it became a simple fishing village before evolving into yet another coastal resort. La Napoule, further east again and also once a Roman settlement, had been favoured by rich visitors since the 1880s. Its ancient fortress was almost in ruins when it was bought by the American millionaire Henry Clews, and his beloved wife Marie, in 1917. Clews was an artist and sculptor and between them the couple recreated the ruin as a medieval château and there lived a fantastical life, often attired in the costume of the Middle Ages, among the gargoyle-like sculptures of its owner. In contrast, Marie's white peacocks would wander frequently onto the nearby railway track, indifferent to the Train Bleu racing to its Riviera destinations from Paris.

At the Hôtel des Bains at La Napoule in 1898, Oscar Wilde and the journalist and publisher Frank Harris ate a breakfast of little red mullet, beefsteak with apple sauce, cheese and a sweet omelette while discussing the relative merits of the male and female body.[11] Wilde would spend several lethargic months at La Napoule admiring and consorting with the young fishermen on the port rather than applying himself to the writing Harris had hoped he would resume. From here he would continue on his weary, itinerant way until his death in Paris two years later. In 1899 Harris built a luxurious belle époque style hotel, Le Cap Estel, on a peninsula below the village of Eze near Monte Carlo, which quickly lost money.

It is at La Napoule that the true romance and glitter of the Riviera begins, spreading east along the curving coastline towards the high altars of Cannes and Nice. Rising up behind the town are the hills of Tanneron where the mimosa trees grow like weeds and puff their evocative scent from their fluffy yellow flowers into the cool air of late winter.

Barry and Eric had come to a Provence which basked in a beauty 'born of the sun', as the novelist Alphonse Daudet felt, although he was himself more of a Parisien.[12] The massif of the Esterel Mountains is of striking beauty from every angle, the volcanic rocks of porphyry being a deep, rich red, as opposed to the schiste and cristalline which make up the wooded Massif des Maures to the west. Dominated by Mont Vinaigre, the Esterels rise to 618 metres, with an overall span of around 19 kilometres before giving way to the grey limestone hills of the Alpes Maritimes which run up to the Italian border to the east. This is a rugged, harsh terrain with deep ravines above which the jagged peaks rise out of dense green pines and tower above vertiginous rock faces which plunge down into the sea. Vegetation consists of the maritime and parasol pines, eucalyptus, mimosa and cork oaks, these last two important for the local economy. The maquis, the shrub land, is dotted with wild thyme, lavender, broom and myrtle – home to scuttling lizards, small black scorpions and darting adders. In summer the heat which shimmers off the russet-coloured rocks seems to throb in time to the rasping of the cicadas, while the warm scent of the maquis envelops the hills. And sometimes, with the heat, come the fires.

A succession of civilisations and conflicts runs through the history of Provence. The region has been inhabited since prehistoric times. First came the Ligurians, followed by Greeks, Phoenicians and Romans. After the fall of Rome, Visigoths, Franks and Moors invaded this land where every Mediterranean race has left its footprint – not forgetting the marauding feet of barbarous pirates. Fear of the Moors and pirates drove the inhabitants of the coast to build the multitude of small towns and villages which punctuate the landscape, perched on their rocky outcrops and bound round with defensive walls. In the eighteenth and early nineteenth centuries the Esterel was the haunt of brigands. The dense undergrowth of the maquis was perfect cover for these outlaws, who descended on their prey as they travelled apprehensively on the only passable road through the hills. In *A Book of the Riviera*, S. Baring-Gould remarked: 'Should a parched traveller venture to pluck a bunch of grapes, it is well for him if this slight indiscretion does not bring on him blows of a cudgel, a stone, or a shot from the gun of the owner'.[13] But all that would change by the turn of the century. Far better roads were made through the hills and by 1905 Baring-Gould could pronounce that 'The Esterel may be traversed even more safely than Regent Street'.[14]

It was below this wild region that Barry and Eric, with the help of Eric's mother, bought their 6,000 square metre peninsula, a couple of coves and a small beach of crushed red rocks accessible only by sea or by clambering down the cliff face. The sun-kissed summits of the mountains rose high into the sky above, changing tones along with the light, while down below in the deep blue of the Mediterranean the rocky inlets pushed their fingers towards the shore. Three rocks, surrounded by water, spread out from the base of their cliff like the prongs of a red, fossilised spearhead. They had found the name of their villa – Le Trident. The plot was as much of a challenge as any enterprising architect could wish for, and the home in which they would live for so many years never ceased to have the illusion of sitting, slightly precariously, on its small plateau preparing to hurl itself into the sea far below.

It is perhaps more on this part of the coast than any other that the Mediterranean is all-pervading, changing its palette of blues and greens through the course of the day to the inky blackness and soft swish of its tiny waves at night. But on occasion its mood can change, its colour become a sullen grey and its tideless waves grow angry and threatening. It is as well not to become too affected by its temperament. Barry and Eric were not. They had come to the Riviera to work, to become successful and sought after, and with great optimism prepared to do just that. But first they had to build a home for themselves.

'The worst has happened. I've BOUGHT THE LAND!!!!!! Only don't say a word to anyone. It's too thrilling.'[15] So wrote Eric from Paris to his mother, Mary, in England. He went on to stress what a fine investment it was: 'worth double in a year or two'. The land had cost 300,000 francs. Paying in instalments, he 'would benefit if the franc goes to pieces in the meanwhile'. This included the cost of a narrow approach road along the cliff. He finished by exclaiming: 'You will adore the place – it is a heavenly spot. Do say you approve'.[16]

What is extraordinary about this letter is that Barry isn't mentioned. Perhaps this was from discretion – for Eric's father may have been ignorant of the relationship between the two men. Eric's enthusiasm obviously appealed to his mother, who undertook to contribute one-third of the price of the construction of the future house at Miramar, enabling Barry to leave for the south immediately. Eric would not move there permanently until 1927, two years later.

The great villas of the coast had to be equipped for entertaining in the new style. Salons had to be large and welcoming and, with the vogue for vacations in the heat of summer, dining on large candle-lit terraces became de rigueur. Barry, instantly in tune with Riviera life, understood this. He also felt that houses should now be designed to be cool. He and Eric became instrumental in encouraging outdoor living, suggesting that every new client should have a swimming pool, although it would be many years before one was blasted out of the rocks at their own home. The constant ebb and flow of socialising from house to house was a way of life that would only come to an end with World War II. It was all, as Edward VII had observed, 'like a constant garden party'.[17]

It was imperative Barry's finished house should act as a showcase for his talents, a place so striking it would draw potential clients to first admire and then commission his designs: Le Trident would demonstrate an accomplished blend of Modern and Mediterranean with Moorish and Classical influences. Although capable of the purest of designs, Barry would be nothing if not versatile. At the request of his clients, details such as round towers were sometimes incorporated. He also used vernacular elements such as roman tiled roofs. However, it is probable that if he had been allowed carte blanche there would have been many more overtly modernist villas gracing the coast. Although his designs demonstrated a range of influences including Art Deco, his villas generally are thought by many to be some of the jewels in the crown of Riviera architecture.

The entrance to Le Trident itself was dramatic. From a narrow path and a modest gate, a sinuous flight of steps descended to reach the house entrance, with its heavily nailed double front door and substantial stone architrave. In front of the door was a stone mosaic of a spaniel, Eric's family crest. The door handle was a sea creature in bronze, the escutcheon the head of a sea nymph flanked by two fishes. The door opened onto an upper floor of three bedrooms (one of them Barry's), a bathroom and a servant's room. Over the stairwell was an exquisite vaulted ceiling, an element Barry was to use in several of his commissions. White walls and ceilings were in vivid contrast to the black tiled floors.

On the lower floor were living quarters, with Eric's bedroom and bathroom leading off the panelled dining room. As well as the office the couple would share for so many years, there was a library and a spacious salon with a fireplace of Arles stone and a beamed ceiling painted white. These rooms were furnished in English style with books, comfortable sofas and armchairs. From the salon, French windows opened onto an arcaded loggia. This dining terrace, the *salon d'étè*, overlooked the sea far below. Barry used both casement and French windows. A first floor balcony incorporated a classical balustrade, again an element he would use in some of his commissions. A small star-shaped pool in the curve of one of the terraces invited guests, in the spirit of the Trevi Fountain in Rome, to fling coins in the hope they would return. In the future this act would gain a more than usual poignancy.

The flat-roofed solarium, mandatory for modernist villas, sported a small bell-gable in the Spanish-American style. A strikingly tall chimney stack was pure Art Deco. The whole house was rendered white, startling against its background of red rocks. The view was spectacular. To the east lay Cannes where, at night, a necklace of twinkling lights, like miniature diamonds, lit up the long promenade of the Croisette. To the west the vast expanse of sea was interrupted by the headland of Cap Roux. And, very rarely, immediately ahead and with the right atmospheric conditions, one could just see the island of Corsica 170 kilometres distant.

A very long, rather tortuous, flight of narrow concrete steps was built below the house, winding its way steeply down the hillside before reaching the two secluded coves where the sea foamed around the fingers of rocks and guests could bathe far from prying eyes. Here too lived sea urchins and, in the deep, jelly fish floated. A small price to be paid for the glory of the wide sweep of the Mediterranean which spread to the distant horizon.

It was in this inter-war paradise that Barry was to establish himself. Like other progressive architects, he had to contend not only with the problem of persuading the powerful mayors of the various communes to grant planning permission for designs with which they had little sympathy, but also the firm ideas and strong characters of his clients. To complicate matters further, an existing law forbade foreign architects to operate except under the auspices of a French practice. He and Eric would work mainly through four cooperative and respected Cannes-based architects, Marc-Pierre Rainault, François Arlac, Pierre Nouveau and Louis Cauvin. This situation continued until 1942 when the law was quashed, establishing a new Ordre des Architects which allowed foreigners to practise, presumably to permit German architects to work in the country they hoped to govern far into the future. Barry's clients were usually American or British who, though delighted to be able to discuss their aspirations with another English speaker, were extremely rich, much travelled and used to having their own way.

When all was completed in 1927, they carved an emblem of a trident into the keystone above the front door. It was all an extraordinary achievement. Not only was it the first house Barry had ever designed, as it was situated precariously on its steep and rocky cliff, Eric's engineering skills had been vital. From the following year, when he came to the south for good the couple would always work together, with Barry as architect and Eric as business manager, surveyor and landscape designer. Although Eric is seldom mentioned in records he was indispensable to the practice.

Now Barry had been awarded his first contract on the Riviera. On a peninsula 45 kilometres to the east, he was commissioned to create La Mauresque.

The author Somerset Maugham wanted a new home.

2

La Mauresque – 1926
Somerset Maugham

I bought it cheap because it was so ugly ... there was nothing
to do but to pull it down and build another in its place.
Somerset Maugham, Strictly Personal

Cap Ferrat is one of the pearls of the Riviera, its rocky peninsula
thrusting itself into the sea between Nice and Monaco –
more precisely between the smaller towns of Villefranche and
Beaulieu. Originally an ancient hamlet considered part of
Villefranche, in 1904 it became an independent district. In
spite of its rocky contours it has a verdant beauty dotted with
cypresses and umbrella pines and embracing the sea. It was
here, in 1927, that Somerset Maugham bought 40,000 square
metres of land in the Sémaphore, or lighthouse, area of the
Cap. And it was here he asked Barry Dierks to remodel the
existing house. In the manner of a game of whispers, many
biographers have attributed the work to Henri Delmotte, a
Niçoise architect. But the detailed records of François Fray of
the *Patrimoine de France* make it quite clear that it was Barry
who was responsible. Delmotte would, in fact, do restoration
work on the house after damage inflicted by troops during
World War II.

By 1927 Maugham was 53. A small man at five feet, six
inches, his face had not yet become creased and reptilian

with age, but the stutter which had begun in childhood had not been cured and would still cause distress. As his parents wanted his birth to be on British territory he was born, the youngest of three brothers, at the British Embassy in Paris. His father, Robert, was a Paris-based lawyer who advised the staff of the Embassy. His mother was Edith Snell, a fragile beauty who would die of tuberculosis when Maugham was 8. Two years later his father died of cancer. Orphaned by the time he was 10 Maugham was sent to live with an unsympathetic uncle, Henry Maugham, the vicar of the town of Whitstable in Kent. Henry would eventually appear thinly disguised as the snobbish and remote uncle in *Cakes and Ale*, Maugham's wonderfully waspish novel written in 1930.[1] Schooldays at the King's School, Canterbury, were no happier than home life with his uncle and aunt, and he demanded that he be allowed to leave King's at 16. After a more enjoyable year studying in Germany, where he formed what was probably his first satisfying physical and emotional relationship with a German youth, he began to cast around for a suitable profession. Finally deciding on medicine, rather than following in the footsteps of his family in the law, Maugham enrolled in 1892 at St Thomas's Hospital in London. Practising as a doctor, the surroundings and patients in that vibrant and impoverished part of the city would provide fertile ground for his first novel *Liza of Lambeth*, published in 1897. This was an immediate success. Maugham had found his true profession.

Always a disciplined and prolific writer, by the outbreak of World War I Maugham was already famous, having written ten plays and published ten novels, including *Of Human Bondage*, *The Moon and Sixpence* (a life of the painter Gauguin) and *The Painted Veil*, set in China. Now considered too old at 40 to enlist, he joined a British Red Cross ambulance unit based in northern France and attached to the French Army, becoming one of the 'literary ambulance drivers'. A more interesting assignment arose in 1917 when he was sent by the Secret Service Bureau to Russia in an effort to connive in keeping the provisional government in power. In this they failed but his experiences would give rise to *Ashenden*, an account of the adventures of a spy with a conscience – and a precursor to the genre of the British spy novel.

It was while he was with the ambulance unit in France that Maugham met Gerald Haxton. Brought up in San Francisco, Haxton, who would remain the centre of Maugham's life for 30 years, was, like Barry Dierks, outgoing, sociable and charming. Unlike Barry he was also promiscuous, a drinker and a gambler. The relationship was a mutual dependency. Maugham, shy by nature but craving company and adulation, needed Haxton to act as travelling companion, secretary and to make contact with those Maugham wished to meet for both social and private reasons. Misbehaving in London – as he would do increasingly on the Riviera as the years went on – Haxton was eventually deemed persona non grata in England. Frederic Maugham, Somerset's elder brother, was by now an eminent lawyer who would eventually become lord chancellor at the end of the 1930s and this didn't mix well with a Maugham/Haxton ménage. Maugham had been much affected by the 1895 trial of Oscar Wilde for 'gross indecency'. Homosexuals in France were permitted to live their own lives in the midst of the, often disapproving, French bourgeoisie among whom they dwelt.

Initially bisexual, the great female love of Maugham's life was said to have been the actress Sue Jones, the model for Rosie Driffield in *Cakes and Ale*.[2] His elegance and rather enigmatic air made him attractive to women and a subsequent liaison with the married Syrie Wellcome would make him a reluctant father. Syrie was the daughter of Thomas Barnardo who, although he never qualified as a doctor, founded the Dr Barnardo's homes for destitute children. When she met Maugham, Syrie's husband was

Henry Wellcome whose pharmaceutical company would eventually become Burroughs Wellcome. This was an unhappy marriage during which Syrie had several affairs, including one with the American Gordon Selfridge, the founder of Selfridge's department store in London. As soon as Syrie's baby, Liza, named after Maugham's novel *Liza of Lambeth*, was born Wellcome sued for divorce, citing Maugham as correspondent. Maugham, doing the honourable thing, married Syrie in America in 1917 and quickly regretted it. The state of marriage appeared to bring an end to his diversions with women and confirmed the exclusively homosexual life he would now lead. Their rancorous divorce, finalised in 1929, coloured Maugham's life, eventually affecting his relationship with Liza. Noel Coward would say that Maugham had no illusions about people 'but in fact had one major one, that they were no good'.[3]

Although a passionate traveller, whose journeys would take him to the furthest outposts of the British Empire in order to find material for his novels and stories, Maugham nevertheless had to have some kind of home. For the perfectionist he was, this had to be impressive, charming and with a level of comfort to entice guests. He desired warmth and beauty, spoke excellent French and felt at home in France.

Nearly two kilometres in length at its furthest tip, Cap Ferrat splits into peninsulas, one of which is the smaller Cap de St Hospice and the other Cap Ferrat itself. It is Cap Ferrat which has a lighthouse at its tip and most of the grand villas, but it is St Hospice that has the history. Here, in the year 560, a cluster of stone huts made up one of the first Christian settlements in this part of the Mediterranean. St Hospice was a missionary who led his few followers to this spot. He was said to have had the gift of miracles and prophecy, warning of the savage fate which would befall the south at the hands of barbarians. Having frightened himself thoroughly he retreated to an ancient tower on the Cap to live as a hermit until his death. When he died in 580 he was buried by his abandoned followers at the foot of the now vanished tower. Somewhere at the tip of the Cap lie the bones of St Hospice.

Of closer relevance to Maugham and his new home was the story of the odious King Leopold II of the Belgians. Remembered mainly as the creator and owner of the Congo Free State, Leopold was known not only for his immorality but above all for his brutality. From 1885 he ruled the Congo through cruelty and terror. If quotas were not met, executions and mutilations were freely meted out by his paid mercenaries. Great wealth flowed from this misery, mainly through the collection of ivory and rubber. This merciless regime was allowed to continue for 30 years, until international opinion eventually obliged the Belgian government to concede the Free State to Belgium itself in 1908. As he grew older, and probably for spiritual insurance purposes, the King decided he needed a father confessor close at hand. He appointed a retired missionary by the name of Monseigneur Felix Charmettant to be his chaplain and in 1900 set him up comfortably on the Cap. The Monseigneur had spent much of his working life in Algeria and an unknown architect created an overtly Moorish-style villa complete with horseshoe windows and a cupola on the roof. Not being particularly self-effacing, he named it after himself – the Villa Charmettant. The views from the grounds of the house, perched on its small outcrop of rock, were magnificent, the eye following the glittering Mediterranean in a wide sweep from east to west. The mountains of the Alpes Maritimes, adorned with their perched villages, rose high in the background.

Charmettant's neglected villa was not, in fact, pulled down as Maugham wrote in his memoirs, but was extensively remodelled by Barry. While Maugham lived at the Villa Lawrence on the Antibes ramparts, Barry swept away the facade, creating a two-storey house centred around a courtyard open to the sky. Around the courtyard ran a gallery of two stories with an arcade at ground floor level. A vaulted ceiling and black marble floor tiles, characteristic of Barry's work, graced the entrance hall. From here a marble staircase led up to five bedrooms, each with large light-filled windows, and three bathrooms. Downstairs were more bedrooms. In the long high-ceilinged drawing room, with paintings by Zoffany on the walls, was a large fireplace of Arles stone. A staircase tower, housing a library and service rooms, was built onto the side of the building and had a roof of Roman tiles. Beyond the tower was a flat roof, upon which was built Maugham's very private box-like writing room. Inside, French windows ran along one wall and bookcases filled the other.

From the gate of the villa a curved drive led up to a double door, visitors being greeted by a sign that warned 'Beware of the agapanthus!' This door was a copy of that at Le Trident except, instead of Neptune's trident on the keystone, there was a symbolic engraving of the hand of Fatima, designed to keep out the evil eye. This symbol was also carved in red on the entrance wall to the property and would be printed on Maugham's letter heading, table napkins, in his first editions and below the title of the film adaptation of his book *The Razor's Edge*.

The garden was planned by Eric. It rose in steep terraces planted with, in addition to the agapanthus, orange, lemon and avocado trees as well as oleanders – those obedient flowering shrubs which edge the drives of so many gardens in the south of France. Mimosa scented the air in February and jasmine and roses in May and June. On the top terrace a 16-metre marble swimming pool was surrounded by lush vegetation, with a lead pineapple at each corner and, at one end, a mask of Neptune, carved by Bernini, its mouth gushing water. For Barry, a pool would always take precedence over lawns and flower beds, although lawns there were. Maugham would say that the great luxury on the Riviera was grass. These were the days of plentiful labour. The thirteen servants, which included seven gardeners, were housed in apartments in a separate building, probably part of the former estate.

Barry and Eric worked quickly, and by the time Maugham was settled at La Mauresque at the end of 1927 he was able to live his life as he wished, being finally divorced from Syrie in 1929 on the grounds of incompatibility. He was a rich man and could maintain his status among the beau monde of the Riviera. Among his neighbours in the great houses on the Cap were Prince Arthur, Duke of Connaught, the third son of Queen Victoria, who had the villa Les Bruyéres on the same road as La Mauresque. A widower and president of the Boy Scouts Association the Duke was held in high esteem by all who knew him. Accompanied by his mistress Leonie Leslie, the sister of Winston Churchill's mother Jenny Jerome, he would dine occasionally at La Mauresque.

Others were Thérèse de Beauchamp who had built her stunning Italianate Villa Fiorentina, pieds dans l'eau, in 1917 on the point of the Cap St Hospice. At the beginning of the 1920s, before going on to buy La Leopolda at Villefranche, Thérèse sold Fiorentina to an Australian, Sir Edmund Davis, a mining millionaire and art collector. It is Davis whom one must thank for creating much of the littoral path around Cap Ferrat, which walk gives pleasure to so many people. Davis also owned Chilham Castle in Kent in England. The lovely Lady Kenmare would buy Fiorentina in 1939 and promptly leave as the Germans swept across Europe. With her son, Rory Cameron, she returned after the war to restore and create one of the most stunning houses and gardens on the Riviera. It was from a small house on the estate that her son wrote his best-selling book The Golden Riviera. At the Venetian-style Château St Jean, Vilma Lwoff-Parlaghy, an acclaimed artist and a Hungarian princess, took long walks with her lion cub, Goldfleck. Paris Singer, son of Isaac Singer of sewing machine fame was at his new villa (later called Les Rochers) on the Cap. Now separated from the dancer Isadora Duncan, he had married Annie Bates, an English nurse from Devon. The ex-Duchess of Marlborough, née Consuelo Vanderbilt, rented the Villa Lo Scoglietto (on what is now the Place David Niven). Consuelo was newly married to the aviator Jacques Balsan – an extremely happy union, in stark contrast to her former life with the Duke of Marlborough at Blenheim. And at the Grand Hôtel du Cap Ferrat, built in 1908, the rich and aristocratic came and went throughout the years.

Not universally liked, but much sought-after, Maugham settled down to hold court at La Mauresque. In spite of the fact that he was known to be sexually avaricious, certain of his guests chose to ignore this fact, so highly prized was an invitation to La Mauresque. Others felt quite at home. Politicians, authors, artists, actors, socialites, as well as the odd title, all came for the splendid meals created by Maugham's cook Annette and the comfort provided by the rest of the 13-strong staff. From Harpo Marx to Evelyn Waugh to the Duke and Duchess of Windsor they came, along with Churchill and Prince Pierre of Monaco, for whom Barry would remodel a house on Monaco's rock. Matisse, Chagall and later Picasso were guests.

Elegant dinners on the terrace were enjoyed on soft, balmy evenings graced by fireflies and the wafts of scent from orange blossom. Guests also came to admire the important collection of Impressionist and Post-Impressionist paintings and other objects of interest and beauty that Maugham had collected over the years. During the day there was tennis on the garden court and swimming in the pool. As Bryan Connon in his *Maugham Dynasty* wrote: 'Beautiful but obscure young men were part of the scenery'.[4] Bathing was invariably in the nude unless women were present. And, as Beverley Nichols in *A Case of Human Bondage* remembered: 'A young Noel Coward made his exits and his entrances in a flurry of white flannels'.[5] Nichols, ever courteous, was, apart from one breach of house etiquette quickly forgiven, always welcome at La Mauresque. For as long as guests behaved *comme il faut* and didn't irritate their host, visits were enjoyed and most left hoping to be invited again. On Christmas day of 1936 an unpopular and besieged Wallis Simpson drove over from Lou Viei, her temporary home in Cannes, and joined the house party for lunch.

Throughout these years, Gerald Haxton played the triple role of secretary, lover and enfant terrible. While Maugham strove, in spite of his own promiscuity, to create some sort of atmosphere of decorum at La Mauresque, keeping his own liaisons as discreet as possible, Haxton was a loose cannon. Frequent visits to the casino at Monte Carlo and the ports of Nice and Villefranche to encounter willing young men were accompanied by embarrassing bouts of drinking. In spite of this behaviour Maugham was consistently loyal, even when Alan Searle, a young Englishman from the East End of London whom he met in 1928, began gradually to supplant Haxton in usefulness.

The crash of 1929 and Britain's withdrawal from the Gold Standard in 1931 affected everyone, with the exception of some of the very rich. Maugham weathered the storm due to a constant stream of royalties and his relentless output of work. And apart from frequent trips abroad, life at La Mauresque continued in this pleasurable vein during the last golden years of the Riviera. However, it was now difficult to ignore the ebb and flow of European politics. The Russian Revolution of 1917 had been a rude shock to the aristocracy and bourgeoisie alike, not only in France but across Europe. The enduring fear that the old order could be brought down around them contributed to the rise of many right-wing and fascist organisations who felt they were acting in defence of civilisation against communism. There was one common wish in France – that they should on no account be drawn into another bloody war. But in 1939 fresh hostilities loomed ever closer. Now, wishing to contribute in some way to the war effort, Maugham was given a project by the Ministry of Information in Britain to write a series of articles on the French war effort and the attitude of the French towards the British. He visited London for several months before returning to tour France and assess the general feeling among the populace. In April the German Army invaded Denmark and Norway and day by day France grew more confused and unsettled. When German forces swept into and occupied the ill-prepared nation, Maugham became a refugee, escaping with hundreds of other Britons on one of two overcrowded coal boats which left from Cannes for England in July 1940. An extremely unpleasant experience which he related in *Strictly Personal*.[6] Gerald Haxton, as an American whose country had not yet entered the war, stayed on at La Mauresque to pack up Maugham's precious collection of paintings and ornaments. Stored safely away from the villa, they would survive the war intact.

Maugham spent the following years in the United States, first in Los Angeles and then South Carolina, script writing for Hollywood films, composing articles and giving interviews and propaganda talks in favour of the Allies. In November 1944 Gerald Haxton died of tuberculosis in New York, aged 52. Although grief-stricken, Maugham quickly summoned Alan Searle to be Haxton's replacement and general factotum. Finally in 1946, they returned to a hungry and exhausted Riviera.

La Mauresque had suffered badly during the years of war. Although occupied by the Italians and the Germans, it was the Allied Fleet who had caused the most damage while shelling the lighthouse on the Cap St Hospice. In a letter to Noel Coward, Maugham wrote sadly: 'The Italians occupied the villa and took my cars, the Germans occupied it next, took the yacht, emptied the wine cellar and mined the property, and then the British fleet shelled the house.'[7] It was now that he recruited Henri Delmotte to tackle the damage, replacing the shattered windows, mending holes and the roof and restoring the interior to the charm of Barry's original design. While this was being done, Maugham stayed at the small Voile d'Or hotel on the Cap, owned by Captain Powell, whose son was the British film director Michael Powell. Maugham had not asked Barry and Eric to do this work, perhaps because they had only just returned to the coast themselves, their own war experiences having been substantially more dramatic than Maugham's. And, over the years, they had become very expensive.

Life settled down to the disciplined and elegant rhythm of La Mauresque. Annette, Maugham's treasured cook, had not left the house during the war, in spite of its unwelcome guests. Now, using what supplies could be found in the markets, she produced meals to the best of her renowned ability. Alan Searle did his job well, running Maugham's life with considerably less style than Haxton but more capably and, above all, more soberly. Maugham began to travel once more, including regular trips to a Swiss clinic for rejuvenating injections of sheeps' cells and, when in residence at Cap Ferrat, guests came and went as before.

In April 1949 the designer and photographer Cecil Beaton wrote to his hopeless love Greta Garbo that he was:

Writing this propped up in bed with the three pairs of tall windows open onto a brilliant garden where the gardeners are clipping the grass, raking the gravel path, bees are buzzing at the blossom and two black poodles are rushing about causing consternation.[8]

He feels the garden is looking 'quite unreal' and describes the rows of cinerarias, the masses of magenta and mauve stocks, roses, tree peonies and wisteria covered walls. Guests sit on the blue terrace where all the flowers are blue. In spite of the fact they 'do nothing all day and go to bed very early' he is feeling quite exhausted. He has gone to La Mauresque to write his play but 'can hardly get out of bed'. He feels the climate makes him dream vividly – Garbo appears in these dreams and he wakes up in the morning 'absolutely worn out'. However, Marc Chagall is expected for lunch and the orange blossom is out. In the midst of this beauty and comfort he also feels there is a sad nostalgic atmosphere. The former prosperity of Cap Ferrat has given way to 'poverty and decay'. The village is very 'communistic', most of the big houses have been sold and the few lovely gardens that remain look dormant.[9] This was post-war France.

In the same year Graham Sutherland, who would later buy the architect Eileen Gray's modernist house Tempe à Pailla in the hills above Menton, painted a portrait of Maugham at La Mauresque. This was Sutherland's first portrait and for it Maugham endured ten sittings of one hour each day. The general feeling was that it made him look like an elderly mandarin. Maugham pronounced it 'magnificent'.[10]

In 1954 Maugham was made a Companion of Honour, but sadly, the last years were hard. He deteriorated mentally and Searle, in a state of terror that he would be left with nothing when his master died, endeavoured to manipulate Maugham's relationship with his daughter Liza, resulting in a partial estrangement. He persuaded a willing Maugham to adopt him legally, a move challenged by Liza and thrown out by the court at Nice. Through all this Searle continued to care devotedly for an increasingly senile and difficult master. In these declining years Maugham undertook an autobiography, never published in book form, called *Looking Back*. In this he attacked his now dead wife Syrie with such venom, that friends and critics turned against him and he was received so coldly on a trip to London that he would never return there.

The end came in 1965. Twice he had been nursed back
to health from pneumonia at the Queen Victoria Hospital
in Nice. The matron Elsie Gladman, who had stayed on
to support the small Anglo-American Hospital in Cannes
throughout the war, remembered Maugham in her book
Uncertain Tomorrows. It seems he was a good, co-operative
patient but 'rather stubborn'.[11] This worthy lady described
in her autobiography that, on her days off, she was often
summoned to elegant house parties along the coast to
apply enemas to relieve discomfort suffered by certain
guests.

Maugham had always made it known to Miss Gladman
that he did not wish to die in the hospital but at La Mauresque.
During his last stay at the hospital, an ambulance was kept
in readiness so his wish could be honoured. The building
was besieged by journalists and it was 'a round the clock job
to keep them from entering the hospital'.[12] Every morning
at 10 a.m. Dr Michel Rosanoff (Maugham's personal doctor
and a Resistant during the war) accompanied by Maugham's
specialists, would stand on the steps of the hospital and
make an announcement on their patient's state of health.
At 2 a.m. on the morning of 16 December the waiting
ambulance, followed by a pack of journalists, took him
back to La Mauresque where he died of congestion of the
lungs. This is the version given by Miss Gladman which is in
contradiction to other accounts, particularly that of Searle's,
that Maugham had actually died at the hospital and, to
avoid tiresome involvement with the relevant authorities –
mandatory with hospital deaths – was whisked away in the
small hours. But it seems unlikely that Miss Gladman would
have risked her position by allowing a dead patient to be
removed and breaking French law in this respect.

After cremation in Marseilles as he had requested,
Maugham's ashes were taken to England and interred in the
grounds of the King's School, Canterbury, where he had been

far from happy but where he could now return complete with honours. Perhaps in a spirit of 'So there!'

In spite of their difficult relationship, in his will Maugham left Liza, as well as various financial settlements, the shares in the company which owned La Mauresque. Alan Searle need not have worried for, apart from various bequests to staff he was left, among other assets, the contents of the villa, Maugham's fortune and the royalties from his work. Those objects not kept by him were auctioned by Sotheby's in 1967. In the same year Liza sold La Mauresque to an American socialite from Houston. The new owner engaged a Nice architect, Marcel Guilgot, to make changes and La Mauresque entered another era. A rich but lonely Searle moved to an apartment in Monaco. Suffering from increasing ill health he died in 1985. Some of his beautifully made evening clothes went to a fair in aid of the Sunny Bank Anglo-American Hospital of Cannes, where they were quickly snapped up. Sunny Bank played an important part, both medically and socially, in the English-speaking expatriate community.

In countless articles, biographies and autobiographies the fascination with the Maugham years and La Mauresque lives on in the accounts of that enchanting house and garden presided over by its complicated and enigmatic story teller.

3

The Glamorous Years

You have to be thoroughly human to enjoy the French
Riviera, with a nice mixture of virtues and vices the place
will cater for both.

Peter Churchill, *All About the French Riviera*

By 1927 Le Trident was completed, the salon furnished in the
white-on-white style embraced by Somerset Maugham's ex-
wife, Syrie, who had become an influential and sought-after
interior decorator. The first of many much-loved dogs were
bought, frequently small and white, and almost all called
Peter. Hospitality was offered to friends and visiting family.
Photographs show that Mary, Eric's mother, was staying at the
villa as the house was being finished, and in the summer of
1928 Barry's sister Elizabeth visited with her husband, John
Anderson. Friends and family mixed and mingled but when
the guests were friends alone there was a greater degree of
relaxation. Beside the aquamarine waters of the coves below
the house, handsome young men sunbathed on the tiny
beach. Other photos show groups of male friends ranged
along the terrace walls, small towels draped modestly over
loins, or at mealtimes on the loggia. Entries in the visitors'
book, begun at this time, demonstrate how people from all
backgrounds found life at Le Trident delightful. There was

good food. Cocktails at lunchtime tended to be composed of fresh fruit juice plus around 90 per cent vodka or, for the more delicate, vodka and tonic with a dash of Campari. Vodka martinis were for the evening. With meals they drank the local Estandon wine. There was a constant aroma of untipped Balto cigarettes, a French *cigarette blonde* of the era, with its origins in Baltimore. Not here was the constant tension for guests which reigned at Somerset Maugham's La Mauresque – an uneasy mixture of pleasure in their surroundings, coupled with fear of condemnation by the host when behaviour did not measure up to his standards. It seems the atmosphere was always pleasant at the house at Miramar.

Drama is never far from the relaxed and sensuous atmosphere of the Riviera and in the dry August of 1927 more serious fires than usual broke out all along the coast, flared through the mountains of the Esterel and descended to leap the railway line that ran above Le Trident. On the Corniche d'Or all traffic was halted for a time, the tar on the surface having caught fire. But Le Trident and the other buildings at Miramar were untouched, although thousands of valuable cork oaks and pines on the hills above were destroyed. Life returned to normal in the golden days of September, the cicadas sang once again in the pines and the tranquil waters in the bays below no longer reflected the terrifying mingling of smoke and flames.

Although they found the expatriate life of the south of France enticing and became involved with it as rapidly as time and introductions allowed, Barry and Eric would never be among those on the coast whose sole purpose was socialising. Their friends and acquaintances were from a select circle which would serve them well both socially and as clients, but they themselves did not have independent fortunes and, furthermore, they enjoyed the challenge of making their architectural mark on the new Riviera. For them, the south of France was not a holiday indulgence but their permanent home and place of work – and work hard was what they did. There is little evidence they were involved with the Gerald Murphys and their *bohème chic* set on the Cap d'Antibes. Apart from the odd actress, singer or well-placed French client, they worked and played mainly with industrialists, descendants of these, and successful businessmen, all of whom could further the couple's ambitions and among whom, perhaps, they felt most at ease. Their clients were their friends and journals of the time find Barry and Eric dining or partying frequently with them. While Eric was rather less extrovert, as became an ex-colonel of the British Army, Barry was the party animal; devastatingly attractive and witty, he was often the centre of attention. Eric, when the company was appropriate, was a fount of risqué jokes. They both felt it expedient to be well received, while thoroughly enjoying the process.

For the fortunate few the 1920s are considered an era of affluence and consumerism. Along with peace and the growing prosperity of the Allied countries had come better opportunities for travel and, for the British and Americans, the post-war exchange rate with the French franc was favourable. When Barry arrived in the south in 1925, great ocean liners were bringing an increasing number of tourists to Europe from the United States. If they came via England they could continue their journey by train – a luxurious and exciting journey. The Golden Arrow to Dover became the Flèche d'Or at Calais, which raced on to the Gare du Nord in Paris. From the Gare de Lyon one could board the PLM (Paris-Lyon-Méditerranée) Pullman Express. Le Train Bleu was the first of its kind with metal carriages manufactured by the Leeds Forge Company of Birmingham in England. This first-class-only train, which ran from Calais to Menton, was launched in 1922, its restaurant and *wagons-lits* decorated with exquisite Art Deco marquetry by K. Morisson and René Prou. The paintwork, blue with a gold trim, heralded its destination – the azur waters and golden sun of the Mediterranean. The train was the inspiration for the 1924 ballet *Le Train Bleu* for which Jean Cocteau wrote the scenario and Darius Milhaud the music, with the stage curtain painted by Pablo Picasso. Coco Chanel designed the costumes of thigh-length knitted swimsuits and head-hugging bathing caps.

For those who preferred to travel by motor, the wonderful cars of the decade, the Bugatti Decapotables, Minervas, Hispano-Suizas, Lagondas and Rolls Royce Silver Ghosts with their new combustion engines, cruised across France and bore their occupants to the delights of Cannes and Nice and along the corniche roads to Beaulieu and Monte Carlo. It was the age of the coachbuilder. New inventions abounded. In May 1927 Charles Lindbergh flew his Ryan monoplane between New York and Paris in the greatest solo flight in air history. Sir Frederick Banting discovered insulin, Alexander Fleming penicillin and Philip Drinker invented the Iron Lung. Radio came into its own. Cinema, trying desperately to find a firm footing in this new world, began to move from silent pictures to talkies.

Cannes, the writer Stéphane Liégard felt, 'can boast a sun forged especially for duchesses'.[1] Liégard also coined the term La Côte d'Azur to complement the deep summer blue of its sea along the coastline. Although Barry and Eric would never live in Cannes, the town was important to them. Curving around its wide bay, it has a gentler climate than Nice, protected as it is by its amphitheatre of hills. At the western end is the old port, flanked by the Quai St Pierre and overlooked by Le Suquet, the original village perched on an outcrop of rock. During most of its history Cannes was no more than a simple fishing village. Discovery of its charms in the mid-nineteenth century by Lord Henry Brougham, an ex-Chancellor of the Exchequer of the British government, transformed it into one of the most elegant and sought-after resorts in the world. By the end of the 1880s the author Guy de Maupassant would write laconically of what was now a town: 'Des princes, des princes, partout des princes.'[2] In the early 1920s the small port was still filled with the wooden fishing boats and spread nets of the fishermen who frequented the bars on the quay above. Nearby, the pretty white Municipal Casino of 1907 was the gate lodge for the palm-lined Croisette, which began life as the 'Path of the Little Cross'. This elegant promenade, flanked by its famous hotels, runs for around two kilometres along the shoreline. The Carlton Hotel, with its wedding-cake stucco-work, would serve as Barry and Eric's club and letter box and the Carlton terrace, crowded to capacity at cocktail hour, replace the Ritz Bar as the place to see and be seen. At that time the Carlton boasted five tennis courts which hosted competitions entered by champions such as Suzanne Lenglen and Jean Borotra. Other hotels, the Gallia, Metropole and the Beau Site all had their own tennis courts.

It was a heady time for the young, particularly young women. The war liberated them to an extent undreamt of before 1914. White American women finally gained the vote in 1920, with African-Americans and Native Americans continuing to be marginalised. In the United Kingdom votes for women over the age of 21 would not happen until 1928. Women in France had to wait until 1944. But now, compared with their, often disapproving, mothers most Western women were wonderfully free. They cut their hair short, hairstyles ranging from the Shingle to the Marcel-Waved Bob. The privileged drove sports cars, perched on stools in cocktail bars, smoked cigarettes in long holders and danced with abandon. Along with the cigarettes, opium, *le dérangement de tous les sens* was available for those who desired it. Sauciness abounded in postcards, revues and in Hollywood films.

The hotels and restaurants of the coast were filled with voices of diverse nationalities. These included *le gratin* (the royalty and aristocracy of Europe, the Russian contingent being often impecunious), business moguls, playboys and celebrities. These chattered to the accompaniment of the clinking of ice in newly created cocktails and the tinkling of Irving Berlin or Jerome Kern tunes on a baby grand. Later in the evening there would be dinners in private houses or at fashionable restaurants. From designers such as Poiret, Molyneux or Vionnet the women chose their *garçonne* look: loose drop-waisted gowns, which grew shorter as the decade wore on. These were worn with silver hose and, against the chill of a Riviera winter evening, cloak-coats edged with fur. For the young, and sometimes not-so-young, it was mandatory to spend the rest of the night dancing in one of the newest creations of the 1920s – the nightclub – which Jean-Louis de Faucigny-Lucinge in his *Un Gentilhomme Cosmopolite* called 'the fever of the age'.[3] How better if one had the means to forget, even for a moment, those lost forever?

Periodicals such as *La Saison de Cannes* and *Le Journal des Etrangers* detailed the arrival of rich visitors to the coast. These visits were an opportunity for glamour, sophisticated entertainment and the chance to meet old friends and make new ones. Enjoyment was enhanced by starlit nights beside the rippling Mediterranean and the frisson of a Latin environment. It was not for nothing the couturier Jeanne Lanvin named her perfumes, created in nearby Grasse, My Sin, Scandale, Rumeur and Prétexte. There was no Prohibition. Glamour, style and romance were the name of the game.

This new young set began to realise there was much pleasure to be had either exercising vigorously in the sunshine or lying languorously on a beach. Although many different nationalities now returned to the coast after the war, this was the era of the Americans. During the war many thousands of young servicemen from the United States had been cared for and convalesced in the great hotels of the Riviera, requisitioned as hospitals and nursing homes – and many would return as tourists. In 1921 Cole and Linda Porter rented the Château de la Garoupe on the Cap d'Antibes, an estate with which Barry Dierks would later become much involved. The Porters invited another American couple, Gerald and Sara Murphy, whose subsequent sojourns on the Cap have passed into Riviera history. From their Villa America on the heights overlooking the lighthouse, the Murphys entertained and gave beach parties on the small beach at La Garoupe, playing host to the Picassos, Rudolph Valentino, the Hemingways and other such artistic luminaries. Scott Fitzgerald's *Tender Is the Night* was born when he and his tempestuous Zelda joined the group and set the astonishing trend for summers in the sun. The body beautiful became almost an obsession, the beaches along the coast playing host to exercise and dance classes. Golf, tennis, polo, swimming and sailing were pursued with great enthusiasm. The freedom of a lightly clad tanned body, caressed by the sun, was a new and voluptuous experience, dignified by Coco Chanel who acquired a glamorous tan of her own. Chanel and her lover, Bendor, the 2nd Duke of Westminster, did not ask Barry Dierks to design La Pausa, their Riviera love nest, in 1928. Instead they chose a young French architect, Robert Streitz, who built for them one of his charming ochre-coloured Italianate houses at Roquebrune Cap Martin near Menton. Streitz would later become an admirer of Barry's work.

Among the many names which feature in the history of the Riviera of that time was Isadora Duncan. Claimed as being the originator of modern dance, she lived spasmodically on the coast with her various lovers, giving performances and dance lessons. Dogged by tragedy, increasingly eccentric, debt-ridden and notorious for her bouts of drunkenness, in 1927 she met her end in an appropriately dramatic fashion. Driving away from her studio on the Promenade des Anglais in Nice in an Amilcar Grand Sport driven by the handsome racing driver Benoit Falchetto, her voluminous shawl flew back and caught in the spokes of the rear wheel. The shawl throttled her and she was flung onto the road and died instantly.

Also in 1927 Josephine Baker, the 'Black Pearl' from St
Louis, an erotic dancer and civil rights supporter, performed
her 'chocolate arabesques', as Scott Fitzgerald described
them, as well as her version of the Charleston in her famous
Revue Nègre in Nice.[4] And with the Americans came jazz
– music whose influence has endured on the Riviera to the
present day.

On the coast and in the back country the artists dreamed
and painted. It was not long since Renoir had died at his
hillside farmhouse, Les Collettes at Haut de Cagnes. Matisse
had settled in the Regina Palace apartments in Cimiez in
Nice and painted the town and its interiors frequently during
his 'Nice period' of the 1920s. In 1926 Pierre Bonnard
bought the villa Le Bosquet at Le Cannet, above Cannes,
his home for the rest of his life. Colette went native in her
villa La Treille Muscate on the Baie des Canoubiers by St
Tropez, resenting anyone who encroached on her beach. Marc
Chagall roamed the coastline painting the contrast of sea,
rocks and vegetation he admired so much.

In 1925, *Mare Nostrum*, a silent film based on the war,
was being shot at the Victorine Studios in Nice, run by
the multi-talented director Rex Ingram along with a young
Englishman, Michael Powell. Powell would later join Emeric
Pressburger to make the acclaimed Powell-Pressburger films,
such as *The Red Shoes*.

From Antibes to Juan-les-Pins the pine woods run parallel
with the sandy beaches and here, in 1925, the American
millionaire Frank Jay Gould built his 254-room Art Deco
Hotel Provençal. Buying into and modernising the newly
successful casino Gould, along with his wife Florence, would
establish the small town under its *pins parasols* as a young and
lively summer resort. Florence would later proclaim: 'everyone
slept with everyone. It was amusing, it was practical.'[5] A lover
of all water sports, she established the first water skiing centre
at Juan-les-Pins, and here the first beach pyjamas were worn –

to the despair of the old guard of Cannes. In 1926 Jean Patou invented the first sun cream – Huile de Chaldée. It was all very glamorous.

The contrast between the coast and the hills which rose behind was never more marked than at this point in time, and there were those in the hills who did not go down to the coast during their lifetime. While, for the well-off, the towns below sparkled with electric light, running water and gleaming bathrooms, a short motor ride to a hill village would reveal lighting by paraffin lamps, cooking on small wood-fired ranges and, for many households, water fetched from the village pump. Clothes washing was still done in the communal washing trough and flush lavatories did not appear, in some cases, until the early 1960s. In lives which were then intensely rural, even primitive, the peasants took their animals into the lower rooms of their homes in winter, as they would for many years to come. Conditions of life were as spartan as they had been over the past centuries.

Art Deco, known first as the *style moderne*, evolved slowly in France at the beginning of the 1900s but would reach its apogee in the 1920s and 1930s following its enthusiastic adoption in America. The movement was drawn to the attention of the public in France through the thrilling Art Deco costumes of Serge Diaghilev's Ballets Russes. Even more of a turning point was the Exposition Internationale des Arts Décoratifs et Industriels Modernes, a world fair held in Paris in 1925. It was from this that the term Art Deco would emerge. Stunning graphic art posters for advertising and fashion proliferated – the emphasis being on luxury and opulence. The historian Bevis Hillier defined the movement as: 'an assertively modern style that ran to symmetry rather than asymmetry and to the rectilinear rather than the curvilinear; it responded to the demands of the machine and of new material and the requirements of mass production'.[6]

The Art Deco style was enthusiastically embraced by those who built the grand palaces of this period, including Frank Jay and Florence Gould. Their Hotel Palais de la Méditerranée on the Promenade des Anglais at Nice opened to great acclaim in January 1929. Designed by Professor Charles Dalmas, working with his son Marcel, it was the epitome of Art Deco glamour and a departure for Charles, who had built the domed and encrusted Carlton Hotel in Cannes. The facade of the Palais, with the strong rectilinearity of its arcades surmounted by the fenestration of the windows, was decorated with large bas-relief figures by the sculptor Antoine Sartorio. The interior with its splendid entrance hall was breathtaking, with enormous stained glass windows and white marble staircase, illuminated with crystal chandeliers. Mainly conceived as a gaming house with rooms, its accompanying theatre attracted the music hall stars of the day such as Maurice Chevalier and Edith Piaf. But if one had been walking along the Promenade des Anglais in the 1980s hoping to catch a glimpse of this splendour, all that would have been seen behind the silent facade were piles of rubble in an enormous void. Badly managed and losing money from the 1930s onwards, the building deteriorated steadily until 1978 when the remaining contents of the hotel were sold off and the interior entirely demolished, although the facade was spared. As the result of tortuous disputes which brought no credit to Nice, the shell remained empty for 26 years. But it would enjoy one happy and vivacious period before its demolition when it was requisitioned as the commissary for the American troops in 1944 after the liberation of Provence.

In 1928 the ubiquitous Charles Dalmas, along with several other architects, began the construction of the Miramar Hotel on the corner of the rue Pasteur and the Croisette at Cannes. Working with him, François Arluc, architect and engineer, created the first artificial sandy beach on the

Croisette. Eventually, as the years went by, all the beaches of the Croisette would lose their rocks and be covered by soft and cared-for sand. The Miramar opened its doors to the rich and famous in January 1929 but only survived as a hotel for 17 years. In 1946 it became one of the cavernous apartment blocks created from great old establishments such as the Winter Palace in Menton, once beloved of Russian aristocrats, or Le Regina on the hills of Nice, built as the Hôtel Regina to tempt Queen Victoria away from Menton and Grasse to the town.

At the end of the 1800s, Francis II, the exiled last king of the Deux Siciles, sold his Villa Marie-Thérèse at 73 La Croisette in Cannes to his half-brother, Prince Alfonso. In 1927, Emmanuel Martinez, son of an Italian baron from Palermo in Italy and chairman of the Societé des Grand Hôtels de Cannes, bought this belle époque building and demolished it. In its place rose the enormous Art Deco Hôtel Martinez, designed by architects Palermo and Mayer. Beaten by one month by the Miramar, the Martinez opened its doors in February 1929 and would always remain a hotel. It was fortunate that, on his day of glory, Monsieur Martinez did not have a crystal ball to reveal the anguish and formidable problems, in war and peace, which would befall him and his hotel in the years to come.

In 1931 the most important hotels of the region would hold a meeting during which a collective decision was made to open for the entire year, rather than just the winter months. No longer would the coast have a tranquil summer season.

In 1929 the remains of the Fort de la Croix were demolished to make way for the Palm Beach Casino on the seafront at Cannes, built by the Nice architect Roger Seassal. This 'summer casino', with its enormous swimming pool, was a kitsch mixture of a Hispano-Mauresque exterior and an Art Deco interior, and now began its reign of costume balls, dances and receptions. There were those who rejected the modern style of Art Deco decoration feeling, as did Le Corbusier, 'modern decoration is no decoration'.[7]

Two years before Barry arrived on the coast, the French architect Robert Mallet-Stevens had designed the Clos St Bernard (also known as the Villa Noailles) at Hyères in the Var, for Count Charles de Noailles and his wife Marie-Laure, patrons of the Surrealists. A large, severe house of grey reinforced concrete it overlooked a splendid view of the old town and was a striking example of Modernism, one of the first on the Riviera. The interiors were decorated by the luminaries of the contemporary Art Deco world. Their neighbour, who had a right of passage through the property, was the American novelist Edith Wharton who wintered in her, very different, Castel St Claire keeping in touch with America from afar every year until her death in 1937. It was at Hyères that Wharton wrote *The Age of Innocence*, which won her the Pulitzer prize, making her the first woman recipient.

In 1927 the Anglo-Irish designer Eileen Gray created at Roquebrune-Cap-Martin, near Monaco, what was perhaps the most iconic of early modernist villas on the coast – the ill-fated 'E1027'. Gray was influenced by Le Corbusier, one of the pioneers of Modernism, and his concept of 'new beauty'.[8] Intended as a summer home, she designed the villa on a terrace above the sea in collaboration with her lover, the Romanian architect Jean Badovici, creator of the journal *Architecture Vivante*. The obscure house name was a code: E for Eileen, then a set of numbers relating to their names, out of sequence so intertwined like the lovers they were at this time. Like the Villa Noailles, the house was in the shape of an ocean liner. This accomplished example of Modernism caused Le Corbusier to become consumed by jealousy. At the end of the 1930s, Eileen Gray being absent, he would enter the house and, naked, deface the interior with sexually explicit murals, much to Gray's chagrin. In

1933 the architect René Darde built a perfect Art Deco hotel and casino, Hôtel L'Arbois, on the sea at St Maxime, near St Tropez.

Pre-dating this period was the belle époque Carlton Hotel, the Grande Dame of the Croisette. This was where Barry and Eric began almost all their evenings with cocktails on the terrace, before moving on to shows or dinner parties. In 1927 they dined at La Terrasse at Juan-les-Pins, 'la plus belle plage de la Riviera' along with Prince George, the son of King George V and Queen Mary. Prince George, who was bisexual, led a rather wanton lifestyle, and would redeem himself by joining the RAF in World War II and dying in a plane crash in Scotland in 1942. On another occasion they attended the Ambassadeurs Casino at Cannes for the Gold Standard Ball (presumably intended to cheer everyone up as the Great Depression loomed). Here along with the beau monde, they watched a *ballet d'or* amid illuminated fountains (presumably gold). During those glamorous years the galas, dinners, cocktail parties, regattas, *concours d'elegance*, firework displays and sporting events were relentless – but it is clear from the journals of the time how the same people saw one another again and again. In that respect expatriate life has not much changed. But there were other social occasions to which only the Gotha, the crowned heads and princes of the world were invited. These lists dripped with royal titles, and to these few of Barry and Eric's set were invited.

After the Wall Street Crash of 1929, the Depression settled on the United States and in Britain the subsequent collapse of sterling, as Britain came off the Gold Standard, had the same effect. Unemployment, in both countries, was widespread and soup kitchens were in full swing. The dust bowl droughts hit the prairies of America and thousands fled to California in search of a new life. Herbert Hoover, elected president of the United States in 1929, had stated in the previous year: 'We in America today are nearer to the final triumph over poverty than ever before in the history of any land.'[9]

The second Spanish Republic was elected in 1931 leading to civil war five years later. In 1933 the National Socialists took control of Germany, under the chancellorship of Adolf Hitler. In England there were hunger marches and in the same year that Hitler came to power the Jarrow Marchers, 200 men from an area of mass unemployment and extreme poverty in North East England, walked 300 miles to London to beg for business which would bring employment back to their town. Little was done for them. In October 1935 Italy, without declaring war, attacked and eventually conquered Ethiopia. In France, right-wing riots in Paris in 1934 organised by L'Action Francaise, a Nationalist–Monarchist group, led to the election in 1936 of the Socialist Popular Front government of Léon Blum, supported by the Communists. This reinforced, for many, the underlying fear of the fall of the old order, as had happened in Russia in 1917. Although France took a little longer to be hit by its own depression, the failure of Germany to pay its war reparations would add to the economic problems. The French republic was in trouble.

In spite of social upheaval and happily for the economy of the coast, at this time the city-dwelling middle classes of France realised they did not have to take a chance on the weather in northern resorts such as Deauville and Le Touquet. With the growing acceptance of a golden skin they turned their faces to the south, and in 1936 the government of Léon Blum created *les congés payés*, paid holidays, together with subsidised train fares – and, to the distress of many, changed the ambiance of the Riviera for good.

Although the great hotels of the Riviera had too many empty rooms for a few years after the crash, in 1933 the dollar strengthened against the franc and a *New York Times* correspondent in the Paris of the time remarked: 'rich Americans will remain rich and will travel'.[10] The twenties had often been declared an era of wonderful nonsense, but as the 1920s passed into the 1930s the general mood became more sober, as did fashion. The fringes, swinging necklaces and straight, low-waisted dresses gave way to longer, less racy pleated skirts, worn with sailor blouses or jumpers and lace-up shoes for informal wear, all more appropriate in the Depression years. Breasts reappeared and well-fitting suits with slim skirts came into vogue. Evening dresses became long and slinky, the metallic look found favour – long sheaths of glittering material clinched by belts around invariably slim waists. Hair was grown longer. Hats were still important, now often perched on top of the head, or brimmed and tilted fetchingly over one eye, more flattering than the former tight cloches. Trousers for women began to creep into some sort of acceptability. And the often frenetic dance music of the 1920s began to be replaced by the smoother melodies of swing bands.

4

The Casa Estella – 1931
Beatrice Mai Cartwright

Young people, slim and beautiful of line, flash rock to sea,
cleave the sea with their strong arms, and come from the sea
in a sparkle of diamonds.

Grant Richards, *The Coast of Pleasure*

By the beginning of the 1930s, Barry and Eric were well
established. Charming and personable, accompanied by
the frisson which went with their relationship, they were
immensely sociable and accepted virtually everywhere
among the international set. Almost every evening would
see them, elegantly attired, climbing the 30 steps from Le
Trident to the lane above and into their large Chevrolet. The
international gatherings were always convivial and lasted
long into the small hours. Apéritifs were followed by wine
throughout the meal, the whole rounded off with liqueurs.
Family lore tells of the couple returning home from Cannes
after such a gathering when Barry, who was driving, almost
hit an oncoming car. Eric remarked: 'You only just missed
that!' To which Barry replied: 'Good God, am I driving? I
thought you were!'[1]

It was around this time that virgin land on the Cap
d'Antibes became sought-after and Barry, also actively
sought after by English speaking expatriates, would build

or remodel 21 houses there. This Cap is a peninsula which, like Cap Ferrat, stretches out into the Mediterranean and has the advantage of several attractive bays. It would become the smartest seaside location on the Riviera and always more lively than sedate Cap Ferrat. The writer Anatole France described it as 'the most enchanting place to stay on earth'.[2]

The history of Antibes is, like the rest of the southern coast, one of shifting settlements, invasion and violence. In the fifteenth century Provence became part of the Kingdom of France, with Antibes as a border town. In the seventeenth century Louis XIV commissioned the great military architect Vauban to redesign the fortifications of the town, a major project of which the fort and some of the walls remain. Unlike Golf Juan and Cannes, in 1815 Antibes refused to join forces with Napoleon on his return from Elba, earning the gratitude of Louis XVIII.

In 1870 the Villa Soleil had been built on the tip of the Cap d'Antibes, as a writer's retreat, by Auguste de Villemessant the founder of the journal *Le Figaro*. In 1887 the hotelier Antoine Sella discovered the then neglected villa, restored it and in 1889 named it the Hotel du Cap Eden-Roc. The peninsula never looked back. The hotel grew in size and luxury over the years contributing to the allure of the Cap, particularly for summer visitors.

The house Barry remodelled for Beatrice Cartwright was, appropriately, on the Bay of Millionaires within a stone's throw of the Hotel Eden Roc and not far from the Château de la Croë rented by the Duke of Windsor and Beatrice's old friend Wallis Windsor, formerly Wallis Simpson. The Casa Estella had been built in the late 1920s by the American author Lloyd Osbourne, the stepson and collaborator of Robert Louis Stevenson. He sold it to Beatrice in 1932 and Barry and his team must have worked very rapidly to complete the major remodelling, for Beatrice was already writing from there at the end of the year. The single storey house was approached by a long drive shaded by umbrella pines, with terraces and steps to the sea cut into the rocks. Set in over two acres of woodland and lapped by scented bushes of thyme, rosemary, cistus and lavender, it had a wide terrace overlooking the bay. Barry painted the original ochre facade white and the shutters green. Inside, the long all-white salon was decorated by Syrie Maugham. The furniture was restrained contemporary, complemented by one of Barry's signature beamed white ceilings. A flamboyant touch was the wrought iron balusters in the form of the opening notes to Debussy's *La Mer*. Nestled among its trees the house was a charming picture when seen from the sea.

Alexander Woollcott, essayist, drama critic and member of the Algonquin Round Table in New York, was amusing about this period on the Cap d'Antibes. In an article 'The Owner of Ben Finney', written in 1932 for *The Big New Yorker Book of Dogs*, he writes of the days before the rush to populate the peninsula when:

> The silence of the Antibes nights was broken only by the sweet music of the nightingales and the cries of the wounded borne faintly on the wind from the Casino at Juan les Pins.[3]

If the name of Beatrice Cartwright is rarely recorded in the pages of books about the south of France it is because she was a butterfly, flitting between cities, houses and husbands. It was not at all surprising that Beatrice, née Benjamin, would desire a holiday home on the Cap. She was one of the rich, rather feckless nomads who roamed the Western world at that time. Self-indulgent and sensual, she lived for pleasure. She would have four husbands and, although she had three children, her world was of the nightclub rather than the nursery. Over the years her various abodes were in New York, Rhode Island, London, Leicestershire and Paris. If she was not in any of these she could perhaps be found in one of the best hotels in Rome, Biarritz or Zermatt. She was both highly strung and sociable, having many friends in her own circle. Attractive rather than beautiful, she was an accomplished skier and swimmer, with a penchant for driving elegant cars. Along with her slim figure, her best features were her lovely tapering hands.

Beatrice's father was William Everts Benjamin, a publisher and rare book collector, who used his wife's money to control his family and indulge his taste for fine things. In 1886 he had married Anne Engle Rogers, one of the three daughters of Henry Huttleston Rogers who, along with John D. Rockefeller, was a founder of the Standard Oil Company. Rogers was one of the last of the robber barons of the age. Accumulating great wealth, he was a combination of ruthlessness and philanthropy. Among his friends he numbered Mark Twain and Helen Keller. Keller, who though blind and deaf from birth, was taught to communicate by her tutor Ann Sullivan to such an extent that she was able to obtain a bachelor of arts degree from Radcliffe University, for which Rogers paid the fees.

As Beatrice was Rogers' granddaughter, all assumed she was on the receiving end of a stream of Standard Oil money, but for much of her early adult life it was her father who supplied or withdrew her inherited allowance as he saw fit. Her first husband was Alexander Dallas Bache Pratt, a stock broker and clubman. He was the son of Dallas Bache Pratt, a New York banker, Dallas being the family name. The couple married in 1909 when Alexander was 26 and Beatrice was 20. Their homes, usual for their set, were a New York town house and a Newport, Rhode Island 'cottage'. Their daughter Cynthia was born a year later and their son, Dallas Jr, in 1914. But Cynthia and Dallas lived with relatives in America for most of their childhood while their mother lived in Europe. The person who acted as surrogate mother to the children was an English woman, Maud Duke, whom they called 'Dear'

– and indeed they would always love her dearly. Dear would stay with the family for 50 years.

In 1918 the children's father was drafted to fight in France where he was both injured and gassed. His family stayed at their house in Newport where Beatrice and other society women formed an aid group called The First Fifty. One of the recorded aims of the group, in a bid to help the food programme, was 'to cut their midday meal to two courses and their evening meal to three courses, or vice versa'.[4] Beatrice was 'bored to extinction' until she met the chairman of The First Fifty, a handsome New York socialite and former Yale University athlete called Preston Gibson, one of the most dashing figures in local society.[5] Gibson was endeavouring, without much success, to establish himself as a playwright. When at the end of 1918 Beatrice sued Alexander for divorce, citing 'desertion', in spite of her husband still being enlisted in the army, the divorce was granted and Beatrice married Gibson almost immediately.[6] Her parents were furious, and with good reason, for Gibson had already been divorced by two heiresses, eloping with one while still a student at Yale, and having 20 co-respondents cited by the other. It made no difference that, as an ambulance driver on the front in the recent war, Gibson had won the French Croix de Guerre and was twice cited for bravery under gas and enemy fire.

The newly married couple, with Beatrice's children and Dear in tow, rented a house on East 63rd Street in New York before moving to Hollywood where Gibson hoped to become a screen writer in the new and burgeoning film industry. Here they mixed with the stars of the day, including Douglas Fairbanks and Mary Pickford. While living in a rented house in Santa Barbara, Beatrice began a lifelong friendship with Wallis Spencer, then married to her first husband Earl Winfield Spencer, an abusive aviator based in San Diego.

But the Californian idyll came to an abrupt end when Beatrice's parents, determined to put an end to what they considered a 'gold-digging marriage' suddenly cut off her allowance.[7] With little or no income the couple were beset by creditors. For several weeks, along with the children, they hid in a hotel in Newark, New Jersey, until Beatrice, able to stand it no longer, gave in to her parents. She agreed to take the children to France and begin divorce proceedings in Paris. Beatrice, Dear and the children sailed for Europe on the RMS *Celtic* in spring of 1921, Beatrice writing tearful letters to Gibson during the voyage. Cheerful, yet enduringly lazy and improvident, Gibson would have one more unsuccessful marriage to another heiress, eventually dying penniless of tuberculosis.

With her debts in America still outstanding, Beatrice became virtually exiled in Europe and in a state of constant friction with her father, who continued to keep her on a strict allowance and prevented her taking possession of her mother's jewellery when the latter died in 1924. In spite of this, Beatrice still managed to stay in the best hotels in the smartest cities in Europe. Her two children had become an encumbrance and were sent to boarding school in America. As a result, her son Dallas would always feel keenly the absence, even indifference, of his mother during his childhood. In December 1922 Beatrice married again, this time to an Englishman of 39, Charles Cartwright. Cartwright was a naval officer from a landed family in Leicestershire and used to being in command. This time her parents approved but, 'would have preferred an American', but at least Charles had money of his own.[8] Beatrice joined him in his posting to Malta where he was in command of a ship in the Mediterranean. While describing him as: 'devoted, such a comfort and joy, so handsome and distinguished in his full dress uniform with decorations and ribbons, very sweet and sympathetic and gentle', she became bored with the monotony of being a navy wife in Malta and was relieved when Charles retired.[9]

Although seemingly happy in her marriage, her letters to her family now seem to have been an endless complaint about lack of money. Most were addressed from the Hyde Park Hotel in London, the Excelsior in Rome, the Carlton in Biarritz and the Crillon in Paris. If they are not complaining about her poverty they are full of news of the international set she is now moving among. Strangely, she does not omit to give details of the couture clothes she adorns herself with, an O'Rossen suit, a Callot pleated crepe black dress, a brown Reville sport suit. And here, 'all wear cloche hats'.[10] Her Rolls Royce had a black cabriolet body, yellow basket weave on the rear panels and a rooster as a radiator cap. In 1923 she bought a flat in Stanhope Gate off Park Lane in London, and furnished it from her previous homes in America, explaining in detail the elegant decorations she was planning throughout. Her health was a constant preoccupation. She seldom mentioned her children.

Now that Beatrice and Cartwright were often together, the relationship gradually became tedious: 'The English are so reserved they are sometimes baffling and it is hard to follow their thought processes, one feels like a child learning a new alphabet.'[11] During this time the children would spend several weeks each summer in various resorts in Europe in order to see their mother. But while she and Charles always stayed in the grandest hotel in town, the children and Dear would be lodged in more modest accommodation nearby.

In spite of her constant pleas of poverty Beatrice, presumably with the help of Charles, now bought a town house in Curzon Street, Mayfair, and the unfortunately named Sludge Hall in Leicestershire – both amply staffed with butlers and handsome footmen. To these were added an elegant Paris flat in the rue Constantine and later, fortunately for Barry, the Casa Estella on the Cap d'Antibes.

Sludge Hall was bought mainly for Charles in order to indulge his love of hunting. Beatrice disliked the

Leicestershire countryside but occasionally entertained there, her guests including Wallis Simpson. Wallis, now married to the Englishman Ernest Simpson, was slowly working her way towards the Duke of Windsor.

Although scarcely remembered now, during the 1920s and 1930s Beatrice was a flamboyant and glamorous member of the international set, a noted hostess in her splendid houses and a sought-after guest at others. In spite of the feeling of indifference which now pervaded the marriage between her and Charles, they had always wanted to have a child and at last, in July 1930, Aubrey Cartwright was born. Babies held little interest for Beatrice, but her son Dallas, now in his teens, became of use as an occasional escort, a role which he was delighted to fill. He became particularly useful in the south of France, when Beatrice moved into Casa Estella in 1932.

The marriage with Charles was coming to an end. Impatient with each other and their different ways of life, they eventually began divorce proceedings. It is not known exactly what Beatrice had done to infuriate her husband, but he was determined to prevent her from having custody of their son. The 9-year-old Aubrey was made a Ward of Court, only to be cared for by Charles or his Cartwright relatives. He was to be brought up as an English gentleman and eventually sent to Eton College, while his elder brother Dallas was educated in America.

Beatrice now spent the summers on the Cap d'Antibes among the many friends who also congregated on the coast during the long, hot, sunlit months. In 1938 she treated herself to a new car, a specially commissioned Talbot Lago T23 Coupé with 'teardrop' bodywork designed by Figoni and Falaschi, a beautiful car, still remembered today. Dressed in beige and black, the colours of the car, she won the 1938 Concours d'Elegance in Nice in the Coupé category.

In February of 1940 Beatrice's father died, thus releasing the control he had retained of her portion of the Standard

Oil inheritance. She was now a very rich woman. When war was declared in September of that year, Charles Cartwright joined the British navy, his old service. In May, ambushed on a land mission in Holland, he was killed. Although Beatrice immediately applied to the English courts to have custody of her son Aubrey, this was refused. Her consolation prize was her fourth, and most disastrous, marriage. Freddy J. McEvoy was an Australian racing driver, big game hunter, gambler and bobsleigh champion so fearless he was known as 'Suicide Freddy', also as 'Tiger' because of his great strength and piercing eyes. McEvoy had taken part in eight European Grands Prix, usually driving Maseratis. He was also a rogue and a playboy and close friends with the film actor Errol Flynn, another Antipodean. The comparison went further, for not only did he look very like Flynn, he too was a womaniser and hard drinker. He was on the periphery of a notorious case when two young women accused Flynn of statutory rape committed in McEvoy's Los Angeles apartment. Although Flynn was acquitted and supported by his many friends, the trial did not enhance his movie career.

It seems that Beatrice always insisted on marrying her lovers because, in her mind, there was no question of her ever taking the role of permanent mistress. So, in Paris in March 1940 as the threat of the German advance grew ever nearer, she married Freddy McEvoy. He was a very different proposition to Cartwright. Beatrice was now in her early fifties, nearly 20 years older than McEvoy and already twice a grandmother. After the marriage, and ignoring the coming danger, they went to Antibes to spend the summer in the Casa Estella. They stayed on as Denmark, Norway, the Netherlands and Belgium fell to the Germans, as the Battle for France was fought in the north, after the evacuation of Dunkirk and through the signing of the Armistice which made the south an 'Unoccupied Zone' under Field Marshall Pétain.

While Somerset Maugham and other expatriates left from Cannes in their overcrowded coal boats in the heat of August 1940, Beatrice and Freddy stayed. Coal boats were not for her. She wrote to Dallas:

> The British are sadly missed here. Cannes looks depressed as compared with other years ... Pyjamas and shorts are forbidden in public. The War and its complications have upset everybody. The weather is divine.[12]

They waited until the cooler month of October before leaving via Lisbon. Along with Jeanne, Beatrice's faithful maid, they managed to load a mountain of wardrobe trunks, Vuitton suitcases and themselves onto an overcrowded train to Portugal, even using a lavatory as storage. Only arrogance, overbearing personalities and liberal tipping could have accomplished this. They crossed the Atlantic to New York on an American export ship, and once in the city established themselves in a suite at the Waldorf Astoria.

Meanwhile, on a now almost deserted Cap d'Antibes, Beatrice's butler, Antheme, went to work on the Casa Estella. To protect against requisition he stripped the bathrooms of their plumbing, sent the furniture and valuables to a barn in the mountains and put up a sign saying the house was under the protection of the Finnish minister who, fortuitously, was a friend of Beatrice's.

Back in America, Beatrice was happy to indulge McEvoy's whims and they lived well. She bought him a 104-ton yacht, the ill-fated *Kangaroo*, and settled a $250,000 trust fund on him. But the one thing she had always expected from her husbands was faithfulness and by 1942 she suspected that McEvoy was having affairs. She had him watched, and when she was told by her private detective that her suspicions were correct, she succumbed to the first of several strokes, which would eventually affect her speech and movement. In

October 1942 Beatrice divorced McEvoy on the grounds of adultery – but allowed him to keep the yacht. She would not marry again.

Consolation this time was the purchase of a spectacular apartment in New York on the top floor of 820 Fifth Avenue. As well as the grand main rooms, there were seven bedrooms for servants and a servants' hall. She would also buy a house on Banyan Road, Palm Beach, home of the international set in Florida. This she called Estella, re-creating happy memories of the Cap d'Antibes. In the spirit of beginning again, she changed her name, now calling herself Mrs Beatrice Benjamin Cartwright, as the widow of a war hero, rather than the divorcée of a philanderer. In memory of this third husband she had a monument to Charles Cartwright installed in his parish church in Leicestershire. She now got on far better with her children, and was allowed closer contact with a growing Aubrey Cartwright.

As for McEvoy, he quickly married Irene Wrightsman, the 18-year-old daughter of the president of Standard Oil of Kansas, a marriage which lasted two years. An accomplished yachtsman, with an ever-growing FBI file, he spent his time smuggling between Mexico and California, while conducting a long-running affair with 'poor little rich girl' Barbara Hutton, the Woolworth heiress. Barbara would buy him a ski chalet in New Hampshire. His wives and mistresses always seemed to want to leave him with some small token of their McEvoy experience. His third marriage was to a pretty French girl of 26, Claude Stephanie Filatre. It was on the schooner *Kangaroo*, his gift from Beatrice, that disaster struck. Sailing to Morocco in 1951 with, as the story goes, a load of smuggled whisky, a storm struck and the yacht foundered. He lashed his wife to the mast and, with some other members of the surviving crew, swam to shore to get help. Finding none he returned to the yacht and, with Claude, began the swim back to shore. Their bodies were found together on the rocks the following day.

Beatrice did not return to the Casa Estella until 1947. When she did she found it almost exactly as she had left it when she walked out of the door seven years earlier. Her butler had replaced the furniture, ornaments and silver as they had always been. There were even pre-war cigarettes in their box on the table. The house had been left untouched when the German Army occupied the south in 1943, perhaps because it was not in a particularly strategic position. Beatrice's last years were spent travelling between her apartment in New York and the Casa Estella, during which time she suffered more strokes which left her increasingly incapacitated. On the Cap, every day her butler would carry her down the steps and place her into the sea. Here she could swim and float with an ease she did not feel on shore. Her iron will forced her to continue to entertain at her dinner table, beautifully dressed and bejewelled by her maid Jeanne, but unable to hold a conversation. She was spending the summer at the villa when, in August 1955, she died. The daunting effort to be a glamorous socialite was over.

The Casa Estella was bequeathed to Aubrey, the son who had been withheld from her throughout his childhood. Aubrey used the villa as a holiday home and became involved in the local British community. He married and had two children but, plagued by depression, died in a Swiss clinic in 1972. Cynthia, Beatrice's daughter from her first marriage to Alexander Pratt, also married and had two children. She and her elder brother Dallas had always been very close and her death in 1985 touched him deeply.

As for Dallas, he became a practising psychiatrist, animal rights activist and collector of precious books, manuscripts and antique maps. An excellent biography of his life from cradle to grave, *Dallas Pratt: A Patchwork Biography*, by his friend Richard Chapman describes how, with his partner

John Judkyn, Dallas founded and furnished the splendid American Museum of Britain at Bath, Somerset. In the 1950s he would also buy the ancient Castello in the village of Opio above Cannes, where he spent many happy summers. A philanthropist, his life was active and fulfilled.

A memento of Beatrice is left in the form of a sculpture of her beautiful tapering hands by the American sculptor, Mario Korbel. In white marble, this is held in the Franco-American Museum at Blérancourt in the north of France. Beatrice herself lies in the Sleepy Hollow Cemetery, New York. The Casa Estella seems to have been subject to only minor alterations over time and remains, as it has for over 80 years, serenely overlooking the boats which pass by in Millionaire's Bay.

Le Château de l'Horizon – 1932
Maxine Elliott

The house has to please everyone, contrary to the work of
art, which does not. The work of art is a private matter for
the artist. The house is not.
　　Adolf Loos, in Joseph Masheck, *The Art of Architecture*

One summer's day in the 1930s the politician and author
Winston Churchill lay on his back, head first, on a slide 25
feet long and shot down into the Mediterranean. The slide
in question led from the edge of a salt-water swimming pool
in front of a striking, all-white villa at Golfe Juan, between
Cannes and Juan-les-Pins, and had been designed cunningly.
The actress, once strikingly beautiful, who had commissioned
the villa from Barry and Eric had become extremely large
in her old age, particularly in her nether regions. Anxious
to ensure the slide would fit her comfortably, the couple
devised a plan. All three would go to the edge of the
unfinished terrace and the lady in question would be asked
to contemplate a detail on the rocks below. This she did,
whereupon Eric whipped out a tape measure and, without
touching, swiftly measured the breadth of her derrière. The
plan worked perfectly and the slide, flanked by two steep
staircases, would comfortably accommodate both her and,
occasionally, Winston Churchill.

Maxine Elliott, now only a footnote in the memoirs of others, would bring the Edwardian era with her to the sleek modernist house, with its Moorish touches, which Barry built for her at Golfe Juan. It would be one of the 'jewels in his crown'. Born Jessie Dermott in 1868 in Rockland, Maine, Maxine was one of six children of a sea captain Thomas Dermot and his wife Adelaide Hall. Having been born with an adventurous spirit, she would often join her father on his large sailing ship on the high seas. She began her acting career at the age of 15 at the Notre Dame Academy in Roxbury, Massachusetts, and when she moved to New York to continue her studies, she changed her name to Maxine Elliott. In the city she fell in love with and, too rapidly, married a handsome but dubious lawyer, George MacDermott. A disastrous relationship which did not last and, some would say, broke her heart.

But it was not long before her dark statuesque beauty, beguiling 'midnight eyes' and strong personality drew attention to her, rather than her pedestrian acting talent. Her grandmother had been Moravian from Central Europe, which probably accounted for her unusual gypsy-like looks and luxuriant dark hair. From 1890 to 1920, Maxine acted almost constantly. Many of her performances are long forgotten but they included plays by J.M. Barrie, Oscar Wilde and roles as Shakespeare's heroines. In 1895 she joined the Augustin Daly touring company, which took her to England for the first time in Shakespeare's *Two Gentlemen of Verona*. But it was the Nathaniel Goodwin company, which she joined a year later, that would change the course of her life. First, because she would marry Nat Goodwin as the third of his four wives and then, in 1898, because he would buy her a house in England, a country to which she seemed constantly drawn. This was the mock-Elizabethan Jackwood House, near Woolwich, a borough then outside London.

So began Maxine's constant touring in America and abroad, involving trips to Australia and criss-crossing the

Atlantic between her acting career in America and her English home. In London in 1905 she took the lead in *Her Own Way*, a play by Clyde Fitch. This was an instant success and would make her a star, earning her the theatrical acclaim that had so far eluded her in England. So much so, that in August 1907 she was invited to lunch at Buckingham Palace by the long-suffering Queen Alexandra. An invitation almost certainly prompted by Alexandra's philandering husband Edward VII, the son of Queen Victoria. Maxine was the first actress to be so honoured and began to be accepted into society, where she was determined to shine. She became socially ambitious, a venture she pursued with her usual spirit and determination.

Becoming weary of touring, in 1908 she opened the elegant Maxine Elliott Theatre at West 39th Street near Times Square in New York, its classical facade and interior designed by Maxine herself.[1] The facilities for its performers were groundbreaking in their comfort. She attended to every detail, for she was a perfectionist. It was rumoured that the funding for the theatre was a gift from the banker J.P. Morgan with whom Maxine seemed to have a closer friendship than she would ever openly admit. And in the same year, with sealed papers thus avoiding a scandal, Nat Goodwin filed for divorce in Reno, Nevada.

Now gathering adulation as she went, in the forefront of those who were known to admire the curvaceous beauty with her wasp waist was Edward. But, in spite of the lunch with Queen Alexandra, no one would actually introduce her to him – the one person who could ensure she scaled the social heights. It was known that Edward favoured summer trips to the Marienbad Spa in Czechoslovakia, so in 1908 Maxine calmly laid a plan. She took a hotel room in the spa hotel when he was in residence and, dressed exquisitely all in white, placed herself on a seat in one of the parkland walks where the King and his entourage could not fail to miss her. Armed with a book she professed to be reading, she slowly raised her

famous dark eyes to his as he passed. It worked admirably
and in August of the following year the *New York Times* would
report from the spa town: 'King Edward smiles on Maxine
Elliott'.[2] She was now officially part of the King's entourage
and accepted by the circle which surrounded him. The same
newspaper also mentioned that she was a very wealthy woman
who had invested her profits in property in Texas, 'which
paid one hundred per cent'.[3]

Maxine's sister Gertrude, six years younger, had also
become an actress. Almost a carbon copy of Maxine, but
gentler and more delicate in appearance, she was always
in thrall to her strong-willed sister. In 1900 Gertrude had
married one of the finest actors of the British stage, Johnston
Forbes-Robertson, and so become part of the theatrical set
in England. The courteous Johnston would find Maxine's
attempted domination of the couple's domestic life a trial
for many years. The Forbes-Robertsons would have four
daughters, the youngest of which, Diana, would write an
affectionate 'warts and all' biography, *My Aunt Maxine*.

In the year following her first meeting with Edward VII,
Maxine left Jackwood House (later sold by Nat Goodwin)
and, in addition to her London residence in Regent's Park,
bought Hartsbourne Manor at Bushey Heath, Hertfordshire,
within reasonable distance of London. In the early nineteenth
century Hartsbourne had belonged to the Baronet Sir
Thomas Thompson who was one of Horatio Nelson's 'Band
of Brothers', serving with him at the battle of the Nile and
Copenhagen. Here Maxine set about turning the house into
a charming and comfortable home. Here too, she created a
private wing for the Forbes-Robertsons and their growing
family, and expected them to use it.

Maxine had arrived socially and, good actress that she was,
now took on the role of society hostess to perfection. She was
a quick learner. Where the King went so did his circle. They
came first because the King bade them and they returned

to enjoy Maxine's personality, her wonderful meals and the comfort of her house, as well as those they would meet there. Just as all was going so well, inconveniently in 1910 the King died. But Maxine was able, with her intelligence and charm, to continue to entice the 'right people' to Hartsbourne. She loved a title and when this was coupled with a successful political career, it was even better. As well as having enjoyed the favours of Edward VII, it was now Lord Curzon, ex-viceroy of India and later foreign secretary (with a penchant for American women) who paid court to her, as did Lord Rosebery, an ex-prime minister. Both of these men were widowers, but the adoring Duke of Rutland was not. Probably the last great love of her life was the 27-year-old New Zealand tennis champion Anthony Wilding. A solicitor and barrister, he had the looks of a Greek god and a disposition so faultless that others had nothing but praise for his character. The fact that Maxine at 42, although still handsome, was 15 years older than Wilding appeared to make no difference to either. Theirs was a loving and mutually respectful relationship, perhaps kept alive by the frequent partings due to Maxine's theatrical commitments and Anthony's tennis tournaments. He would win four singles championships in a row at Wimbledon.

By 1911 Winston Churchill, then First Lord of the Admiralty, was staying at Hartsbourne with his mother, the beautiful Jenny Jerome. Jenny, the daughter of a financier, was an American from Brooklyn. She had married Lord Randolph Churchill, a son of the 7th Duke of Marlborough, a politician and Winston's father.

This would be the first of many visits Churchill would pay to Maxine's comfortable homes. But his wife Clementine, not at ease with her and her social gatherings, would often make an excuse not to join them. Lady Diana Cooper, socialite and 'the beauty of the age', wrote affectionately about Maxine in those Hartsbourne days: 'In her house near London she gave us dazzling fun'.[4]

During the years leading up to World War I Maxine socialised more and acted less. When war was declared in 1914, unwilling to be left idle while those around her donned uniforms of every description and changed the pattern of their lives, she evolved an aid scheme which would both suit her and contribute to the common good. Not for her the endless toil of nursing amidst mud and blood, with sparse rations and a dearth of comforts of any kind. She decided to fund a barge to be taken to the canals of Flanders, equipped with food and other necessities for refugees and the dispossessed. Being rich, she could contribute handsomely. Bringing money over from the States, she went to Calais and bought a large vessel called the *Julia*. Her lover, Anthony Wilding, was on hand operating a fleet of armoured cars for the Royal Navy and able to give advice and practical help. The *Julia* was towed to the Belgian canals and became an amply provided supply barge which, together with a large lorry, distributed much needed goods to 'my poor refugees' in the surrounding areas.[5]

With her peremptory style and commanding air Maxine became known in Belgium as 'Lord High Admiral', a title which displeased her not at all.[6] A journalist on the Boston *Sunday Herald* of April 1915 now reported her as: 'a portly woman of forty-five [she was 47] clad in a purple sweater with skating cap to match' and was amazed at the home comforts she had created in her barge – cabins with beds, lavatories and baths plus a cosy sitting room. And the socialising, in a rather different form, continued. By the time the operation was closed down in May 1916 around 350,000 of the needy had been fed and clothed. The Belgian people and their king were deeply grateful and the latter bestowed upon Maxine the title of Knight of the Order of the Crown.[7]

In May of 1915 Captain Anthony Wilding was killed by a shell during the Second Battle of Ypres. He was 32. Perhaps they would have married, perhaps not, but it was felt by

Maxine's friends that after his death she was never quite the same vital person again.

Feeling she must top up her capital following the outlay on the barge project, Maxine returned to the stage until 1920. During this time she made two films for Samuel Goldwyn, an experience she disliked thoroughly, realising that audience preferences had moved on and her particular type of acting did not suit modern tastes. She was out of sympathy with life in America and acting in general. Deciding finally to retire, she was asked whether she would miss the glamour and replied: 'I'll miss it about as much as the early Christian martyrs missed the man-eating lions in the arena.'[8] From then on she mentioned the theatre and films rarely. In 1923 she sold Hartsbourne, where she had reigned as 'Queen of Hearts' for 14 years, and moved to London, remodelling a large house at 20 Abbey Road at Maida Vale. It was now she decided to abandon any attempt at glamour and to accept middle age. Unfortunately this included finding comfort in food – a lot of food. Rich cakes, butter, cream and sauces would begin to play a necessary part in her daily life which, combined with lack of exercise and long sessions at the bridge table, would turn her into the old lady with the generous derrière who would become familiar to Barry and Eric.

Striving to find new interests, at the end of the 1930s Maxine moved to Paris to the Avenue Saint-Honoré d'Eylau, where she remodelled an apartment. More practice for her next and final move. In *My Aunt Maxine*, Diana Forbes-Robertson wrote that 'Purpose, happiness, and beauty returned to Maxine in the last decade of her life.'[9] She moved to the Riviera and, with her close friend Charlotte Boissevain, scoured the coast for a suitable plot on which to build a house. Charlotte, as Charlotte Ives, had also been an American actress, had married well and now owned the Villa Hou Zee in large grounds on the Cap d'Antibes, where Barry would build an elegant swimming pool pavilion. It is debatable as to whether the plot Maxine found in 1931 was suitable, but it was certainly challenging. At Golfe Juan, between Cannes and Antibes and with Juan-les-Pins as a neighbour, it consisted of a narrow strip of rocky land behind which lay both the railway line and the main coast road. In front, rocks edged a steep drop into the wide expanse of the Mediterranean. Maxine, like Barry and Eric, wanted to be as near to the sea as possible.

Golfe Juan itself, like virtually all the Riviera and its hinterland, has a turbulent history. It was first inhabited by a Celtic-Ligurian tribe, around 200 BC, before becoming a Roman village, although by the fifth century all trace of habitation had disappeared. Around the eleventh century there was some sort of resettlement, causing the area to come under the control of the monks of the Cistercian monastery of the Isles de Lerins, off the coast of Cannes. At the beginning of the sixteenth century began the construction of what would be the village of Vallauris. In the act relating to the establishment of this new habitation, it was decreed that pottery and glass should be made and sold by the inhabitants of the commune. In March 1815 Napoléon Bonaparte, after escaping from Elba, landed at Golfe Juan with 600 men. He moved east to Cannes and bivouacked on what is now the rue de Belges, next to an old, deconsecrated chapel called Notre-Dame de Bon Voyage, then remote and surrounded by shingle. From here he began his '100 Days' trek northwards, on what is now the Route Napoleon, a journey which ended with his defeat at Waterloo. In 1948 the artist Pablo Picasso gave Vallauris an enormous boost when, for seven years, he chose to live and create his own pottery there.

It was Charlotte Boissevain who introduced Maxine to Barry and Eric. The plans for the house Maxine envisaged, so different to any she had lived in previously, demanded constant compromises on both sides. Maxine knew what she wanted – and she wanted to be involved. Living in a cottage on the site, she supervised every detail of the building work. Barry and Eric's prudence and good humour stood them in good stead. They were ever braced for the command: 'It won't do, rip it out'.[10] Even the escalating cost, as endless details were changed or added, did not dissuade Maxine from striving for perfection in what she intended to be her last home. A pencilled note on a scrap of paper, in Maxine's rather unsteady hand, lists her demands, including a direction that the salon should be 50 feet long. The Château de l'Horizon would be one of Barry's most important works. The rocks above the sea had to be blasted out and levelled before building could begin. In projects of this kind Eric's knowledge of engineering was indispensable. The villa was on four levels with the centre flanked by two projecting wings. Rendered white, its flat roofs and arcaded galleries gave it an aspect of the casbah, although on the lower floor was an American bar, always primed for cocktails. Each of the bedrooms had their own bathroom and private balcony, where guests were expected to take their breakfast. Servants were amply accommodated for, with 12 bedrooms.

As the whole was on a slope, the entrance to the villa was on the first floor and visitors used a bridge to cross the railway line which ran in front of the house. A bridge which Maxine, with her indomitable will, cajoled the authorities into allowing her to build.

The entrance hall was in strict contrast to the crisp white exterior, for here were two grand curved staircases and a marble flagged floor. The hall led to a suite of reception rooms and the enormous salon giving onto the terrace, which was built around several maritime pines. This in turn overlooked the *pièce de résistance*, the great sea water swimming pool, then the largest private pool on the Riviera, and sporting the famous slide down into the sea. The English magazine *Punch* would describe it as: 'a white palace floating on the waters'.[11]

Eric had managed to create a garden on this reluctant site, with a small English-style lawn to one, more shaded, side. Walls were draped with climbing roses, and banana, mimosa, palm and carob trees softened the surrounding terraces. Oleanders flanked the steps down to the small jetty below. A great wall was built behind the house to keep out the noise of the passing trains – with limited success.

Barry's usual urbanity collapsed when he saw the furniture from Hartsbourne Manor being unloaded. Maxine's niece, Diana Forbes-Robertson, wrote that he burst into tears when he first observed all the goods and chattels of a comfortable English home being carried into Horizon. But he recovered quickly, remarking: 'This is her personal world, and if my house can't contain heavy upholstery, tasselled lamps and silver-framed photographs it hasn't succeeded.'[12]

Barry and Eric became frequent visitors to Horizon and Diana Forbes-Robertson felt that Barry loved Maxine dearly. He had always cheeked her and knew this had caused her to love him in return. But in a letter to Winston Churchill, Maxine, when writing of those on the Riviera at that time, felt: 'It was an Adam-less Eden ... only pansies grow here in profusion and they are not my favourite flowers.'[13] Presumably she made an exception for Barry and Eric.

At Hartsbourne, her English home, Maxine had been part of the political and aristocratic life of the country. But the Hartsbourne years were in the past and many of her former guests had grown old or died. Those she gathered round her on the Riviera were a more eclectic crowd and her guests there were often more café society than aristocrats. But there was one who shared the memories of the Hartsbourne days and his visits would bring her more joy than all the others. Winston Churchill, cast into the political wilderness after the defeat of the Conservative Party, was now spending his days writing his great biography of the soldier and statesman the Duke of Marlborough and painting landscapes and gardens. Theirs was a platonic friendship of great warmth.

Maxine organised her household with Fanny Vandystaedt, who had been with her on the Belgian barge as her housekeeper. Those who live on the Riviera do not lack visitors, and they came to Horizon from near and far – 30 for lunch or dinner was far from unusual. The guest bedrooms were frequently full. The rules of the house were: guests should take their breakfasts on their individual balconies and then don swimming costumes or similar and gravitate to the pool. Maxine herself had a cleverly designed swimming costume which draped like a dress when she was out of the water, concealing her ever-increasing girth. The splendid lunches and dinners where held in the cool rooms inside. Everyone wanted to visit this spectacular house and swim in its splendid pool.

As in other large villas on the Riviera, where the hosts did not appreciate their houses being used as hotels, individual excursions were frowned upon. Guests either went out to invited meals or cocktails as a group or stayed around Maxine at Horizon. Creeping out to the casino after dinner was performed with bated breath. The most favoured visitors were those who would spend time playing bridge, backgammon or six-pack bezique with Maxine. Soon her increasing age and weight meant the only feature which recalled her years as a beauty were her large, compelling brown eyes.

An addition to the household was a vicious lemur monkey called Kiki. The beloved Kiki was allowed the run of the otherwise immaculate house, appearing unexpectedly, causing havoc as he romped among the guests, attacking anyone who approached Maxine and, his greatest enjoyment, nipping at women's ankles. He ruled supreme and was heartily disliked by everyone except Maxine herself. There were some who found Kiki too much of a hurdle to overcome and did not return, but most did, keeping a wary eye out for sudden attacks by needle-like teeth. Even Maxine did not escape, her hands and ankles liberally swathed with iodine, until eventually she had his lemur teeth filed down.

The one person who was allowed to come and go as he pleased was Winston Churchill. His trips to the casino (gambling was a source of great enjoyment), into the hills to paint, and to lunch and dine with friends such as Lord Rothermere, were treated with indulgence. Rothermere, Harold Harmsworth, was owner of the London *Daily Mail* and *Daily Mirror*. Estranged from his wife, who kept their Mas de Pibonson in Mougins, he was a frequent visitor to Horizon from his villa La Dragonnière at St Jean-Cap-Ferrat. At Horizon he appreciated the company of both Maxine and the nubile and scantily dressed young women who were often among the guests.

In 1936 Maxine was asked to let her house, for the month of August, to the then King Edward VIII, soon to become Duke of Windsor when he abdicated in December 1936 in order to marry his American mistress, Wallis Simpson. He was planning to visit the Riviera, together with Wallis, under his travelling name of the Count of Chester. He had visited Horizon and liked it, saying: 'the long marble chute from the lower terrace down to the sea. Zzzzzip! Splash! Wonderful!'[14] Maxine began, reluctantly, to prepare the villa for the King and his party. She was loathe to move out of her comfortable home. However, the fear of the proposed visit being leaked to the press, plus the election of the Popular Front Socialist government under Léon Blum in France, caused a radical change of plan. Edward was advised the Riviera was 'blazing with red flags'.[15] The proposed visit now became a cruise along the Dalmatian coast in the luxury yacht *Nahlin*, a romantic voyage with his beloved Wallis. Maxine breathed a sigh of relief.

But she was delighted when stars such as Douglas Fairbanks Senior stayed and when 'Tarzan', Johnny Weissmuller, dived from the top terrace over the dining area and into the pool. The English artist Graham Sutherland was also a visitor. The interior designer Elsie de Wolfe, who gained a title when she married the English diplomat Sir Charles Mendl *en blanc*, was another spirited American woman. She would chide Maxine for her laziness and lack of exercise, showing off her own thin figure and demonstrating her headstands beside the pool. They crossed swords over whether the trains racing along walls behind the villa could be heard or not, Maxine denying this vehemently, her protestations sometimes drowned out as one rattled by.

Churchill himself was often indifferent to the mix of guests around the dinner table and, in any case, usually visited in the winter months when life was quieter. He loved the Riviera and he loved comfort – Maxine provided both. He came virtually every year throughout the thirties to write and paint, and it was a mutually satisfactory arrangement. She would write to him: 'Your *joie de vivre* is a wonderful gift and on a par with your other amazing gifts. In fact you are the most enormously gifted creature in the whole wide world and it is like the sunshine leaving when you go away.'[16] Her letters frequently entreated him to return when he could.

But when he was staying there in January 1938, the now Duke and Duchess of Windsor were dinner guests at Horizon, and this event was prepared with care. The others in the small party were David Lloyd George, the former British prime minister now urging conciliation with Adolf Hitler, Diana Forbes-Robertson and her husband the American journalist Vincent Sheean. Churchill deemed the dinner 'a great success'.[17] Sheean, slightly overwhelmed, described the evening in his book *Between the Thunder and the Sun*. The men of the party discussed politics and the welfare and conditions of Welsh coal miners, 'in the exquisite little room, gleaming with glass and silver, over the flowers and champagne – one who had been King, one who had been dictator [Lloyd George] and one who was to be [Churchill].'[18] And, a rare event, that night Kiki the lemur was locked up.

As the decade wore on, Churchill became increasingly concerned about the situation in Europe. In a letter to Maxine of February 1938 thanking her for his stay in January, he added: 'I do not find things any better ... Now the whole place is in the hands of the violent party men and I fear very much lest something should happen in Central Europe.'[19] In 1939 came the increasing expectation of war along with the deterioration in Maxine's health. In June she wrote to Churchill: 'This is my first attempt to hold a pencil but my fingers are fairly itching to tell you how heart warming I found it that you are so concerned about my illness.' And: 'I shall look forward more than I can say to your coming here in August! Or September if you prefer – whenever you can spare the time, and know, dear Winston, that I am always your grateful and utterly devoted Maxine.'[20] But as war grew closer Churchill would not visit Maxine again.

Warned by the much esteemed Dr Brés of Cannes, who 'cared for everyone' to keep to a strict diet, or else, Maxine continued to eat enormous meals, deserts and cakes. Even the professional hostess, the American Elsa Maxwell, who was far from sylph-like herself, remonstrated with her, to no avail, as she watched Maxine consume a multi-course lunch. It is said that Maxine may have been one of the models for Somerset Maugham's story *The Three Fat Women of Antibes*, possibly that of Beatrice Richman, as the description fits her closely.

When France mobilised its soldiers, as it did in September 1939, it did so from one day to the next, often leaving families in confusion and distress and the soldiers badly equipped. Maxine, increasingly unwell and refusing to leave France, did what she could, organising sewing parties to clothe needy children in her local town of Vallauris, and putting together comfort parcels for the regiment of the *chasseurs alpins*, the elite mountain troops. Among the many expatriate aid programmes that sprang up along the coast during 1939, it was the much-admired *chasseurs alpins* who were supported the most. That year, Christmas in the small Communist town of Vallauris was lightened by Maxine's gift of a Christmas tree and presents for the children. Many of the expatriate aid groups organised trees and presents for the children of local villages in that last year of peace.

In the early part of 1940 Noel Coward, staying at the Carlton Hotel in Cannes, hired a speed-boat, 'recklessly at a fabulous price' and raced along the coast to a silent Horizon.[21] He stayed with a now bedridden Maxine, speaking of the past, until she became weary. Once in his boat, preparing to return to Cannes and a little way from the shore, he turned to look back and saw that Maxine had dragged herself from her bed and was leaning against her balcony waving her handkerchief:

> Her white hair, her white night-gown and the handkerchief were tinged with pink from the setting sun. I waved back and then the lovely picture became blurred, because I knew in that moment, that I should never see her again, and my eyes were filled with tears.[22]

On 5 March 1940, Maxine collapsed and died in her bathroom. Barry was the first friend to arrive. He passed the entrance to Maxine's bedroom where a *chasseur alpin* soldier stood guard, his head bowed over his rifle. In tears, Barry knelt by her bedside to say his final farewell. Others followed, although many had already fled the Riviera. Winston Churchill asked Lieutenant-Colonel George Keppel to represent him.

Maxine was buried in plot 331 in the Protestant section of the Grand Jas cemetery in Cannes. A group of *chasseurs* played the 'Last Post' then fired a volley of shots over her grave. She lies in the same section as Lord Brougham, a British Chancellor of the Exchequer, who was responsible for discovering the little fishing village of Cannes in 1834 and turning it into one of the most sought after winter resorts of Europe. Maxine would have been pleased; she had always loved a lord.

Maxine left one million dollars in her will, to be divided among her family. Horizon was left to her sister Gertrude, but no member of the family would ever live there. As soon as France fell, her housekeeper, Fanny Vandystaedt, closed up the villa and took off for her small house in the hills. Diana Forbes-Robertson wrote that Fanny took with her the silver and all the paintings by Winston Churchill.

In November 1942, in Operation Torch, the Allies landed in North Africa and the Germans occupied the Free Zone. Horizon was requisitioned by German troops. At the liberation of the south of France in August 1944, the American Army took over the villa as an officers' club.

In 1945 Air Chief Marshal Sir Arthur Harris (known as 'Bomber Harris') wrote to Churchill, describing a visit to the villa. He found it 'relatively undamaged' except for water leaks and the garden being full of mines.[23] Fanny told him the Germans took nothing except Churchill's painting of the pool and the volumes of *Marlborough* which he had presented to Maxine. Harris wrote: 'It all looked somewhat sad' and added, 'The local French are terribly hungry.'[24]

In a now defunct publication, the *Reading Eagle* of May 1945, a journalist records that 'Churchill's painting of Chartwell hangs in the caretaker's cottage of Château de l'Horizon'.[25] Fanny had told him that she hid the painting when the Germans demanded the books and paintings. There have been several different versions of the fate of the paintings Churchill presented to Maxine.

Barry, Eric and Frantz Philippe Jourdain, a young architect, were asked to restore the house to its former state. The family then rented out the villa until it was bought, in the late 1940s, by Aly Khan, the handsome playboy son of

the fabulously rich Aga Khan III. The Aga owned the Villa
Yakimour at Le Cannet, above Cannes. Aly Khan loved and
appreciated Horizon and took good care of it, even ensuring
that Maxine's bedroom should be kept as it had always been.
When he married the beautiful but troubled film star Rita
Hayworth in Vallauris in summer 1949, the thrilled mayor
of the town presided over the ceremony at the town hall.
One hundred and twenty policemen were needed to control
the crowds as Rita, wearing an ice-blue chiffon dress and
hat by Worth, rode with Aly in a white Cadillac convertible
to Horizon. There, hundreds of guests were serenaded by
musicians on the terrace while the intertwined initials A and
R, spelt out in carnations, floated on the pool. It was an ill-
fated marriage which ended four years later and produced one
fought-over daughter. The shy Rita hated the social life of the
Riviera, a fact that was not helped when Fanny Vandystaedt,
kept on as housekeeper, waspishly never failed to remind
her that Maxine would have done things differently. Aly's
constant infidelities helped not at all. Rita's lawyer in the
divorce four years later was Maître Suzanne Blum who would,
controversially, exert considerable control during the last
years of the ailing Duchess of Windsor.

For two years in the 1950s it was the turn of Aly's new
love, the actress Gene Tierney, to walk the halls and garden
of Horizon. They became engaged but Aly's father, the Aga
Khan, refused to accept Gene as a daughter-in-law. She
returned to Hollywood where she was treated, voluntarily,
for mental illness. Aly Khan died in a motor accident,
driving his new Lancia in a suburb of Paris in May 1960
with his latest lover, the French model Bettina. She was
unhurt. Aly was later taken to Horizon and buried in a
grave in the small lawn next to the villa. Intended to be a
temporary resting place, it was not until 1972, 12 years later,
that his remains were finally reinterred in a mausoleum in
Syria. His eldest son, Karim, became Aga Khan IV and kept

the villa until it was sold to the future King Fahd of Saudi Arabia in 1979.

Enlarged, enveloped in concrete by other buildings, changed beyond recognition, Barry's wonderful slide swept away and replaced by a wall, the splendid Château de l'Horizon, one of Barry Dierks's finest achievements, is no more.

6

Villa La Reine Jeanne – 1933

Paul-Louis Weiller

Friends called him Paul-Louis Quatorze, a joking reference
to his kingly collection of villas, châteaux and palaces.

Jane S. Smith, *Elsie de Wolfe*

At the beginning of 1932 a slim determined Frenchman of 39
years of age piloted his light aircraft along the Mediterranean
coast. He concentrated on the wilder area around the islands
of Hyères in the Var, seeking the perfect location for a house
for his lovely bride. Refused nothing by her adoring husband,
she yearned to find a piece of Greece in France. He eventually
tracked down 70 hectares of uncultivated forest where ancient
pines and cork oaks loomed over an undergrowth of juniper,
myrtle and thyme. The land was near the town of Cabasson,
in the district of Bormes les Mimosas, below the Maures
Mountains. The husband was Paul-Louis Weiller, World
War I flying ace, industrialist, philanthropist and citizen of
the world. His new, and second, wife was 20-year-old Aliki
Diplarakou, a Greek beauty and former Miss Europe. Aliki
felt the land at Cabasson, which swept down to two private
beaches beside which umbrella pines grew out of cracks in
the rocks, came close to the atmosphere of her Greek home.
The house was intended to be a refuge from their other,
worldly, existence.

Weiller was an extraordinary person. He was the son of the industrialist and senator Lazare Weiller and his second wife, Alice Javal. It was a family, on both his father's and mother's side, which had risen from the ranks of the ancient Jewish community of Alsace to wealth and a degree of social standing. After graduating as an engineer from the École Centrale in Paris at the beginning of World War I, Weiller joined the French Air Force as a reconnaissance pilot, flying his lightweight aeroplane over enemy lines to observe German artillery movements. The 'Squadron Weiller', formed of two Breguet 14 squadrons, used the wireless telephone techniques he had developed for mapping, which empowered the final successful offensives of 1918. Intrepid, he had been wounded several times while flying. For his achievements he was showered with decorations, including the Croix de Guerre, the order of the Chevalier de la Légion d'Honneur and the British Military Cross for gallantry.

Once the war was over Weiller joined the Societé Gnome et Rhone, an aero-engine company and, as a pioneer in civil aviation, organised the first air routes between Europe and Africa. When in 1935 the French government nationalised private airlines, creating Air France, Weiller became a board member.

In 1922 he had married Princess Alexandra Ghika, the daughter of Jean Ghika, a Romanian prince, and Hazel Singer, a minor heiress, whose father was Charles J. Singer of Chicago. Unusually for international aristocrats, the Ghikas made their permanent home at the Villa Primavera in Cannes and became much involved in the town.

The marriage between Weiller and Alexandra Ghika produced a daughter, Marie-Elisabeth, but ended in divorce ten years later. Weiller was then free to marry Aliki, a beauty queen with adventurous tendencies who, later in the 1930s, would dress as a man and have herself smuggled into the monastery of Mont Athos in Greece where no woman was permitted to tread. An escapade which resulted in a lively scandal. Cultivated and multilingual she would be the love of Weiller's life. This marriage produced a son, Paul-Annik, who would, in an enduringly competitive relationship, be as talented, determined and successful as his father.

It was at Cabasson that Weiller asked Barry Dierks to build a house at the edge of the estate, as close to the beach as possible. He wanted it to be part of the natural setting, respecting the landscape and the trees which surrounded the plot. Weiller decreed that none of these trees were to be cut down and must be incorporated into the design. Once the building was finished, one tree would appear to grow out of the house itself and the terrace overlooking the sea was built around several others. Here Barry designed a house in an eclectic mix of styles but given unity and a distinct Provençal character with the use of local materials, the villa and its dependencies being all faced with rough stones.

The house was built around a central summer dining room open to the stars, a rustic version of that built at La Mauresque. A round tower at one end housed the dining room and some of the many bedrooms. In the salon, giving onto the long terrace, Barry again used a beamed ceiling, along with a great chimneypiece. The layout was such that each bedroom was accessible from both the interior and exterior of the house, due to a long terrace and connecting bathrooms, enabling nocturnal comings and goings reminiscent of Edwardian country houses. A guest house in the guise of a *pigeonnier* was built at a short distance, the cooing of its avian occupants merging with the soft swish of the waves. Other guest houses were dotted among the trees and shrub land, the whole unified by the repeated use of Roman arches. The Batchelor's House contained games of all kinds, including a boxing ring. In all, around 30 guests could be accommodated.

Lady Diana Cooper, now married to the diplomat Duff Cooper, who 'knew everyone' and loved almost all, would describe La Reine Jeanne as, 'Babylon of beauty, of shame, of flesh and hedonism'.[1] She would also write: 'Paul-Louis Weiller had come into my life two years before and would, I knew, stay to the end,' a slightly ambivalent statement as she could also be teasing when speaking of him and his social aspirations.[2] He would present her with a fur coat by Dior, which she called her 'coat of shame'.[3]

The villa was named La Reine Jeanne, perhaps in honour of Jeanne, the first Countess of Provence and Queen of Naples, who landed at the nearby island of Brégançon in 1345. Her tempestuous life may have appealed to Weiller's own adventurous spirit. Taking refuge in Provence after the death of her first husband, whom she was accused of murdering, and accompanied by the second of four others, Jeanne built as refuge a palace in the Place des Aires in Grasse, of which only a few fragments remained in the 1920s. Restless in the extreme, endlessly plotting, racing between Provence and Naples – 'a beautiful and passionate woman, she traversed the shores of the Mediterranean like a whirlwind' so wrote Sir Frederick Treves in his *The Riviera of the Corniche Road*.[4] Exasperated by her behaviour, her kinsman Charles of Durazzo put an end to it by strangling her in 1382.

During the 1930s friends and acquaintances came and went, appreciating the tranquillity of the surroundings, always perfumed with the scent of pines and accompanied by the sound of the sea. Meanwhile a growing fear of the threat of Communism spreading from the east, together with anxiety as to Germany's intentions, ran like an unpleasant current through everyday life. Each week that passed seemed to bring Europe closer to war.

Being of Jewish descent, when France fell in June 1940 Weiller was in danger. By September the Vichy regime, under Field Marshall Pétain, was already beginning to persecute Jews and Freemasons and invoking the Statut des Juifs which excluded Jews from owning businesses and practising professions. In October of that year Weiller was interned at a convent at Pellevoisin in the Indre in the centre of France before being sent to Marseilles under *résidence surveillée* (house arrest). But with his combination of bravery, wealth and connections he was not an easy man to incarcerate. He had put La Reine Jeanne in the care of his sister-in-law and her husband, but the Vichy government quickly requisitioned the villa and turned them out. As with so many properties during the war years, it was ill used, in particular by the Italian Army. The surrounding forest became an ideal terrain for the local Resistance fighters who, by killing a German officer on the estate, put the whole area in grave danger of reprisals.

Escaping to Cuba via Morocco, Weiller immediately set about making money, there becoming the 'King of Sugar'. Here a young Richard Nixon became his business lawyer and an enduring friend. He then travelled to North America where he made contact with the Free French, but prudently stayed out of France for the rest of the war. He was not idle in America, becoming involved with Paul Getty's Standard Oil and amassing more riches in oil and banking. It seems that virtually everything he touched turned to gold. The exception to this was his marriage to Aliki. At the beginning of the war Weiller had sent Aliki and their son, Paul-Annik, to safety in New York, himself going to Canada in 1943. It seems as if the disruption caused by the war gave Aliki the perfect opportunity to free herself from his demanding character, relentless social climbing and, in spite of his devotion to her, his constant unfaithfulness. As soon as he arrived in North America she travelled to Reno, Nevada, divorcing him rapidly and causing Weiller an emotional shock from which he would never totally recover. In 1945, Aliki married Sir John Russell, a future ambassador – a marriage which lasted and produced two children.

The south of France was liberated by American and French troops in August 1944 but Weiller did not return to his villa in Provence until 1947. He was now 54. His wealth, philanthropy and hospitality had already been of note before the war and now, perhaps to fill the void left by Aliki's desertion, they became legendary, aided by the vast fortune and business interests he had amassed during his stay in the Americas.

Weiller had interesting neighbours at La Reine Jeanne with whom he did not fail to socialise in the holiday season. At Cap Nègre were the Bruni Tedeschi family whose fortune came from the Italian tyre manufacturing company CEAT founded by Virginio, grandfather of Carla Bruni-Sarkozy, who would become a first lady of France. At the Tour Sarrazine at Cabasson were the Grand Duke Henri of Luxembourg and his large family. So constantly did they socialise that in later years Prince William of Luxembourg would marry Weiller's granddaughter, Sybilla.

The nearby Fort de Brégançon, a rocky island among the Iles d'Hyères, owned through the centuries by the royal families of France, was restored by the state in 1963 and became the official summer residence of the presidents of France. De Gaulle lasted one night there, rendered sleepless by a too short bed and the tireless onslaught of mosquitos. But the Pompidous and Giscard d'Estaings enjoyed the Fort's history and privacy. The Mitterrands used it rarely and the Chiracs only intermittently, Jacques Chirac preferring more exotic locations.

The list of those who visited and re-visited La Reine Jeanne in the post-war years is long. Delages, Rolls-Royces, Bentleys and similar purred through the wooden entrance gates into the private forest. Weiller was fascinated by royalty and had the means and sensitivity to entertain them as they expected. Along with French presidents they would dine beside the cream of Hollywood and French cinema stars, actors, writers, artists and musicians. Greta Garbo would call him 'Paul-Louis XIV', to others he was 'The Commander'.[5] At the villa Elizabeth Taylor and Richard Burton holidayed alone, in rare privacy. Vivien Leigh indulged in her affair with the Australian actor Peter Finch, only to be discovered there by her husband, Laurence Olivier. Brigitte Bardot, the actor David Niven and soon-to-be president, Richard Nixon, stretched out on the small beaches or strolled in the shady woodland around the house. Yul Brynner, an accomplished photographer, found excellent subjects at La Reine Jeanne. In 1965 Paul-Annik, Paul-Louis's son, married Princess Olimpia Emmanuela Torlonia di Civitella-Cesi who was connected to the Spanish royal family. Together they would have six children. It was on their yacht in 1968 that Audrey Hepburn would meet her second husband, the Italian psychiatrist Andrew Dotti.

Games, water sports and relaxation were all encouraged but, as with the Count de Noailles of the Villa Noailles at Hyères, and Maxine Elliott at the Château de l'Horizon, the day revolved around the wishes of the host. Although the house rules were generally more relaxed at La Reine Jeanne, each day at noon guests were expected to gather at Weiller's water skiing session in order to observe and admire. Excursions outside the estate were to be made in groups, if at all. Independent exploring was not encouraged.

Weiller collected beautiful objects – many houses around the world among them. He bought and restored these buildings, filled them with rare and precious treasures and allowed his friends to live in them free of charge. On one occasion this included the Duke and Duchess of Windsor living rent free in his luxurious house on the rue de la Faisanderie in Paris. He needed friends and he needed to bestow generosity. Among his many philanthropic ventures, Weiller was a benefactor of the Château of Versailles. Also at Versailles, he commissioned the Parisian architect Patrice Bonnet to build the villa Le Noviciat, a house he lent on two occasions to General Eisenhower. Of greater interest was the villa Le Trianon on the edge of the château grounds, which Weiller had bought from the interior designer Elsie de Wolfe in 1935. Although she was sole owner of Le Trianon when Weiller bought it from her in 1935, with the proviso she could occupy it for the rest of her life, she had not always been alone there. From almost the beginning of the century Le Trianon had also been the home of two other extraordinary American women, making up The Magnificent Triumvirate of Versailles. A lesbian enclave of great style, enhanced by the American Minna King, Marchioness of Anglesey, who lived next door. As well as Elsie was Elisabeth Marbury, the first female impresario, and Anne Morgan, daughter of the banker J. Pierpoint Morgan. During World War I Anne had founded and worked tirelessly with the American Committee for Devastated France in the department of the Aisne.

Weiller had first met Elsie after the war and when, after the Armistice, the ladies of the Triumvirate resumed their lavish, sought-after parties at Le Trianon, he was a frequent guest. He never failed to admire Elsie in spite of her foibles, such as selling back to him items from the villa which were included in the original purchase price in 1935. In 1951 he bought and restored the dilapidated seventeenth-century Hôtel des Ambassadeurs de Hollande, a town house in the Marais in Paris. It was one of the great mansions of the city. Although he did not live there himself, he entertained the beau monde lavishly in its elegant salons.

In 1965 Weiller was gratified to be made a member of the Académie des Beaux-Arts and in 1989, when he was 96, he was awarded the Grand Croix, the highest honour of the Legion d'Honneur. Although losing his sight, when on holiday in Provence he still water skied for the delectation of his guests. He was 100 when he died in Geneva in 1993, his mind and memory intact.

Still lived in by his descendants, of all his many houses it is perhaps to La Reine Jeanne that Weiller's spirit returns, wafting among the cooing of the doves and the soft wash of the waves on his shore.

Villa Le Roc – 1934
George Cholmondeley

It was very much Rock's house ... The house and its style
were his idea.

Peter Stansky, Sassoon

Orders for Riviera villas and remodelling work flooded into
Barry and Eric's in-tray. In 1934, one of these commissions
was from George, 5th Marquess Cholmondeley, who asked
Barry to build him a villa *pieds dans l'eau* at Golfe Juan. The
piece of land the Marquess had purchased was less than 220
metres along the rocky strip from Maxine Elliott's Château
de l'Horizon to the east and similarly backed by the road and
railway. On the plot stood a Gaudiesque faience-clad and
turreted edifice built by the Parisian architect Georges Massa.
This was the Manoir Eden Roc (nothing to do with the hotel
of the same name) and the first thing Barry did was to pull
it down.

Before acceding to the title of Marquess of Cholmondeley
in 1923, Lord Cholmondeley was Earl of Rocksavage, always
known as Rock, a name that stuck. Old enough to have fought
in the Boer War he would nonetheless, under the influence
of his wife Sybil Sassoon, embrace the twentieth century with
enthusiasm when commissioning the Bauhaus-influenced
Villa Le Roc.

Barry designed an asymmetrical flat-roofed building that combined curves with cubic shapes. The numerous curved balconies were supported by slender piloti. He was asked to provide five bedrooms, salons, and a dining room as well as five rooms for staff. As in all Rock's homes there was a gym, and on the flat roof of Le Roc he would exercise naked, his well-honed, tanned body exposed to the sunshine and sea air. In contrast to the exterior, the interior was entirely Art Deco. Much of the furniture had been bought in 1925 at the Salon des Arts Decoratifs in Paris. This included some striking pieces designed by Rene Prou who also created the mahogany and rosewood marquetry panels for the carriages of the Blue Train. In the summer sitting room was a mural by the French artist Camille Roche. A footbridge was built over the railway tracks to create access to the house. As with the Château de l'Horizon, the railway was omnipresent.

The pool house with its indoor salt-water pool was particularly striking, its curvilinear form and long horizontal lines of windows wrapping around corners influenced by the designs of the German architect Erich Mendelsohn. It was centrally heated, an innovation in indoor Riviera pools of the time.

The narrow terraced gardens, designed by Eric, were planted with bright flowers such as zinnias and plumbago which brought colour to the rather austere facade of the house above. Elsewhere, santolina and lavender softened the rocky ledges. The trees were brought in by sea on rafts. The Cholmondeleys would use the villa for spring and late summer holidays, Rock often visiting alone in winter, when the soft golden light of that season would stream in through the many windows. The couple embraced the vogue for a tanned skin with enthusiasm. But when the Mediterranean became rough and angry the waves would rush foaming up to the top of the steps which led from the water's edge, so close were the buildings to the sea. It was a house to which one went to luxuriate in the open air, to enjoy the pleasures of the sea and indulge to the full the fashion for fitness and exercise. They called it Le Roc, which was no pun on Rocksavage, but a simplified version of the Manoir Eden Roc, the original building on the site.

Along with the title of Marquess of Cholmondeley came the holding of part of the ancient office of Lord Great Chamberlain of England, and with this the responsibility for royal affairs in the Palace of Westminster, an office which Rock held in 1936 and 1937 and from 1952 to 1966 for Queen Elizabeth II. The holder is bound to be present on ceremonial occasions, such as the State Opening of Parliament, to ensure the well-being of the monarch. The uniform, belted, tasselled, glittering with silver and gold threads, suited Rock admirably.

An accomplished player of golf, polo and tennis, Rock had been visiting the Riviera since the early years of the century. In 1923 he played mixed doubles with the French champion Suzanne Lenglen on the clay courts at the Parc Impérial at Nice, once the property of the Russian royal family. Lenglen, 'The Lady in the White Silk Dress', was the tennis phenomenon of the age, a sort of Isadora Duncan of the tennis world but without Isadora's rapid professional decline.[1]

In the early years of the century Rock had been a guest at Maxine Elliott's sought after parties at Hartsbourne. Lady Diana Cooper wrote of meeting him there where she felt he was: 'the most beautiful of all young men of his day. We see a lot of Rock. I think he's probably Apollo – anyhow some god.'[2] So it was rather strange that when Maxine realised he was to become her very near neighbour on the Riviera, she felt less than pleased. Her nephew-in-law, the American journalist and author Vincent Sheean, wrote of this:

> He [Rock] had built it after hers ...; but instead of considering imitation to be the sincerest form of flattery I think Maxine was rather annoyed at this. She consoled

herself by thinking that Lord Cholmondeley's house was less successfully contrived than her own ... 'It's hardly possible to hear the trains here' she would say, 'whereas in Rock's house the moment a train goes by all conversation ceases'. I heard her say that one evening at dinner just as a train maliciously hurtled by and the end of the phrase was lost; all conversation had ceased.[3]

Perhaps Maxine didn't welcome social competition on what she considered her own piece of coastline. She needn't have worried. In general the Cholmondeleys rented out Le Roc in the summer. They had their own, rather private, lives and proved to be no threat to Maxine's position as queen of Golfe Juan.

The main family seat of the Cholmondeleys was Houghton Hall, the supremely elegant Palladian-style house in West Norfolk surrounded by gardens and a deer park. Houghton was built in the 1720s by Sir Robert Walpole, the first, although not formalised, British prime minister from whom the Cholmondeley family has descended. Houghton Hall was designed by the architects James Gibbs and Colen Campbell, with William Kent engaged to create the magnificent interior intended to host grand receptions. The estate of Houghton included six villages in Norfolk. Important paintings and exquisite furniture adorned the rooms. But to help fund the increasing cost of maintaining the house, in 1779 Sir Robert's grandson, the 3rd Earl of Orford, was obliged to sell his treasured collection of Old Masters. These were bought by Catherine the Great of Russia, where they found a home at the Hermitage at St Petersburg.

If the Cholmondeley family wished for a change of scene, they would travel to the nineteenth-century Cholmondeley Castle in Cheshire, surrounded by almost 5,000 acres of land. The houses, estates and responsibilities never ceased to be financially draining, works of art continuing to be sold over the years. But rescue and initiative came in 1913 in the form of an unusual and spirited woman. Sybil Sassoon was an Anglo-Jewish heiress, the only daughter born in 1894 to Sir Edward Albert Sassoon, the 2nd Baronet, and Aline Caroline de Rothschild, who was French and the daughter of Baron Gustave Salomon de Rothschild. A famous poised beauty, in 1912 Sybil was presented at the court of King George V and Queen Mary and the following year married Rock. Around that time her friend, the American artist John Singer Sargent, painted her portrait as a wedding present. In this she is gazing calmly away from the observer and holding a golden shawl loosely around her white shoulders.

Sybil had a fascinating family background. The Sassoons were of Iraqi descent with business interests in India, China and England. Immensely successful merchants, they were also heavily involved in shipping and the opium trade, combined with much general philanthropy. From David Sassoon, the gowned and turban-swathed patriarch in India, to his grandson, Sybil's father Edward, the Liberal Party MP for Hythe in Kent, was a progression full of intrigue, romance and great wealth. The family home in London was 25 Park Lane. As well as Sybil, Aline had a son, Philip, four years older than his sister. But Aline died of cancer in Paris in 1909 when Sybil was 15, and their father died three years later as the result of a car accident in Cannes, leaving Sybil and Philip alone and always very close. Philip grew up to become a politician with aesthetic tastes. Sybil and Philip's cousin was the writer and poet Siegfried Sassoon. Siegfried's father, Alfred, was disinherited by the Sassoon family for marrying, out of his Jewish faith, the sculptor Theresa Thornycroft. Homosexual like his cousin Philip, during the 1914–1918 conflict Siegfried became virulently anti-war but was nevertheless awarded the Military Cross for 'suicidal bravery'. His poignant war poems were, and still are, greatly acclaimed.

The marriage between Rock and Sybil was not embraced warmly by either of their families and put a strain on Sybil's relationship with her Rothschild relatives. For their honeymoon they took a six-month trip to India. This was a country with which Sybil's family had close connections and with which Rock was familiar, having served there in his army days as ADC to Lord Minto, the viceroy and governor-general. The present viceroy was Lord Hardinge. Here they were obliged to socialise with various colonial officers, events which Sybil endured rather than enjoyed: 'Lady Hardinge who was having a high old time with Rock and waggling her Benares work earrings at him in a most engaging manner.' And 'The Wiborgs are here. 3 flashy girls ... They left tonight so Rock hasn't spoken to them. Hooray!' At one reception Rock danced only with Sybil and, 'we had great fun, quite like old times (only without the previous heart burnings!)'[4] It was not easy being married to the most handsome man in the room.

Sybil brought appreciation of art, music and literature to the marriage, particularly music. Like her brother who was an avid collector, filling his houses with precious objects, she loved beautiful things. Using her sense of the aesthetic and Sassoon and Rothschild wealth she would always feel great responsibility, as its châtelaine, to care for and improve Houghton Hall. But unlike her brother, who was enduringly sociable and a renowned host, Sybil, and certainly Rock, would lead quieter lives and often separately from each other. She preferred the company of artistic rather than high society. Rock, with his self-contained air, concentrated on improving Houghton and the estate where, according to the photographer Cecil Beaton, they rarely invited guests (Beaton being an exception). But there was much mutual respect and affection and the interests which brought them together were Houghton, their children, sport and cars, particularly Bugattis. Their children, born from 1916 to

1920, were Aline, Hugh (who became the 6th Marquess) and John.

Although Rock did not approve of the indulgent lifestyle of Edward, Prince of Wales, and even less Edward's growing dependence on Wallis Simpson, in 1935, the year after the villa's completion, he agreed to allow Edward to have Le Roc for a fortnight in mid-summer. Edward's holiday excursions were booked in the name of the Earl of Chester. As he was not allowed to accept gifts from his subjects, he paid Rock a token rental fee of £5. The Duke of Westminster's yacht *Cutty Sark* was at their disposal. Wallis wrote in August 1935 to her Aunt Bessie in America: 'We got here Monday to find a lovely villa in the water – our own rocks and all the privacy in the world but very hot.'[5] Edward, as reluctant heir to the throne and with an ailing father, was determined to have a spell of uninterrupted time with his adored Wallis and this was a temporary solution, a testament to the progress of their affair which had developed steadily over the past couple of years. Much effort was made to hide the holiday from the international press, with only a small house party of seven as guests. Wallis's letters from Le Roc at this time, while Edward was still in England, show how she is already organising his social life, arranging seating, choosing the wine and making sure there is a green vegetable on the menu for his dinner parties. The letters to her 'darling Aunt Bessie' are far warmer than those to poor yearning Edward, those to the latter ending, at that time, with such endearments as, 'Perhaps I'm quite fond of you' and 'Hallo!' although in one case she softens and writes 'I love your eyes'.[6] A proposed cruise along the Dalmatian coast on the Duke of Westminster's yacht was abandoned in the face of Mussolini's designs on Abyssinia, and replaced by stays in Budapest and Vienna, returning via Salzburg, Munich and Paris, accompanied by a group which included the ever-present Herman and Katherine Rogers. Wallis was disappointed: 'You would think Mussolini had planned this mess just to break up the yachting trip.' But she is perceptive – 'I suppose it means war eventually'.[7] Wallis was now balanced on the middle of a seesaw with her husband Ernest Simpson on one end and the Prince on the other, a balancing act which suited her, but which she would not be able to maintain.

For Christmas 1935 Edward ordered a present of a gold and gem-set cigarette case to be made for Wallis by Cartier of London. Twelve tiny precious and semi-precious jewels, used repeatedly, marked their journeys together in 1934 and 1935. By this time Edward was passionately in love with his, now suddenly hesitant, Wallis. On the death of his father in January 1936 he became king. He would never be crowned, abdicating 11 months later. So it was for the coronation of Edward's brother, who became George VI, that Rock, looking splendid in uniform, carried the Royal Standard, perhaps with more enthusiasm than would have been the case for Edward. Edward himself returned quickly and permanently to the arms of his Wallis and what seems to have become, for him, a long life of boredom.

For both Rock and Sybil, an enduring passion was their splendid Bugatti cars, which they kept in England and France. Ettore Bugatti, Italian-born and French-naturalised, took care to give personal attention to clients such as the Cholmondeleys and thus became a friend. In 1924, when the Cholmondeleys were staying at the Villa Caldana near Cannes, Rock won the prestigious hill-climb event at La Turbie, in the hills above Monaco, in a Type 35B. The couple would own seven Bugatti cars over time – sports tourers and saloons – on several occasions competing in the Monte Carlo Rally. In France, an Englishman Paul Hardy became their personal mechanic/general handyman. Bugattis were notoriously expensive to maintain.

At the outbreak of war Cholmondeley Castle park in Cheshire became the first camp for the Free Czechoslovak troops under the Czechoslovak government-in-exile. Rock became a member of the Civil Defence Force, running an Air Raid Precautions post in the basement of their London home. Sybil joined the Women's Royal Naval Service becoming the chief staff officer to the director and finishing as superintendent. She worked hard and travelled extensively, being awarded the CBE (Commander of the Order of the British Empire) in 1946.

When the Germans and Italians took over the south in November 1942, the Cholmondeley's left Le Roc in the hands of Paul Hardy and his wife, who cared faithfully for the villa as it was occupied successively by Senegalese, Italians, Germans and, on Liberation in 1944, Americans. Liberation came too late for Paul's wife, who died of the malnutrition which afflicted so many in the south of France. A little later Paul himself was killed in a motorcycle accident.

After the war Sybil and Rock settled down to lead a contented life together at Houghton in Norfolk. Rock now engaged in improving the decoration of rooms in the House of Lords, which he felt had hitherto been rather bleak. In the year of their golden wedding anniversary he wrote to his friend, the poet William Plomer, of how lucky he had been to have Sybil as a constant companion at his side for 50 years. Suffering from worsening health he died in 1968 aged 85. Noel Coward, always solicitous towards his friends, visited Sybil in London six months later and recorded:

> I lunched on 28 March with dear Sybil Cholmondeley who suddenly broke down over Rock. I was dreadfully sad for her. She is such a loving old friend. She soon recovered herself and I felt somehow glad that I had been there and touched that she should have trusted me enough to give way in front of me.[8]

During the war one of her tasks, owing to her good French, had been to liaise with the staff of General de Gaulle in the offices of the Free French in Carlton Gardens. But it was not until 1984, when she was 90, that the French in the person of President François Mitterrand, awarded her the Légion d'Honneur. This was pinned on Sybil's jacket after lunch in the State Dining Room at Houghton Hall where, as it was President Mitterrand's birthday, he was presented with a chocolate cake complete with candles.

Living for 20 years after her husband Sybil continued to be active, taking great interest in the progress of Houghton, giving an annual lunch party for the Queen Mother, seeing friends and travelling widely. She died at Houghton in December 1989 – she was 95.

Le Roc was rented out, although still used occasionally by the family. In August 1950 Mrs Norman Winston, Rosita, the wife of an American property developer, took the villa for a house party. It was said by some of Rosita that she was a social climber who gathered dispossessed aristocracy of all nations to her table. At one of her house parties her usually patient husband, weary of dining constantly with strangers, took to having his meals at the Eden Roc hotel in Antibes.[9]

Rosita's party at Le Roc in 1950 would become the scene of a dramatic jewel robbery. While she and her guests, who included the professional hostess Elsa Maxwell, played bridge downstairs a young Italian cat burglar Dante Spada, known as Tarzan, climbed the wall of the villa and entered through a small window, stealing jewellery worth around £20,000. Some of the jewels belonged to the avant-garde couturier Elsa Schiaparelli, who had invented the perfume Shocking. Dante was caught and brought to trial in Nice where some of the haul was recovered. According to the *Pittsburgh Post* of 17 August, Madame Schiaparelli, on the way to her house in Tunisia ten days later, was stopped by customs officers at Nice airport. As the result of a tip-off her luggage was searched and two small clips she had reported as stolen were found. Madame Schiaparelli maintained that she had discovered these jewels after the robbery, and had told the other guests in the villa although not the police. She was questioned by the Nice police for six hours before being allowed to go on her way 'on provisional freedom'.[10] One wonders who had tipped off the customs. Independently of all this, Schiaparelli Haute Couture did not prosper in the post-war era and closed in 1954.

At Rock's death Le Roc was inherited by his three children. In 1974 it was all sold to the new owners of the Château de l'Horizon along the coast and immediately neglected. Over the years the fabric of the house gradually deteriorated and the dramatic indoor swimming pool became unusable. In contrast to Maxine Elliott's Horizon, Le Roc has not been engulfed and changed beyond recognition, simply allowed to fall, shamefully, into decay. Barry Dierks's modernist creation is still flanked by the prow-like and neglected swimming pool. Protected by no one, with an indifferent owner, around these distinctive buildings undesirables regularly break through from the road above for various disreputable rendezvous in the garden Eric planned with such care. A murder of several years ago added to the degradation. Such has been the fate of the stylish, avant-garde Le Roc.

8

Le Moulin – 1935
Eric Cipriani Dunstan

The most talented and versatile man of our English colony
... was draped in apricot crêpe-de-chine and had gilded his
wavy white hair with metal paint.

Winifred Fortescue, *Laughter in Provence*

One January day in Mexico Eric Cipriani Dunstan, ex-BBC
announcer, 'the man with the golden voice', stood clutching
a bunch of wild flowers and watched with horror as the car
containing his wife of three months careered down a steep
incline before bumping to a stop at the bottom. It was 1938
and Flora Stifel, from West Virginia, was in the car with her
maid. Their chauffeur, who had not engaged the hand brake
properly, remained standing among the wild flowers with
Dunstan. The incline down which the car slid, near the town
of Cuernavaca, was known as The Death Drop. Her maid was
unhurt, but Flora broke her ankle in the accident and it was
thought at first that this was the extent of her injuries but,
taken to hospital in Mexico City, she died several days later
from internal complications, aggravated by pneumonia. As a
result, Eric Dunstan became a rich man.

In 1935 Dunstan had asked Barry Dierks to restore an old
mill house in the hills almost 13 kilometres above Cannes.

Although the house itself was tumbling down, it was set
in a virtual Garden of Eden. Fifty acres of water meadows
were flanked by hills of cistus, cork oaks, mimosa and vines.
On limestone soil, wild flowers such as marsh orchids,
Canterbury bells and anemones flourished. The six-metre-
wide Mourachonne River flowed through the property, clear
and sparkling in the sunshine, with its own small cascade.
Sluices would ensure that Barry and Eric were able to create
wide expanses of lawn, evoking an English garden. Dunstan
counted Barry Dierks and Eric Sawyer among his friends for,
as he recorded later, 'rare is the architect like Barry Dierks who
combines his own taste with a capacity to satisfy the personal
taste of his client'.[1] Various events in Dunstan's life during
the following years slowed down the work but eventually the
new house, built within the walls of the ancient mill, was large
and comfortable. Outside it had the air of a traditional French
country house, ochre-coloured and roofed with Roman tiles.
Only Barry's large, many-paned windows differentiated it from
a typical Provençal dwelling. The wide sitting room, both
elegant and welcoming, had the usual large stone fireplace to
guard against damp, cold winter nights. Virtually the only nod
to Modernism was a striking narrow stone staircase, flanked by
solid supports rendered white. Slender piers of narrow bricks
were placed at the turnings, this latter feature being echoed in
the large pergola on one of the terraces behind the house.

The land itself was a blank canvas. Eric used the water
in many ways – gushing out of the mouths of fauns and
satyrs, in shady pools and under bridges and, in a lower part
of the garden, a round swimming pool with a pool house
echoing the traditional design of the main house above. A
stone arched bridge led to the upper part of the land and
the cascade above the river meant that one always heard the
gentle sound of falling water.

Eric Dunstan and Flora Stifel must have been a
fascinating couple. Although their marriage was short

by any standards, they had known each other well for several years. Dunstan shared his exotic middle name with the composer Philip Cipriani Potter who, in turn, was named after his godmother, the sister of Giovanni Battista Cipriani, the painter and engraver of eighteenth-century Florence. The connection was through Dunstan's mother Edith Turner, who had been a friend of Philip Potter. Edith was herself a talented painter of landscapes. In 1891 she married Malcolm Dunstan, who would have a distinguished career as director, first of the Midland Dairy Institute and then of Wye Agricultural College in Kent. Their son Eric was born in 1894 at Hamilton Drive in the shadow of Nottingham Castle. A tiny baby, he would grow to over six feet. Dunstan would have no children but his two sisters, Joan and Hester, ensured the continuation of the Dunstan line.

Sent to Radley College school in Oxfordshire which, at that time, his prep school considered the 'Home for Lost Dogs', Dunstan, in his engaging, unpublished autobiography of 1951 wrote that his years there were uneventful: 'At games I was a wreck.' His final report on leaving said he had, 'A positive genius – for doing the minimum of work and escaping detection.' But he had a good voice, good enough to gain a singing scholarship to Magdalen College, Oxford, where, in 1912, he became an academical clerk, singing bass with a grant of £95 a year, having beaten 14 other candidates to the post. An academical clerk became a member of the choir but was also expected to attend lectures, tutorials and to graduate like other students. So one damp October evening in 1912, searching for his rooms, he found his way through 'the dim-lit foggy cloisters to my door'. Here his path was partially blocked by packing cases containing glass and silverware – Edward, Prince of Wales, was moving into the rooms next door. Dunstan and the Prince would become casual friends at Magdalen.

Dunstan thrived at Oxford. With the respected Dr John Varley Roberts as choirmaster and organist he grew to love the music and liturgy, a love which remained with him throughout his life. When war was declared he, like so many other eager young men, joined up two days after the declaration of hostilities, abruptly leaving his studies. His first posting was as 2nd lieutenant with Kitchener's 2nd New Army. After training he spent six months on the Italian Front. But it was not long before he was writing to the president of the college, 'Magdalen seems like a vivid dream', asking that his place be kept open in the event of his return. Back in England he transferred to the 7th Service Battalion East Kent Regiment, known as The Buffs, and was sent back to France with the rank of captain. Posted again to the Front, he went on to run a bombing school as brigade bombing officer: 'A perilous experience, but I was lucky and so were my pupils.' Tuberculosis put an end to his time in the army and probably saved his life, for in 1916 he escaped the first day of the Somme where his battalion lost 22 officers and many men. Accepted back into Magdalen, he finally graduated in 1917.

Meanwhile, where was Flora Stifel? She was born in 1877 in Wheeling, West Virginia, where the family owned a large Victorian mansion on Main Street. The family firm of J. L. Stifel was founded by Johann Stifel, Flora's grandfather. Stifel was a German Jew who had emigrated to America in 1833 and, true to the American dream, gradually built up one of the most important calico printing companies in the Central States. Her father was William Stifel, Johann's son, and her mother Emma Schandein from Philadelphia. The couple had three children, Ann, Flora and Arthur. William Stifel was a director of many of the important companies in Wheeling, and the family was respected in the community. In 1903 Flora moved to Des Moines, Iowa, where she married Porterfield Krauth Witmer, a founder of one of the city's insurance companies. This was a marriage that lasted for 18 years until

Witmer's death, and of which little is known. There were no children.

Flora would never be beautiful. Strangely, she had a striking resemblance to her future friend, Wallis Simpson. Now a rich widow, Flora must have done some thinking. She set about metamorphosing herself into a chic figure of the international set and fundamentally changed her appearance and her life. Her ambition was to live in society and in a world away from Des Moines. What she lacked in good looks she made up for in extravagance, to the despair of William, her down-to-earth father in Wheeling. She travelled to Paris, where she took an apartment in the Crillon Hotel (a former palace of Louis XV) on the Place de la Concorde, and set about meeting the socialites and luminaries of the day.

During these years of Flora's transformation, Dunstan set out to earn his living. It was 1917 and he was convalescing at the Marquess of Bath's stately home of Longleat in Wiltshire, then being used as a temporary hospital, when he spotted an advertisement for, 'Public work in the South of Spain, suitable for an invalided officer'. At the interview in London he was asked if he could speak Spanish: 'Not a word', and glanced at by his interviewers with the pronouncement 'He'll do'. Which was how he became assistant to Arthur Keyser, the consul in Seville. He was 22. He felt that his classical education was: 'as good as, if not better than, any other form of upbringing. It leaves you with a reasonably trained mind, no money, reasonable looks, and a determination to get as much out of life as possible.'

On his way to Seville, Dunstan stayed at the Palace Hotel in Madrid with the governor of Gibraltar, Sir Herbert Miles. Uneventful, except for one evening. Having leant nonchalantly against the bar, the whole counter collapsed showering him with bottles, fried potatoes, glasses and liquid, but leaving him unhurt. Life was destined never to be dull. Installed at Seville, one of his jobs was to grant visas to travellers. Secret markings on the visas gave information to Allied controls at the frontiers. Spain, being neutral, was full of spies. All went well, apart from Dunstan having marked the Lord Provost of Glasgow's passport with the wrong figures, which resulted in the latter being put under close arrest at the French frontier until able to prove his innocence.

When the military attaché at the Madrid Embassy died suddenly Dunstan found himself a temporary diplomat. His stay in Spain was unmarked by further catastrophe, but during the winter he fell ill again and was, via a posting at the British legation at the Hague, sent back to England to convalesce at Hove in Sussex. Here fate stepped in once more through a meeting with Sir Anthony Stanley, chairman of the British Red Cross Society, who offered him a job in Italy. Stanley was the brother of Lord Derby for whom Barry Dierks would later remodel the Villa Sansovino, Derby's Cannes home, and with whom Dunstan would work when another war loomed. As a sub-commissioner in the Red Cross, he was sent to the Italian Front in charge of four ambulances and two X-ray units. His group was run by the Quakers, for whom he had unconditional respect. A sudden attack by the Austrians on Caporetto in north-east Italy in 1917 brought his outfit firmly into the war. The various Red Cross units would lose 80 of their 130 ambulances.

Returning to London, Dunstan was then appointed private secretary to Sir John Tilley, chief clerk at the Foreign Office. But fate always seemed to decree that he should keep moving – he rarely applied for overseas assignments, they always seemed to present themselves. A friend of the imperial secretary to the high commissioner in South Africa wandered into his office in Whitehall one day and announced that the secretary, Sir Cecil Rodwell, had been awarded his first governorship and was looking for, 'a young fellow who wanted to see a bit of the world'. The part of the world in question was the Fiji Islands. Dunstan jumped at the chance. Released from his Foreign Office job, he set sail for Australia on a Union Castle freighter transporting 300 English wives going to join their Australian soldier husbands – an interesting journey during which six babies were born.

Australia was bitterly cold. Billeted at Federal Government House Dunstan had another slight mishap. Seeing a fire neatly laid in the fireplace in his bedroom, he put a match to it before going down to lunch. On returning later he found the fire burning away beautifully but, the chimney being shut, the room full of dense smoke and all his carefully unpacked possessions covered in soot!

It took three months to travel by sea from Sydney to Suva, the capital of Fiji. He was entranced by the country, its beauty and its inhabitants, and his two years there were happy, 'our pleasures are Arcadian', although he feared for the future of the islands. By 1920 he felt he must try at last to earn some real money and make his way in the world – and so began the long journey back to London. Sitting in his club, the Bath Club on Dover Street, he mused with friends as to what sort of job he could do. One made the suggestion he should go to see Gordon Selfridge at his great Selfridges department store in Oxford Street and offer his services. Dunstan didn't see Selfridge, who was in America, but was taken on as a salesman in the basement department at £3 a week, an unusual occupation for an ex-public schoolboy at that time. His friends were embarrassed when they encountered him at his post – after all, he was now 'in trade'. When Selfridge returned and was told of this rather strange new addition to the basement staff, he sent for Dunstan who explained he had just returned from a posting in Fiji. One of Selfridge's first questions was, 'What are the women like in Fiji?', an area in which Dunstan, being homosexual, was not particularly interested. Selfridge needed a private secretary and Dunstan was immediately taken on at an increase of £2 a week. He would stay with Gordon Selfridge for six years.

In his autobiography, Dunstan describes Selfridge as a lovable man to whom his staff were devoted. For someone who had begun his working life by selling newspapers in Jackson, Michigan, Selfridge had done spectacularly well. His one weakness was women, the more expensive and extravagant the better. His long suffering wife had died in the influenza epidemic of 1918 but his formidable mother kept him more or less on the straight and narrow until her death in 1924, thus avoiding the worst of the scandals which would later beset him. Wildly extravagant in his later years, besotted by the ill-fated Dolly Sisters – an all-singing, all-gambling Vaudeville act – in 1947 he would die, almost destitute in Putney, South West London. But in the 1920s Selfridges was the epitome of successful retailing. The enormous store brought sparkle to London. Dunstan spoke to a bright young thing who remarked, in the course of conversation: 'Marvellous, we can come into the store and steal. I've always wanted to swipe silk undies'. He lived with Selfridge and his four children in their rented Lansdowne House on Berkeley Square and became an excellent and supportive private secretary during a period when Selfridges ruled the roost among stores in London. Flamboyant displays and promotions constantly drew crowds to the windows and into the store.

Selfridge also gave important receptions at the grand Lansdowne House as well as at the store. Dunstan organised the first of the six general election parties which would be held in Selfridges. On the night of the wedding of the Duke and Duchess of York (later King George VI and Queen Elizabeth) Selfridge gave a supper party for some of the members of those royal families who had visited London for the wedding. The supper procession, which included King Alfonso of Spain, was progressing to the marquee in the garden, when a figure in a low-cut red dress suddenly jumped the line and flung her arms round the neck of Selfridge, who was escorting a princess of the royal party. The dancer,

Isadora Duncan, dishevelled and drunk, was renewing her acquaintance with Gordon Selfridge. Told to 'Get rid of her, for Heaven's sake', Dunstan pursued Isadora's flight up to the ballroom where the orchestra was playing waltzes and where she was about to launch into dance. He scooped her up and carried her, struggling vigorously, out of the house and into a taxi, from where he deposited her into the care of the housekeeper of her hotel. He was certainly an indispensable private secretary. His social connections grew as time went on and he became a great asset to Selfridge and his store.

At the end of six years Dunstan grew restless, feeling it was again time to seek pastures new. For a brief period he worked as a salesman in the shop of the interior decorator Syrie Maugham, estranged wife of Somerset Maugham and an ex-mistress of Gordon Selfridge. It was not a job he enjoyed and he left it to run a temporary labour exchange during the general strike of 1926. He was a fairly liberal-minded Conservative, had been involved with the Conservative Party at Magdalen and continued to support it. He had no sympathy with the strikers, feeling that the average man and woman were, 'not to be dictated to'. Once the strike was over, and still job-hunting, he visited the office of the impresario Rupert D'Oyley Carte on the Strand, from where the Savoy, Berkeley and Claridges hotels were run. The D'Oyley Carte office was across the street from the BBC and, while in the waiting room, Dunstan spotted a friend enter that building. Abandoning the D'Oyley Carte office, he went into the BBC, then in Savoy Place, and asked his friend for a job. Rapidly, 'I found myself with a Bible, a programme and a newspaper, being tested at a microphone – and I was lucky again.' He would always consider himself lucky.

So began Eric Dunstan's eventful life as announcer, journalist and commentator. In his diary he wrote 'announcing in those far off days was a novelty which gave the person concerned a mysterious glamour, though requiring no more than a clear speaking voice and a modicum of common sense'. A formidable presence in the BBC at that time was the complicated and dictatorial director general, John Reith. Although Dunstan complimented him for having fought for the integrity and dignity of the corporation, his eventual clash with Reith would make BBC history. But there were no such problems in 1926 when two rich Indian cotton merchants decided India needed its own version of the BBC and, together with the Marconi Company, put up the capital to form the Indian Broadcasting Company. Reith appointed Dunstan general manager. In the India Room of the British Library is a large file consisting of correspondence between Dunstan, Reith and Lord Birkenhead, the secretary of state for India. The project begins hopefully enough but underfunding, a population with many dialects and the poor sales of radio licences across the continent follows a trail from optimism to virtual despair on the part of Dunstan. In order to reach audiences to make the project viable they were obliged to broadcast in English, Urdu, Bengali and Gujarati from their two small bases in Bombay and Calcutta. But while he, himself, was well paid to the tune of £3,000 a year (a very large amount in those days) the allowance to run the India project was £2.10 a day. The capital was inadequate to pay running expenses and the company was soon at the end of its resources. The Indian businessmen withdrew their support. From Dunstan's letters it is clear how hard he worked to make the Indian Broadcasting Company succeed and how much and how often he tried to encourage investment, but in vain. After three years he resigned, mortified at the failure of what he felt had been an inspired idea. The company went bankrupt, later becoming the Indian State Broadcasting Company, 'a genuine Indian company', and Dunstan returned once again to England.

There had been highlights, one of which was meeting Mahatma Gandhi at Jehu Beach near Bombay. He found

Gandhi, in his dhoti, washing himself with soap in the sea. They retired to his palm-leaf shack and had a long conversation about broadcasting in India. As he had with Fiji, Dunstan loved the country and its people and would grasp the opportunity to return in very different circumstances.

Once back with the BBC, now a senior announcer due to his 'golden voice', he settled down to his former job before fate played another of the small tricks with which it punctuated his life. The election of 1929 would be won by the Labour Party's Ramsay MacDonald. John Reith, nursing what some considered an over-developed ego, often took part in the announcing for great historic occasions. On this particular occasion, and at the last minute, he proposed to announce the election results himself during the second news bulletin of the evening. Reith was not a natural announcer, and as soon as he got into the swing of things, the telephones began ringing asking for the results to be given out clearer and slower and for 'a regular announcer to be put on'. It was a difficult situation, everyone was in awe of Reith but, perhaps not surprisingly, it was Dunstan who volunteered to tell him of the public's opinion. He said, 'I did my best to politely inform him of the position', but Reith's terse reply was, 'I will not read any slower, I am going on announcing', turning his back on the messenger. Dunstan, furious at being ticked off, told his colleagues of his lack of success. Later that night, as he was leaving the building to go to Gordon Selfridge's election-night party at the store, as luck would have it and while tempers were still hot, he met Reith who asked him where he was going. When told, Reith replied: 'You can go and need not come back till I send for you.'

Arriving at Selfridge's, Dunstan found the party in full swing and headed straight for the supper room and the bar. Asked why he wasn't on duty at the BBC on election night, he told bitterly of the events of the evening. Charles Graves, brother of the author Robert Graves, was a journalist on the *Daily Mail* newspaper and future author of *The Royal Riviera*. Graves sat and listened quietly. Dunstan spent the evening at the party, had no idea how he got home and woke in the morning to, 'a revolving pillow and an outsize headache'. At lunchtime he arrived at his club to be greeted with the news that the *Daily Mail* was sporting large headlines, 'Dispute in BBC Studio' followed by the whole story of his row with Reith. Realising he would now have no future at the corporation, he rang up and resigned. He was replaced immediately, the BBC stating he had left because, 'He used tendentious inflexions in announcing the results.'

Dunstan was out of work for several hours. That afternoon he received a telephone call asking him to visit the editor of the *Star* newspaper, run by the Quaker Cadbury family. He became one of their journalists and the first radio critic on a daily newspaper. Launched in 1888, the *Star* would always be a liberal paper, 'championing the cause of the underprivileged and highlighting the needs of working class families'. This was something new for Dunstan but he had a happy, well-paid relationship with his new employer, a relationship which would last for eight years. He deemed the Cadburys and their associates 'the best employers in Fleet Street' and was gratified to see 'Read Eric Dunstan in *The Star*' twinkling in lights in Leicester Square. Lucky again.

British Movietone News was launched in 1929 and became the first sound newsreel in Britain. The parent company was Fox Movietone News in America and British Movietone went into competition with other newsreels, such as Pathé. Dunstan joined Movietone soon after the launch and so began to present once again. He was now a commentator, providing commentaries on events, national and international, rather than an announcer relaying the news of the day. To present day ears his delivery seems clipped, even staccato, but it was of his time and his voice is very clear. He would say his voice was, 'something between a butler's and a bishop's', which meant he was in demand for solemn occasions such as important funerals and international events. He was commentator on the events of the Abyssinian-Italian War, the Silver Jubilee of King George V in 1935 (which showed the first colour newsreel) and the funeral of the King in the following year. Now famous and admired, he was settled and happy. In 1934 he had acted, as himself, in a Pinewood Studios film, *Death at Broadcasting House*, a mystery with perhaps a touch of irony in the title.

Dunstan took his holidays on the Mediterranean and one year, planning to visit Morocco, he found himself stranded in Marseilles – his boat having been shipwrecked. He took a plane to Tunis and from there travelled to what was then the small town of Hammamet, 76 kilometres south of Tunis and built on the Gulf which bears its name. He found a simply furnished white room and felt it was all perfect. On the long and deserted sandy beach he bathed naked and lay down in one of the dunes for a siesta. He awoke to find an amiable, plump man gazing down at him. This was a French count, Max Foy, and it was through him that Dunstan became involved in the exotic expatriate social scene of Hammamet, and it was here he met Flora Stifel.

It may have been in Paris that Flora, newly transformed into a chic socialite, came across an aristocratic Romanian with light blue, slightly unnerving eyes, and the profile of a Greek statue. Karl Georges Sebastian was 33 and Flora 52, although she professed to be seven years younger. They married in New York in November 1929. This marriage of convenience would produce Dar Sebastian, one of the most stunning private houses in North Africa. Flora's marriage to Sebastian was, for a while, a satisfactory partnership. He was homosexual – a fact which seemed to suit Flora very well. Social life was far easier with a husband in tow. The third person in their marriage was Sebastian's lover, the American artist Porter Woodruff, responsible for many of the covers of *Vogue* magazine of that time.

The couple led an international life, moving constantly between the United States, Paris and further afield. Sebastian had already bought a large stretch of land on the bay of Hammamet and begun the plans for a summer home there. His marriage to an indulgent Flora meant that her money would ensure the house became far more than a mere holiday villa and would be renowned for its style and beauty. Designed mainly by Sebastian and built by an Italian builder, it had all the elements of a perfect Moorish dwelling. Flat-roofed, sharp edged and sparkling white, it contained arches, arcades, courtyards, large cool rooms with wide groined ceilings, terraces, studded doors – in fact, all the romance of North Africa.

Many artists, actors and celebrities visited Hammamet during the 1920s and 1930s, lured by its beauty, simplicity and those expatriates who had built elegant houses on its shores. Sometime during the early 1930s the paths of Sebastian, Wallis Simpson and her husband Ernest had crossed. By 1932 the Simpsons were in straitened circumstances and Sebastian, wishing to show them his Hammamet home, sent them two return tickets from London. The trip was to be in March and would include a journey to the edge of the desert. Wallis wrote to her Aunt Bessie that she would buy only 'One light coloured flannel suit for the trip, which could be used here [in England] in the country afterwards.'[2] But by the time Flora and Sebastian visited her in London in 1934, Wallis was worrying less about clothes. Her affair with Edward, Prince of Wales, was well under way and she had 'bought a coat and dress with the $200 the Prince gave me ... along with some leopard skins'.[3]

Dunstan returned to Hammamet several times but was not at ease with the cosmopolitan, pleasure-seeking set who had built their attractive houses in the bay:

As there so often is with those exquisite beauty spots which attract intelligent, idle people ... the intimate friend of one day is the bitter enemy of the next. I could never be sure from one year to another who would be friends with whom – which was a pity.

But he valued the country for its culture and Roman and Phoenician history, evident in its many classical ruins. He always appreciated the people of the places in which he travelled saying, 'When people say to me "I loathe the French or the Italians or the Egyptians or the Americans" I know that person has mostly himself to blame. Bad manners breed, and vice versa.'

One person who was presumably no longer a friend was Georges Sebastian, for in January 1936 Flora divorced him in the United States, taking her fortune with her, and by September 1937 had married Dunstan, her friend from Hammamet. Flora, lonely and unhappy after her divorce, had gone to England where she saw a lot of Dunstan, still working at Movietone News. One of the reasons she was unhappy was that she kept bumping into people who had known her in lovely Dar Sebastian and Dunstan, always kindly in such cases, was able to comfort her. Sebastian stayed on at the villa, reputedly in more reduced circumstances. At the declaration of war in 1939 he fled to the United States and Dar Sebastian was requisitioned by the German Army, Rommel passing through for a couple of nights. Eventually, finding it impossible to maintain, in the early 1960s Sebastian sold the villa to the Tunisian government. Preserved, it is now the International Cultural Centre of Hammamet. Barry and Eric knew North Africa and may even have visited Dar Sebastian. Certainly Barry was much influenced by Arab architecture in his own designs.

Dunstan and Flora were spending a weekend in Paris to visit the 1937 Exhibition when, one evening over dinner,

Flora mused that she might change her name from Sebastian, with its unhappy connotations. She then asked why she didn't change it to Dunstan. At that stage she was 60 and Dunstan was 43. It was all very measured, Dunstan pointing out that everyone would say he was marrying Flora for her money, and he couldn't very well marry her without it, adding, 'I think you'd be a fool if you did [marry me].' But by September of that year they had married in Paris and set off to visit their respective families.

It seems that Dunstan had no known intimate relationships with women, although it is also evident that throughout his life he had many women friends whom he liked and valued. He was extremely discreet about his homosexual affairs – a necessity anyway in England, where such relationships were illegal. Those who knew him felt that he preferred only brief liaisons with no commitment. It is difficult to know what his relations were with Flora. There is a slight clue in that, in their hotel in New York, at the end of the day they walked to their separate rooms on the 20th floor and he kissed her goodnight in the corridor. He mentions this fact because he felt as if 'Flora had kissed me with a mouthful of pins' – static from the carpets.

Dunstan got on very well with Flora's family in Wheeling, and from there they travelled to Chicago, Des Moines and St Louis and then, in January 1938, on to Mexico – 'I wish we never had.' For it was here that Flora would die of the injuries sustained by the fall of her car over the incline. Many were the rumours that flew around the Riviera for years afterwards. But during the remaining hours of her life Flora apportioned no blame, the inquest recorded accidental death and her family accepted the verdict and remained good friends with Dunstan, with whom they corresponded regularly. Later Flora's brother would donate money towards a restoration project at the Sunny Bank Anglo-American Hospital in Cannes.

In the year of Flora's death Dunstan's father, Malcolm, also died and Dunstan, now virtually retired, took his mother to Cannes where he, Barry and Eric began in earnest, and with more ample funds, to continue to work on the restoration of the house he would call Le Moulin. By now Dunstan had few money worries. At Christmas of 1938 Le Moulin had its house-warming party. It was all idyllic for 18 months before, as Dunstan said: 'That lunatic bastard of a house-painter set the world in flames.'

During the Phoney War which followed the declaration of hostilities in September 1939, the expatriates of the Riviera rose from their sun loungers and began to plan energetically many and various aid programmes. Dunstan quickly organised the Anglo-American Ambulance Service in Cannes as well as being involved in other charities. One day he received a letter from John Snagge, a senior newsreader at the BBC, suggesting he return to the corporation as they were short of announcers. He was delighted to take up this offer, John Reith having resigned in 1938. His first 6 p.m. news reading in London contained Winston Churchill's famous speech on the determination of the British people to fight on regardless, an important occasion. However, next morning he was told he had too much personality and was taken off announcing. The disappointment must have been great. Although the BBC invented a nebulous job for him, he knew there would be no new career for him there. While he was in London France fell, and returning to Le Moulin to put his affairs in order suddenly became an impossibility. There was also tragedy. His remaining family lived in 'Bomb Alley' between Maidstone in Kent and the capital. A German plane, returning to base, unloaded its bombs after a raid on London, and one fell directly on his mother's house. His sister was killed outright, his mother's companion severely wounded and his mother untouched but so shocked she died shortly afterwards. Later in the war his surviving sister, who lived in nearby Offham, would count 890 doodlebugs (the V-1 flying bomb) passing over her house in one day.

Through a cousin Dunstan now became part of a secret intelligence unit and was posted to Egypt, where he lived in pleasant circumstances in Maadi, an affluent suburb of Cairo, for three and a half years. The unit was set up to interrogate German and Italian prisoners but, as Dunstan spoke neither of these languages well, he was put in another 'secret' section and promoted to major. As the war moved west he was sent to an organisation dealing with refugees, sorting the men into various fighting groups. This took him to Palestine, Lebanon, Syria and Turkey.

Back in Cairo, he bumped into Basil Dean, the theatre and film producer. In 1939 Dean, along with the comedian and director Leslie Henson, had formed ENSA, the Entertainments National Service Association. The association was intended to provide entertainment for both home and overseas troops in World War II. It was all a great challenge. Dancers, comedians, singers and actors often travelled uncomfortably and dangerously over unforgiving terrain to find themselves dressing and making up in small cramped tents and performing on makeshift stages in front of thousands of homesick servicemen and terribly injured men in hospital wards. The performers were often either boiling hot or freezing cold and the pressures were enormous, but the greatest actors and entertainers of the day joined ENSA, leaving their comfortable homes and theatres to travel overseas in order to entertain the troops. However, the demand and the area to cover were great and the project over-stretched, causing those less talented to be included in the company. The latter and their programmes were often sub-standard, prompting the alternative label 'Every Night Something Awful'.

It was into this particular theatre of war that Dunstan now entered. Dean needed someone to start up ENSA in South

1. Le Trident, with the trident shaped rocks below

2. Elegant Barry

3. Barry and Eric in their study

4. Barry and friends relaxing

5. The upstairs corridor at Le Trident, with its succession of arches

6. Somerset Maugham in a rooftop folly, built by the previous owner of La Mauresque

7. Maugham and Alan Searle dining in the Moorish patio at La Mauresque

8. Maugham on the staircase at La Mauresque

9. Freddy McEvoy, Beatrice's fourth and racy husband

10. The Casa Estella from Millionaire's Bay on the Cap d'Antibes

11. Beatrice Cartwright painted by Reynaldo Luza. Watercolour 1943

13. An aerial view of Le Roc and its Mendelsohn-style pool house

12. Maxine Elliott in 1908, breaking the ground for the Maxine Elliott theatre in New York

14. The spectacular Château de l'Horizon with its famous slide, beloved of Winston Churchill

15. Lord and Lady Cholmondeley of Le Roc, luxuriating in sun and sea

16. The sinuous lines of the Villa Aujourd'hui on the Cap d'Antibes

17. Eric Sawyer (left) and a fellow driver for the Cannes Anglo-American ambulance service, 1940

18. Isabel Pell and her dog Heine under house arrest at Le Moulin, 1943

19. Jack Warner with two of his most feisty stars: Bette Davis (left) and Joan Crawford (right)

East Asia. Dunstan would be based in India and jumped at the chance of returning there. As was usual with him he fell on his feet regarding lodgings, being offered the bungalow belonging to the Aly Khan and his first wife, Joan Yarde-Buller. From his office in a room in the Taj Mahal Hotel in Bombay he was soon heading up an average of 200 personnel and 300 to 400 visiting artistes. The latter were assigned venues ranging from the Khyber Pass to Burma and all over India. Here they had to put up with torrential rain, sticky heat and filthy billets, with the Japanese Army often unnervingly near. Dunstan's job was to get them all on the road and keep supplying entertainment. He was frequently impressed by the dedication of many of the performers and their kindness to the troops, beyond the call of duty.

In 1944 Noel Coward, on one of his numerous journeys entertaining the troops, narrowly avoided death while being chauffeured around by his old friend Eric Dunstan. The group had been driving along in a limousine belonging to the Aly Khan when the car crashed into a naval lorry which had turned sharply off the road. Ricocheting off the lorry the car then skidded into a palm tree and then the sea wall, losing its back wheels in the process. A frantic Dunstan was unaffected by the crash but Coward was briefly knocked unconscious, suffering from his bruises for many days afterwards.

The actress and comedian Joyce Grenfell was also in Bombay in that year and wrote in *The Time of My Life*:

Eric Dunstan is older than I'd expected [he was then 50] with a long neat head covered in silver white hair ... His blue eyes pop a trifle and he is fairly sure of himself but he is considerate and imaginative and, unless crossed, I feel he will be able to get on with. There is something of the bully in him which I don't fancy and his temper is very touchy. But that may be the climate and he is rather overworked.[4]

Like so many others, Joyce Grenfell had been critical of the ongoing organisation and standards of ENSA, but now felt that the set-up in India would be different:

> I've got to revise my views and prejudices about ENSA. Eric has raised its standard high out here and is determined to keep it that way. He is very ruthless and if a show, although rehearsed and passed by Drury Lane [a London theatre], doesn't pass his standards, he re-orders it and sends home the artists who won't do or who don't know how to behave. In fact he has discipline and enforces it. Long may he continue ... Basil Dean is due here soon.[5]

Basil Dean arrived and Dunstan felt Dean 'had the unhappiest knack of spoiling his own creation by his own personality – it was impossible not to fall out with him', which he promptly did and resigned, returning to England via a trip to the North West Frontier, the Khyber Pass and Kabul.

Just after Victory in Europe (VE) Day on 8 May 1945, Dunstan came again to his peaceful Moulin in Provence. With a competent staff hired to run his house and garden, including a devoted Indian servant who had followed him from India, he settled down to become one of the most agreeable and worthy members of the expatriate community. He became chairman of the committee of Sunny Bank hospital in Cannes which, remaining open under its English matron, had come through the war years of constant deprivation. And there was much to be done among the undernourished population on the Riviera, where everything was still scarce or unobtainable and, due to the various political and military upheavals, morale was low. When his Indian servant eventually returned to India, Dunstan continued to support his family, enabling the young son to attend university and go on to have a successful career in banking in New York.

In his water meadows in the hills, Dunstan was far from the crowds increasingly thronging the Croisette in Cannes and the Promenade des Anglais in Nice. He was busy and popular – silver-haired and golden-voiced. And apart from being given permission to use his 'ceremonial voice' for part of the commentary on the funeral of King George VI in February 1952, he did not work again.

Winifred, Lady Fortescue, author of evocative best-selling books of the 1930s based on her life in the hills above the Riviera, in *Laughter in Provence* describes a *fête champêtre* given by Dunstan, 'the most talented and versatile man of our English colony'.[6] It was to be on a night of the full moon. Everyone was instructed to wear Greek or Roman attire. Dunstan himself was draped in apricot crêpe de Chine and had gilded his wavy white hair with metal paint. He was a noble Roman senator. In the garden of Le Moulin, lit by Chinese lanterns and fairy lights, Winifred Fortescue 'watched shadowy classical figures wandering among the flowers like a dream of the past ... At midnight a huge bonfire was lit in the field in front of the house, and goddesses, gods, fauns, dryads and satyrs danced around it wildly to the strains of a capering gypsy band.'[7] And there were many dim corners in the garden where these ethereal beings could disport themselves.

In 1958, when he was 64, Dunstan sold his beloved Moulin and moved to the more manageable Ferme des Orangers on the Cap d'Antibes. Here he created another garden, a true Riviera one this time. A friend, John Halsey, remembers the party Dunstan gave there for Somerset Maugham's birthday, among the huge drifts of agapanthus bordering paths under orange and lemon trees: 'The scent of citrus blossom was overwhelming and heavenly. Huge terracotta jars were awash with trailing geraniums.'[8] He lived contentedly on the Cap until his death in May 1973, dying peacefully in Sunny Bank Hospital.

In the main it had been a good life and, as he said, he had almost always been lucky.

⊷⟞⟝ 9 ⟞⟝⊶

The Villa Aujourd'hui – 1938
Jack Warner

> Motivated by the sinuous road, the powerful play of curves
> magnifies this daring composition. His masterpiece.
>
> <div align="right">Charles Bilas and Rosso Lucien, <i>Côte d'Azur</i></div>

On an August night of 1958, the film producer Jack
Leonard Warner crashed his Alfa Romeo on the Boulevard
Maréchal Juin, the curving coast road of the Cap d'Antibes.
It was 2 a.m. and Warner, sleek, tough and brash, had just
won two million francs after a six-hour game of baccarat
at the Palm Beach Casino in Cannes. Passing the Aga
Khan's Villa Jane-Andrée on his left he fell asleep, his car
drifted over the road and straight into the path of a coal
truck, then flipped over and burst into flames, flinging
Jack out 40 feet, hitting the road head first. The driver
of the truck was unhurt and Jack was gathered up by the
occupants of a passing car. The impact hadn't killed him
but was severe enough to keep him in the Cannes hospital
of La Broussailles for four months besides causing other,
enduring, problems.

Warner had been going home, and home was Barry's most
spectacular creation on the Riviera. The Villa Aujourd'hui
had been commissioned in 1938 by Mrs Audrey Chadwick
whose then husband was president of the Chicago Towel

120

Company. Unusually forward-thinking for a Palm Beach socialite, described as resembling a dainty Dresden figurine, she was a collector of modern art and a friend of the artist Salvador Dali, owning several of his works. Dali inscribed to her his painting, *Las llamas, llamans*: 'The Flames, They Call'. She encouraged the local museum to buy the paintings of other modern artists and was involved with a sociological work, *The Gold Coast and the Slums* by Harvey Zorbaugh, her section being, rather surprisingly, on the slums. In 1931 she had asked the architect Maurice Fatio to build one of the first Art Deco villas on the Via Bellaria in Miami Beach. She called this Florida house 'Today'. Her favourite Greek key pattern was incorporated into window surrounds and the eggshell lacquer panels of the double entrance doors. These were commissioned from Henri Dunand, who would go on to decorate the luxurious *Normandie* ocean liner.

Linking her two homes, she would call her Riviera house Villa Aujourd'hui. Many of the details of the Florida house were incorporated into the house on the Cap d'Antibes, and the design was an audacious response to the constraints of the site. Rendered in purest white, it undulates in curve and counter-curve along the narrow coast road, the most dramatic modern villa to be built on the Riviera before World War II. Barry, exaggerating, would say that the total space he had to work in was about the size of a grand piano.

On this piece of land, on the very edge of the bay, had stood a small turn-of-the-century villa called Le Bungalow. As he had done with the folly at Le Roc, Barry pulled it down. Inside the new house, corners, windows and doors were curved. In the reception rooms curved plate glass windows overlooked the great sweep of bay, with panoramic views from Juan-les-Pins to Golfe Juan. A great metal-framed glass door gave onto small but charming terraces overlooking the narrow public beach below. A cantilevered staircase, with spindles of twisted green Murano glass led to a curved landing under a glass dome. The name on the front of the villa was picked out in glass studs. Greek key patterns around the windows were not forgotten.

There was a certain amount of *va et vient* between the owners of houses on the Cap and Florida's Miami Beach. Audrey Chadwick of Aujourd'hui, Beatrice Cartwright of the Casa Estella (who also owned 'Estella' on Miami Beach), Lady Norman of La Garoupe and the Duke and Duchess of Windsor from the Château de la Croê, entertained each other in both places.

In 1949 Audrey, now Mrs Le Ray Burdeau, sold Aujourd'hui to the producer Jack Warner. Once Jack Warner became the owner, the fairly discreet socialising of latter day gave way to party-time. Over the years, through the double front door, stepped film stars with household names, particularly during the ten days of the Cannes film festival each year when entertaining was relentless. They came to enjoy Jack's hospitality, recline under the Mediterranean pines around which the terraces were built, to swim from the tiny beach and sunbathe among its fishing boats.

Jack Warner and his brothers were the sons of Jewish immigrants from an area of Poland under the control of the Russian Empire. Benjamin, a cobbler by trade, and his wife Pearl, fled to the United States with their two children to escape the persecution of Jewish communities. Once in America they changed their name to Warner and had more children, five boys and three girls in all. They moved between America and Canada as Benjamin tried to earn a living for his large family. Jack was born in Ontario, Canada, but would grow up in a district of Youngstown, Ohio. Here a grocery store and a bicycle shop were added to the family's acquisitions.

Along with his older brothers, Harry, Albert and Sam, Jack seems to have been drawn to the entertainment industry from a young age. The four began their stellar careers in film in 1904 by buying an Edison Kinetoscope machine, which came with a reel entitled *The Great Train Robbery*. They showed this in small towns around Ohio and Pennsylvania. The reel showed a train rushing silently towards a thrilled, often frightened, audience while bandits fired equally silent gunshots. All this was hard work and made no money, but the idea of film-making was born and none of the brothers would pursue another career. Realising they would never become successful unless they had a permanent home for their Kinetoscope, the family elected to pawn some of their possessions and sell their bicycle shop, virtually their only sizeable asset. They rented a hall in New Castle, Ohio, advertising 'Refined Entertainment for Ladies, Gentlemen and Children'.[1] A sign asked gentlemen not to spit on the floor. Warner Brothers were on their way.

Moving on from their rented hall to a small theatre they called the Cascade Movie Palace, they rented and showed ever more film reels and went on to acquire 15 more theatres in Pennsylvania. Once they began their distribution and film exchange, things moved fast. In a venture headed by the capable business brain of the elder brother Harry, plus the technical expertise of Sam, Albert (Abe) as treasurer and the extrovert, ever-performing Jack as producer, this tightly knit family group, united by ambition and affection for each other, headed to Hollywood.

After a series of dramatic trials and errors, in 1918 the brothers launched their studio in rented sheds on a Hollywood lot. The Warners were trailblazers, producing in 1918 the first full-length film, *My Four Years in Germany*, a war propaganda film. In 1927 they produced the first 'talkie' with *The Jazz Singer*. Al Jolson was the star, and the film brought him eternal fame. The production used the Vitaphone sound-on-disc process, ensuring silent films would begin to disappear into history. During the 1920s their most

successful series was *Rin Tin Tin*, the adventures of a German
Shepherd dog. But two rather different films put Warners
firmly on the map. In 1931 James Cagney starred in *The Public
Enemy* and Edward G. Robinson and Douglas Fairbanks Jr in
Little Caesar. These were tough crime films in which women
were ill-treated and murder was the theme. They made stars
of their main actors and gave rise to a series of fast-moving,
fast-talking and profitable gangster dramas. The motto of the
studios was 'Educate, Entertain and Enlighten'. However,
the productions of this period were frequently titillating and
risqué, so much so that the profession began to get a bad
name and there were calls for 'Hollywood to be cleaned up'.
Many of these films were awash with women shedding their
clothes down to attractive underwear. Few films seemed to
be complete without a scene or two of female disrobing. In
Warner's *Gold Diggers of 1933* Ginger Rogers and her troupe
sang and danced with large gold coins covering strategic
parts. This type of film led to the foundation of the Hays
Code, a form of moral censorship strictly enforced on film
production until the 1950s.

Would the Hollywood of dreams ever have evolved in the
way it did if it hadn't been for the Jews of Eastern Europe?
Their parents came to America and, extraordinarily, many
of their sons understood very quickly what Americans, and
ultimately audiences across the world, wanted and needed
– escapism. Although originating from other lands, they
presented to the world a style of entertainment that was
purely American. Among them were Louis B. Mayer of Metro-
Goldwyn-Mayer who believed in 'wholesome entertainment',
Samuel Goldwyn of Goldwyn Pictures, Harry Cohn of
Columbia, the producer David O. Selznick of RKO; the list
is long.[2] One of the exceptions was Darryl Zanuck of 20th
Century Fox, a Protestant of Swiss descent, who began by
working as a scriptwriter for Warner Brothers before going
into production.

In 1914 Jack had married Irma Salomon, the blond daughter of a prosperous German-Jewish family, and two years later Jack Warner Jr was born. Irma would be a loyal wife and good mother, supporting her husband as Warner Brothers rose through the ranks of successful Hollywood film studios. She believed in her marriage and tolerated her husband's increasing absences from home over the years, although she could not have failed to be concerned by the fact he was constantly surrounded by some of the most beautiful and fascinating women on the planet. However, he seemed to have kept his affairs away from the producer's suite. Bette Davis, who Warners made into a great star, would write: 'No lecherous boss was he! His sins lay elsewhere.'[3]

The cohesive relationship of the four Warner brothers had been vital to their success. Of Harry, Abe, Sam and Jack, Harry the businessman and president was strict and calm. Unaffected by the sensuality endemic in the profession, he had a long and happy marriage with his wife Rea, whom he adored and spoilt. As the years went by, Harry's disapproval of Jack's extramarital adventures, mixed with disagreements over strategy and policy, caused a slow and steady estrangement. Brother Abe was the rough diamond. In charge of distribution, he cared nothing for the niceties of life, which he left to his wife Bessie. His gruff, down-to-earth manner, impatient with inflated egos, meant that increasingly he was obliged to smooth over the conflict between his two older brothers. Sam, head of production alongside Jack, was another peacemaker, charming and fun-loving. A bachelor at 37, in 1925 he married the 18-year-old Ziegfeld Follies star Lina Basquette.

The premiere of *The Jazz Singer*, the film which Sam had done so much to create, was held in October 1927. The opening was a triumph – the audience had heard someone on the screen sing to them for the first time. But none of the Warner brothers were present, for 24 hours earlier Sam had died in hospital from a cerebral haemorrhage leaving the family, and especially Jack, feeling bereft. Now he would bear the burden of being the sole head of production.

In 1931, at a Hollywood party, Jack met someone to whom, although he would not be any more faithful than to his wife Irma, he would always be in thrall. Ann Boyar, who was in the throes of a divorce from her actor husband, was cultured and intelligent with exotic looks. After an affair lasting five years and in the face of vehement disapproval from his family, Jack divorced the faithful Irma and married Ann. The brothers' parents had died two years previously so were no longer there to guide and unite, and the siblings made no secret of their dislike of the sophisticated, self-confident Ann. Harry was even more furious with his brother than usual, which led to violent verbal exchanges and would eventually split asunder what was left of the Warner family ties.

During these years Warner Bothers produced hugely successful films. Many are now classics, such as *42nd Street*, *Baby Face* (a notorious pre-Hays Code film about prostitution) and *The Adventures of Robin Hood*. The studio's stars of that time included Barbara Stanwyck, James Cagney, Edward G. Robinson, Bette Davis, Errol Flynn, Humphrey Bogart, Olivia de Havilland and Douglas Fairbanks Jr. Most of these were, to a greater or lesser degree, in frequent conflict with Jack.

When Pearl Harbor was attacked by the Japanese and the United States entered the war Jack, ever patriotic, managed to become enrolled as a lieutenant-colonel in the Air Force Signal Corps. He threw himself into producing propaganda films, the first of which was a training short called *Winning Your Wings*, narrated by James Stewart. Himself a pilot, Stewart would end the war with the rank of colonel, and be awarded the Distinguished Flying Cross and the French Croix de Guerre. A string of other such films followed, some solely for training purposes, others for public consumption. Warners had 'a good war' during which, in 1942, *Casablanca*, one of the most iconic of Hollywood movies, was made. The studio had played its part, raised millions of dollars for war bonds and, it was widely acknowledged, acquitted itself admirably. But in 1947, terrified of the influence of Communism in the studio system, Jack served as a 'friendly witness' against various employees in front of the infamous House Un-American Activities Committee. This caused many to lose both their jobs and their ability to work in Hollywood.

Ann, who already had a daughter, Joy, from her first marriage, now gave birth to Barbara, Jack's second child, although initially, owing to the timing of the birth, they told everyone Barbara had been adopted. Ann, who had moved into Irma Warner's old home on Angelo Drive in Beverly Hills, quickly transformed it, hiring the Californian architect Roland E. Coate to create a sumptuous Georgian-style mansion. By now she had become almost totally estranged from the Warner family. Her enmity towards them was due to her awareness of their intense disapproval and she did her best to distance herself and Jack from the family circle. Her antagonism was directed particularly towards Jack Jr who reminded her of her husband's first wife, so respected by the family. It became almost a fixation to manipulate an estrangement between Jack and his son, now head of the television department of Warner Brothers. This developed to such a degree that Jack, not wishing to antagonise her, refused to see his son's children – his two granddaughters.

It was because of this fraught situation that Jack decided to buy a bolthole far from Hollywood to where he and Ann could escape. He chose Aujourd'hui – perhaps it was the soda fountain that attracted – and bought the villa from Audrey Chadwick for $160,000. It was 1949 and initially both Jack and Ann spent part of every summer there. Here he could indulge his passion for gambling. Casinos were scattered along the coast, offering his preferred baccarat and chemin de fer, but his usual haunts were the Palm Beach at Cannes and the casino at Monte Carlo. Here he was at ease with fellow gamblers, such as the press baron Lord Beaverbrook, as forceful as Jack himself, the soon to be deposed King Farouk of Egypt, Darryl Zanuck from his cabana at the Hotel du Cap and, occasionally, the Aga Khan. At the Palm Beach, which Barry Dierks had helped to restore after the ravages of the war, one of the chairs bore a brass plaque with Jack's name. His frequent attendances merited it.

The 'hostess with the mostest' Elsa Maxwell was often around, winning and losing alongside Jack. Although, in fact, losing rarely, for in spite of his faults Jack was not ungenerous and tended to cover her losses. Always fulsome to those who supported her, Elsa would write:

> To Jack an act of friendship is as involuntary as breathing. Last summer, for example, knowing that Dickie Gordon [Elsa's companion] and I would be at our farm near Cannes before their arrival there, Jack insisted that we make ourselves at home in their villa, Aujourd'hui. So every day we packed a cold lunch, sat on the rocks in front of the villa, and splashed in the sea in isolated splendour. That is real generosity. To lend money or the like is one thing, but to lend your house is to lend a bit of yourself.[4]

Ann Warner became bored with the life of a movie mogul's wife and began to turn her back on the Hollywood scene, rarely attending functions and instead indulging her love of art and literature. The ubiquitous Salvador Dali stayed at their house in Angelo Drive to paint portraits of both her and Jack. She put on weight and became reclusive. Well aware of Jack's mistresses she was nevertheless defensively confident of her hold on him. They would live increasingly independent lives but never separate. Now she visited Aujourd'hui rarely.

In 1953 their 18-year-old daughter Barbara gave a party at Aujourd'hui during the sultry holiday month of August.

Jack was in Rome and Ann, as usual, closeted in her home in Beverly Hills or at their Arizona ranch. Barbara was unfortunate enough to fall for a handsome, well-built and well-born bad boy. Michael Caborn-Waterfield (Dandy Kim) was the sort of opportunist of which Riviera history is made. Akin to Freddy McEvoy, one-time husband of American heiress Beatrice Cartwright of Casa Estella on the other side of the Cap d'Antibes, he was a sportsman, fatally attractive to women and dabbled in international crime. His pilot father had died during the war. He was educated at Cranleigh School in England, and became part of the Chelsea set in London. He was effortlessly confident. So much so it was not difficult to persuade Barbara to produce the keys to open Jack Warner's safe and allow him to extract several bundles of 10,000-franc notes. She maintained he blackmailed her by threatening to tell her father of events which had happened the previous year. Later, before leaving, he would return to the safe with a friend and help himself to even more bundles of francs, around £23,000 in all. Fleeing to Tangier, where he had 'business connections', and then to London, Dandy Kim was eventually condemned to four years in prison of which he would serve only one. Among his many other activities which, it seems, included a spell of gun-running, in London he founded the lingerie company Ann Summers in 1970, selling it a year later.

The Riviera has been, and still is, a backdrop for dramatic and ingenious burglaries. But it was Paramount, not Warner, who would make the ultimate Riviera movie on this theme – *To Catch a Thief* with Grace Kelly and Cary Grant.

It was the accident on the coast road at Cap d'Antibes that provoked the final rift between the family, Jack Jr, and his father. Cass Warner Sperling in her biography *Hollywood Be Thy Name* described the situation as it evolved. Although Harry Warner was still president of the studios, he was exhausted and suffering from ill health due partly to the often violent

rows with Jack. He longed to spend more time on his ranch
with his racehorses. The powerful 'studio system' had finally
crumbled prompting Louis B. Mayer of MGM to exclaim 'the
loonies have taken over the asylum'.[5] In 1956, under pressure
from his brothers Abe and Jack, Harry agreed reluctantly to
sell Warner Brothers to a Boston banking group headed by
the Hollywood banker Serge Semenenko. However, without
the knowledge of Harry and Abe, who had relinquished their
shares, Jack had first sold and then re-bought enough stock
holdings in the company to entitle him to act as president,
thus fulfilling an ambition of many years. On reading this
news in the journal *Variety*, Harry collapsed with a stroke and
neither he nor Abe would ever speak to Jack again. Following
several more strokes, Harry died in July of 1958. On holiday
on the Cap d'Antibes Jack received a telegram telling him the
funeral was being put on hold to await his arrival. He replied
that he was unable to attend and sent his respects. It was in
the following month that the dramatic car accident on the
narrow coast road occurred. There were those, particularly
one of Jack's three self-effacing sisters, who took the trouble
to tell him it was divine retribution for his treatment of Harry.

The intensive care at the Broussailles Hospital in Cannes
(which still exists) must have been of a high standard. The
doctors saved Jack's life and in his autobiography *My First
Hundred Years in Hollywood* there is not the slightest criticism
of his four-months stay there. The only member of the family
who was in Antibes at the time was Barbara Warner, who
was now married to Claude Terrail of the Tour d'Argent
restaurant in Paris. Barbara contacted the rest of Ann's family
but did not call Jack Jr who heard the news on the radio in
California. Ann, along with her personal lawyer, raced to the
south of France, Jack Jr following on her heels and booking
into the Carlton Hotel in Cannes. Then everything seemed
to go wrong. Ann felt increasingly threatened by Jack Jr's
appearance at his father's bedside, particularly as he had gone

straight to the hospital without paying his respects to her first at Aujourd'hui. An interview Jack Jr gave to a French newspaper was misinterpreted as saying Jack was already dead, giving Ann the ammunition to have him banned from the hospital on the grounds his presence caused Jack's temperature to rise alarmingly. Jack Jr returned to America without visiting his father again.

On his return to Los Angeles for convalescence, Jack barred his son from entering the house on Angelo Drive. He then fired him from his position as head of the television division at Warners. Jack did this by proxy, through Ann's lawyer. He would then erase every trace of his son's former presence at the studio.

As the 1960s progressed Warner Brothers, under its new regime, continued to make critically acclaimed films such as *Splendor in the Grass*, *Whatever Happened to Baby Jane*, *My Fair Lady*, *Who's Afraid of Virginia Woolf* and *Wait Until Dark*. In 1966 Jack sold his interest in the business to Seven Arts Ltd, remaining on the board and beginning another career as an independent producer, financing a couple of projects which failed to be successful. In 1967 his remaining brother, the genial Abe, died at his Miami Beach home in November as *Camelot*, the last true Warner Brothers film, was released.

Jack's story was coming to an end. He retired finally in 1969 and, with Ann in control of their home and a new kind and sympathetic mistress for comfort, he spent his days gambling and playing tennis. In August 1972 he was at Aujourd'hui for his birthday, as was his custom. He was now 80 and was presented with ceramic statues of King Arthur and Guinevere, of the Camelot story – a film which had received mixed reviews. His son Jack Jr was not invited. Although they had led separate lives for years, Ann and Jack had never divorced and now she kept him at home in Miami, caring for him devotedly until he died at Cedars-Sinai Hospital in August 1978. Ann insisted on a small family funeral and had the grace to put Jack Jr on the list of guests. Apart from one brief spontaneous lunch he had not been able to speak to his father for 14 years. Jack left his son $200,000, having been advised that such a sum would prevent Jack Jr challenging the will. Ann's share, which included all the property, ran into many millions. This complicated, antagonistic man created a mixture of dislike and reluctant respect among those who knew him, but many of Warner's thrilling and joyous films live on and it is for these that Jack and his brothers are remembered.

Others now preserve and care for Aujourd'hui, Barry Dierks's gleaming white serpentine villa by the Mediterranean – Hollywood sur Mer.

PART TWO

All Change

Ami, entends-tu le vol noir du corbeau sur nos plaines?
    Ami, entends-tu les cris sourds du pays qu'on enchaîne?

Friend, can you hear the dark flight of the crows over our plains?
    Friend, do you hear the dulled cries of the country in chains?

'Le Chant des Partisans'

$\leftrightarrow \Longrightarrow$ 10 $\Longleftarrow \leftrightarrow$

Méfiance

This is a time when everyone lies, the radio, the government, the newspapers. How do you expect an individual not to lie too?

Jean Renoir, *The Rules of the Game*

During their 14 years on the Riviera, Barry and Eric had built or remodelled around 70 properties, of which 12 were new. Other houses were remodelled or restored to a greater or lesser degree – Dunstan's Le Moulin above Cannes for instance, being so extensively remodelled as to almost qualify as a new house. It was all a phenomenal output which, combined with their many guests at Le Trident and frequent evening sorties in their Chevrolet to cocktails and dinners along the coast, must have meant long days and short nights. But they were disciplined, energetic and hard-working. Unlike their clients they did not possess other properties in Paris or America, the Riviera was their only home and those who knew them seem to have regarded them as totally content.

After a series of worryingly lean years, the Côte d'Azur in 1939 experienced one of its most successful seasons. In defiance of the anxiety and tension that gripped Europe, suddenly festival after festival was organised along the coast

from Cannes to Menton. In February, Cannes held its Fête
du Mimosa, which included the English Dagenham Girl
Pipers swinging down the Croisette. Easter of that year was
pronounced the best ever, with hotels full and traffic filling
the streets. Endless battles of flowers took place. At La Joute
Fleuri (The Floral Joust) in Nice, army tanks were decorated
as 'The Temple of Love', 'The Enchanted Egg' and 'The
Butterfly'. There was a Combat Navale Fleuri among boats
in the bay of Villefranche, and the rowing teams of Oxford
and Cambridge beat Toulouse and Nice on the waterway at
Cannes. Throughout the summer, theatres, concerts, horse
shows and water sports provided entertainment for a wide
range of visitors, and on 13 August a spectacular firework
display was held in the bay of Cannes.

In the spring of 1939, the entrepreneur Philippe Erlanger
had persuaded the French government that the time had
come for France to host its own national film festival and
that the chosen town should be Cannes. The proposed
opening date was 1 September and the venue was to be the
pretty wedding cake casino on the Croisette near the old
port. In spite of the increasing threat of war, Cannes tossed
its head and continued with the preparations. With summer
came the stars. Gary Cooper, Tyrone Power and Edward
G. Robinson strolled the Croisette. In Antibes the film
producer Alexander Korda married the Hollywood actress
Merle Oberon, who had starred with Laurence Olivier in
Wuthering Heights. The Riviera was holding its own. Henri
de Rothschild was at the Villa Meurisse in Monaco, the Aga
Khan on the Cap d'Antibes, and at the Château de l'Horizon
at Golfe Juan Winston Churchill was being cosseted by
Maxine Elliott.

The Duke of Windsor and his jewel-bedecked Wallis had
installed themselves at their rented Château de la Croë on
the Cap d'Antibes – a large villa sumptuously decorated
by its owner Sir William Pomeroy Burton, president of

Associated Newspapers. On 22 August the Duke, not yet bored to tears by life on the coast, presided over the Bal des Petits Lits Blancs, one of the most important charity balls of the French social season, held that year at the Palm Beach Club at the east end of the Croisette. The occasion proved to be a last concerted display of wealth and sophistication. Fabulous fancy-dress costumes and dazzling jewels adorned the rich and famous. The decorations were created by artists Jean Cocteau and Raoul Dufy. Gaiety and laughter filled the great reception rooms, although the guests were somewhat subdued during the course of the evening by an uneasy omen – one of the worst summer storms the coast had ever known. On the following day the non-aggression pact between Germany and Soviet Russia was announced, which boded ill and resulted in a mass exodus of scintillating visitors. Within the week the neon signs announcing the birth of what would one day become the most famous film festival in the world were turned off and would not be re-lit for six years.

Now rumours began to fly. Mussolini, having made tentative stabs at mediation between Britain, France and Germany, signed a pact with Germany which established fascist Italy firmly on the side of the Nazi government. Nice had been French only since 1860, and recovering it was high on Mussolini's wish list. This threw the inhabitants of Provence into a state of fear and confusion. The situation caused particular anxiety among the many Italians. Few were in sympathy with the Fascists and some had been in France for several generations, having sought a better life from the crushing poverty of rural Italy.

A definite order for general mobilisation was issued in France on 2 September and on the following day Britain and France declared war on Germany. In France, requisition of property, animals, cars, aeroplanes and ships was put sweepingly into place. Six million men between the ages of 20 and 45, including every reservist, were called up immediately. For the second time in 25 years, and to the dismay of their families, all across France they left their farms, offices, colleges and small businesses and became military personnel within 24 hours. The 'Waiting Army' took to the roads of France. Vast numbers of men began moving through the Alpes Maritimes towards that part of the Maginot Line which lay near the frontier with Italy. Truck-loads filled the roads going east to strengthen the garrisons and frontier posts. Civilian movement of any kind was restricted and papers had to be shown constantly. The safe, privileged world of the Riviera expatriate became one of unease and bewilderment.

However, during the Phoney War of 1939 to 1940 the expatriates of the Riviera rose to the occasion. There was an official *appel à la générosité* and almost overnight charitable organisations sprang up, mainly in rooms donated by hotels, and almost always run by strong-minded women. Virtually every one who was anyone on the Riviera was involved in an aid programme or on a committee, sometimes on several at the same time. Barry and Eric did not hang back.

Organisations were founded to provide aid for families left bereft by the mobilisation, or to provide comforts for the troops, such as Le Vin Chaud du Soldat, La Soupe Populaire and Les Optimistes de la Riviera. An ambitious Anglo-American Home for French Children of the War was opened, then sadly soon closed for lack of funds. A Cantine Militaire was organised for soldiers arriving at Cannes station on troop trains. At first this was slow going, with a row of increasingly bored women sitting on the platform munching biscuits and bickering among themselves. A grandson of John Taylor, the esteemed estate agent of Cannes, wrote he had heard that one angry woman had hurled a plate of sandwiches at the head of another.

In October of 1939, Barry, Eric and a large committee gathered at the Villa Montfleury on the Avenue des Oliviers in Cannes. They were about to launch a much needed venture. The objective of the Anglo-American Ambulance Corps of Cannes (with a branch at the Hotel Ruhl in Nice) was to provide a fleet of ambulances, each capable of carrying five stretchers or ten sitting cases to be used under the authority of the French military. They aimed at 20 cars, either donated or bought by donated funds, and for this they were also linked to the American Field Service in New York, which had done such sterling work in World War I. They asked for Chevrolet cars to be sent from America but first had to make do with others of various shapes, sizes and origin. These included a Citroen Traction, a Mercedes and one of the short-lived Matford Ford F-81 break de chasse. As the Corps was Anglo-American they invited Lord Derby, for whom Barry had remodelled the Villa Sansovino in Cannes the previous year, to act as patron. Derby was a British ex-secretary of state for war, and had also been appointed as ambassador to France in 1918.

The first ambulances were inaugurated by Lord Derby, dressed in military regalia, feathers flying, and blessed by Monseigneur Paul Remond, the archbishop of Nice. Remond, a supporter of Marshal Pétain, nevertheless would work clandestinely to save Jewish children, organising false papers and ordering the Catholic institutions in his diocese to shelter these children, and often their mothers along with them. Others on the Corps committee were Barry as treasurer plus a handful of his former clients – Comte Sala of the Villa Lilliput, Comte Damien de Martel of La Cassine (both on the Cap d'Antibes), Sir Francis Fuller of the Domaine St Francois at Juan-les-Pins and Eric Dunstan of Le Moulin at Mouans Sartoux.

The first vice president and mover and shaker was Eric Dunstan. The two Erics and Barry were all on the committee of the Sunny Bank Anglo-American Hospital in Cannes. Now they also used the Corps funds to establish a *pouponnière* or nursery, at the Villa St Georges on the Avenue Roi Albert in Cannes, for young children whose fathers had been conscripted and whose mothers were unable to care for their families. Dunstan would say, rather typically:

> Why it should be I don't know, but there's nothing like a 'charity' to bring out the worst in the best-meaning of people, and the war time charitable efforts of us foreigners on the Riviera were no exception. Jealousies and enmities over the pettiest of things spread like a plague. I was glad, early in 1940, when I was appointed Commandant and took the first batch of ambulances up to the 'front' or rather the back of it.

The 'front' was Hagondange, a village near Metz and the failed Maginot Line, and the ambulances four large converted Chevrolets sent from America. The Corps, joining other similar groups, also provided a French mobile field hospital with an X-ray unit, a generating plant and a fully equipped mobile operating theatre. All were sorely needed. But when the Germans broke through 15 miles to the north there was a rapid withdrawal of the ambulances and the hospital, along with a constant stream of refugees, to relative safety in the south. Who eventually took possession of the Chevrolets is not recorded.

Aristocratic patrons were eagerly sought for such charitable ventures, and there must have been an element of healthy competition to acquire one of these prizes. Among those conscripted were Henriette, Duchesse de Vendôme, Princess of Belgium; the Duke of Connaught, son of Queen Victoria and Princess Hazel Ghika, the American ex-mother-in-law of Paul-Louis Weiller of Barry's Villa La Reine Jeanne. Princess Ghika would stay, become involved with the Resistance, be arrested and treated so badly she had to be hospitalised, a fact which saved her life. Princess Gennaro de Bourbon des Deux Siciles was born Beatrice Bordessa of a bourgeois Italian family from Chester in the north of England. Along with her husband, Beatrice did not, even under threat, renounce her anti-fascist principles and chosen home of France.

Fundraising and distribution of aid and money were the aims of these committees and, for as long as they were allowed to exist, they did much good. Tea dances, galas, dinners and sporting events were organised energetically in order to raise funds for their respective causes. Women turned out to these in their slim, bare-backed evening gowns, often decorated with appliqué flowers, or sparkling with diamanté embroidery. Orchestras such as Ray Ventura's played music for foxtrots, quicksteps and the new American dances, while the bars of the grand hotels buzzed with life every evening. There was still hope – of a kind. But many others had fled or were fleeing, almost emptying the cocktail bar and terrace of the Carlton Hotel, where the rich had shown off their bejewelled mistresses, and elegantly clad figures had flirted in the soft evening air. The author Beverley Nichols, a close friend of Barry and Eric, was distraught. He had driven across France to the Cannes he had known so well and proclaimed it 'a lunatic asylum'. In his book *The Unforgiving Minute* he wrote:

> The streets were blocked with cars being loaded up with petrol ... and it was being poured into the cars by hysterical women, some of them still in beach-pyjamas. As soon as they had got their petrol they threw their jewel cases into the boot and fled to the north.[1]

Among the many expatriates who made their way sluggishly along roads overflowing with refugees heading either west to the Spanish border or to ports in the north, it was recorded that those from the Riviera were the most obnoxious. The hotels and restaurants en route were scarcely able to cope with travellers demanding beds and food. At the thronged Chapon Fin restaurant in Bordeaux the journalist Geoffrey Cox, in his book *Countdown to War*, was exasperated:

> In another corner a noisy group of expatriate Britons had just arrived by car from the Riviera ... Now with Italy in the war, they were making a bolt for home. Gold, diamonds, pearls flowed and glittered against suntanned faces above superb Worth and Molyneux gowns. Arrogant, raucous voices rang out across the room, scorning France in defeat, and proclaiming that she had had this coming to her ever since the Reds got power during the Popular Front.[2]

One night, on the Carlton terrace, Beverley Nichols met his old friends Barry and Eric. As they were about to leave, Nichols turned to Barry and said he would like to return to Le Trident and throw a coin into the star-shaped pool on the terrace for luck. Eric laughed and called him a sentimental old ass, but Barry said that of course he must. So they drove to Miramar and Nichols threw in coins which joined others at the bottom of the small pool, coins thrown by those who wished to return to Le Trident. There would be many times, over the next years, when returning would be far from certain.

The *drôle de guerre*, or Phoney War, also known by some in England as the 'Bore War', kept France in a state of suspension over winter and into the spring. Endlessly the radio and newspapers repeated, '*Rien a signalé sur le front*' ('No news from the front'). The situation was bad for the morale of the officers and men of the French military and responsible for a considerable loss of momentum, during which time various political groups seized the opportunity for mischief-making.

In his memoir *Strictly Personal*, Somerset Maugham describes walking around an almost deserted Cap Ferrat, passing closed villas whose owners had fled. Writing of the situation as it was in 1939 Maugham had admired those brilliant and energetic officers. But after the Battle for France he felt rather differently.

> The General Staff was incompetent; the officers were vain, ill-instructed in modern warfare and insufficiently determined; the men were dissatisfied and half-hearted. The people at large were kept ignorant of everything that they should have been informed of; they were profoundly suspicious of the government, and were never convinced that the war was a matter that urgently concerned them; the propertied classes were more afraid of bolshevism than of German domination; their first thought was how to keep their money safely in their pockets; the government was inept, corrupt and, in part, disloyal.[3]

In the Alpes Maritimes the perceived threat coming from the Italian border kept the army there busy with manoeuvres and poised for action. In mid-September the Soviet Red Army invaded Poland and the Polish Army surrendered. Within six weeks Stalin and Hitler annexed Poland and divided it between them. The Palm Beach Club on the Croisette sobered up to become a hospital-in-waiting for the French Army. On 3 October, a month to the day after war had been declared, President Franklin Roosevelt, to avoid becoming involved in another European war, proclaimed the United States was neutral. There was a strong feeling of déjà vu.

The small purple fruit were being shaken from the grey branches of the olive trees on the terraces high above the coast when in November the Red Army invaded Finland, forcing it to sign a peace treaty the following March. In the same month Paul Reynaud, resistant to German militarism, replaced Edouard Daladier as prime minister of France. Both men shared the *politique de fermeté* towards Hitler's ambitions. The Communist Party was outlawed and its leaders either imprisoned or in flight. In December, Mussolini's government had made a declaration of non-aggression towards France, but this did little to reassure those living near the border. The tense early months of 1940 seemed endless. In April the German Army invaded Denmark and Norway.

The coast was in turmoil, not all of it unwelcome. Those refugees who, looking ahead, considered the Riviera safer than the north, had begun heading south during 1939. Now they were joined by others in increasing numbers. These included many Jewish families, both French and foreign, heeding the warnings towards their people already given clearly by the Nazi regime. Many, although by no means all, of these refugees were well off and those that were used the hotels, shops and restaurants, so were welcome as far as the local tourist industry and town councils were concerned. But then things happened very fast. The German invasion of the Low Countries began on 10 May 1940 when Hitler launched 'Operation Yellow'.[4] With overwhelming numbers of Panzer tanks supported by artillery bombardments and the relentless dive-bombing of the Luftwaffe, they swept through the Ardennes, tore a gap in the defences at Sedan and began to push the French Army and its Allies around northern France like pieces on a draughtboard.

Although the word of Mussolini had always been mistrusted, the abandonment of his promise not to attack France and the actual declaration of war by Italy on 10 June 1940 shook the Riviera to the core. Within a few hours 50 per cent of the population of Monaco fled, adding to the chaos on the roads. The town of Menton, the area up to Roquebrune-Cap-Martin, the small mountain town of Sospel and the villages on the Italian border into the upper reaches of the Alpes Maritimes were all evacuated. Those fleeing west from the Italians ran into the hoards of those fleeing south. This caused, particularly in the Rhone area, such a tangled mass of humanity that the military authorities, overwhelmed, were obliged at one point to stop all traffic, leaving everyone to sort themselves out as best they could.

The Italians did little in the first few days, except to send their air force on sorties, dropping the odd bomb along the coast, frequently missing their targets. At Marseilles they lost planes to anti-aircraft fire, as well as six bombers brought down in the space of a few minutes by a solitary French fighter. That some of the French soldiers carried Italian names and may have had a cousin, even a brother, on the other side of the line could matter no longer. The battle began, running from Menton into the hills and on into the mountains, while overhead Italian planes continued to machine-gun and bomb the coastline. In this they had a free hand, for there were no longer any airworthy French planes in the area. At one point the Italians landed troops at Menton and reached Roquebrune-Cap-Martin, seven kilometres to the east of Monte Carlo, but a handful of *chasseurs alpins* and French colonial troops threw them back to the border. High on the Maritime Alps, a contingent of 400 French *eclaireurs-skieurs*, the dashing mountain guides, held the line in the face of heavy bombardment.

As the German Army advanced through northern France, the French government retreated from Paris to Tours and on to Bordeaux. Prime Minister Paul Reynaud shuffled and re-shuffled his ministers and appointed the ageing Marshal Philippe Pétain, the 'Hero of Verdun' in the 1914–1918 war, as minister of state. The commander-in-chief of the armed forces was changed from General Gustave Gamelin (for failure to defend adequately) to General Maxime Weygand (inclined towards armistice). The government now included a younger general and ex-tank commander, Charles de Gaulle, as under-secretary of state for war. De Gaulle's armoured divisions had acquitted themselves with honour but failed in a counter-attack against the Germans.

As the cicadas rasped their songs in the maquis and gardens of the south, France finally fell. The Germans entered Paris on 14 June. France immediately appealed to the United States for help, as well as to Britain – planes, above all, were desperately needed to attack German troop movements from the air. Both requests were refused or stalled, and the remaining British troops, left after the evacuation from Dunkirk, were ordered to return to England. This proved to be excellent propaganda for the Nazi regime, who would make it widely known that 'The English will fight to the last Frenchman'.[5]

Reynaud faltered, then suggested the French troops should surrender and the government move to North Africa. General Weygand disagreed, insisting instead on an armistice: 'A stopping of hostilities by common agreement of the opposing sides'.[6] Reynaud then proposed the 'hypothesis' of an armistice, prompting de Gaulle's resignation and rapidly, in confusion, his own. His government was replaced by one led by Marshal Pétain, with General Weygand as minister of defence. Finally, on 17 June 1940, Pétain, with obvious relief and the certainty he was doing the right thing for France, opened negotiations with Germany. In the south, the French had planned a counter-attack to recapture Menton on the very night the armistice was declared. They were immediately ordered to stop combat. Twelve hours later, in a small blockhouse at St Louis, near Menton, a group of soldiers was still fighting fiercely to prevent enemy troops entering France by that route. It took several French officers of high rank to persuade the six men and their corporal to lay down their arms, evacuate their stronghold and join the New Order.

France was now split into two zones, the northern Occupied Zone and the southern French state – the Unoccupied Zone.

As from 11 July 1940, the southern area was governed from the spa town of Vichy and so known as Vichy France. Marshal Pétain became head of state of Vichy France, considered his region to be France itself and thus virtually independent, and believed he had saved the whole of his beloved country from yet another encounter with devastation. The demarcation line separating the two zones ran from Orthez in the Pyrenees, north to Poitiers then east to Geneva. The Unoccupied Zone encompassed the Alps, part of the Massif Central, the Pyrenean foothills, the Rhone valley and the Mediterranean coastline, the southern part being an area of much aridity. The Occupied Zone encompassed the rest, including the recently annexed region of Alsace and Lorraine and the Atlantic coastline.

The British consuls up and down the Riviera were in rather a quandary. As the military situation deteriorated they were unsure what to do with their remaining expatriates as, it seems, was the British government. The blackout had ceased to be firmly enforced and civilian traffic was allowed to take freely to the coastal roads. The British authorities had done nothing to discourage their subjects from visiting or returning to the region in spite of the Italian menace. From May onwards, when the situation in the north became more dangerous, British refugees from Italy, Belgium and northern France had joined others flocking to the south. F.C. Stone, an employee of the British Consulate in Monaco, a neutral principality, recorded in a long memorandum to Anthony Eden at the Foreign Office:

> Constantly augmented by the dwellers of the towns and villages, soon over two million people were crawling at a snail's pace along the roads of France, engulfing on the way military convoys and fugitives from the front. The columns of refugees were bombed and machine-gunned by the Luftwaffe and they buried their dead by the roadside.[7]

Major H. Dodds, His Majesty's consul general at Nice
(described by Somerset Maugham as 'amiable, without a
great deal of energy') called a meeting of the consular staff
of the Riviera towns on 16 June.[8] A British naval officer,
sent from Marseilles, advised that the evacuation of all
British subjects was imperative, but was not sure how this
was to be achieved, as few suitable ships remained in the
Mediterranean. Prince Louis II, prince of Monaco, offered
to take British subjects under his protection, but this idea
was rejected. The British Embassy, which had moved with
the French government to Bordeaux, confirmed, when
contacted by telephone, that 'All British subjects should be
strongly urged to leave whilst it was still possible to do so.'[9]
How to do so was the problem. And every day more and more
became stranded as they escaped from the Occupied to the
Unoccupied Zone. During the meeting of the consular staff
it became clear that Major Dodds had been instructed by
the British Embassy in Paris to leave his post and escort the
Duke and Duchess of Windsor to a Royal Navy destroyer
and on to safety in Spain.

But hopes rose, for on 17 July two British cargo ships, the
Saltersgate and the *Ashcrest*, were suddenly made available.
The advice to leave now became an order to evacuate. If
this chance was not taken, the British government would
accept no responsibility for the fate of those who remained.
Everyone was to be at the Cannes Customs House early on
the following day. What they did not know was that the ships
were colliers – iron-decked, grimy coal boats from Liverpool,
able to take only 1,000 refugees in total, and not equipped
for those. The evening before the embarkation, the Carlton
Hotel on the Croisette was brilliantly lit and crowded.
Maugham, who had left his Villa Mauresque in the hands of
his American secretary Gerald Haxton, stayed the night there
before joining the exodus next day and found 'They were in
evening clothes, some of them a trifle the worse for liquor,

and there was about them an air of hectic, hysterical gaiety, which was sinister.'[10]

In contrast, the scene at the Customs House on the following morning of 18 July was despondent. Those who could be contacted, and who had chosen to leave by ship, were gathered together in the early morning heat. Each person was allowed one suitcase and told to take a blanket and some food. Although some were rich socialites who had hung on until the last minute, the majority were older and less well-heeled – retired army officers and colonial civil servants, governesses and employees of great villas and various businesses. Among them were a few patients from the Sunny Bank Hospital in Cannes, who had decided to chance the voyage. The other British hospital, the Queen Victoria at Nice, had brought their remaining patients to Cannes, mostly on stretchers, for the hospital had closed its doors that morning, being on the Italian side of the Var River. It was quickly realised it would be impossible for anyone who was ill to embark on such ships, so they were taken up the hill to Sunny Bank which the matron, Margaret Williams, was determined to keep open and which was about to begin four long, lean and anxious years.

Cars were sold for a song or abandoned on the quayside, and Consul Stone of Monaco recorded that, 'A large crowd of French people had come to see this melancholy sight and many were openly affected by the departure of these British whom they had always regarded not only as their patrons but also, in many instances, as their friends.'[11]

On the two ships, of which the largest had quarters for a crew of only 38 men, 1,300 were eventually crammed on board, the iron decks burning from a day at rest in the Mediterranean sun. As Somerset Maugham, sailing on the *Saltersgate*, wrote:

One lady, when she came on board, told an officer that of course she wanted to go first class and another called the steward (there was only one) and asked him to show her where the games deck was. 'It's all over the ship, madam,' he replied.[12]

Rumours circulated about the swift departure of the staff of the various British consular offices. Major Dodds, ordered to escort the Windsors, had left quickly returning only in August as an advisor to the American consul general at Marseilles. According to Consul Stone, Dodds now regretted his rapid departure. The British consul general at Monaco left his office to the care of Stone, without taking leave of the Prince of Monaco or the Monagasque government, an action which was not looked upon favourably. The consul at Cannes announced that he would stay – and was gone by the following day. As Stone reported: 'There were those who felt the consular officers and their staff should have considered their duty required them to share the fate of the people under their protection', and that in this they had been less than loyal.[13] The staff of the Cannes office were particularly criticised.

After perhaps the most arduous journey the passengers would ever know, the two coal boats arrived safely back in Britain. As they had passed along the North African coast they had seen the French Algerian town of Oran blazing with light. Blackout was no longer necessary, for the French colonialists had accepted the armistice and the Vichy regime. But as their clients and friends took cars, trains and ships to freedom, Barry and Eric did not leave. Their world had changed, as had that of everyone else, but they were quite clear about what they intended to do. In the following years, which were to become increasingly fraught with anxiety, *méfiance* – a potent word meaning 'mistrust' – became the order of the day.

The American Train – Barry

Now is the time for all good men to come to the aid of the
party.

Charles E. Weller. *The Early History of the Typewriter*

In their remote white house on the Esterel, Eric kept a low
profile. Being British, and at 52 still young enough to cause
trouble, even early in the war he risked internment as an enemy
alien. After the 1940 retreat from Dunkirk, the remaining
British, once seen as friends, were now regarded by many as
enemies who had abandoned France, so successful was the
German and Vichy propaganda. In July 1940 the destruction
by the Royal Navy of the French fleet at anchor at Mers-el-Kébir
on the Algerian coast, to prevent it falling into enemy hands,
changed dislike into hatred. Eric, in spite of these hazards, was
beginning to make contacts with the, very slowly, emerging
Resistance groups on the Riviera. Clandestine meetings at the
villa now took the place of cocktail parties.

Barry was not in hiding, America was not an enemy
country and he was free to come and go. The work of the
French Red Cross became increasingly ineffective following
the declaration of the armistice, and supplies collected in
Britain could not be sent for fear they would fall into enemy
hands. But the American Red Cross was allowed to operate,

providing aid, particularly for children, and Barry became deeply involved. Even when the United States entered the war in December 1941 they were allowed to continue their work in France. The American government believed in keeping the link to Vichy France open, as it would for some time. Barry's days were filled with visiting hospitals, internment camps and those in need. Countless thousands of the much-anticipated food parcels were made up each week in America and sent by ship to Lisbon or Marseilles. From there they were carried by train to Geneva where they were sent out to the camps and other institutions as well as the families of those who had been deported from France. Typically, American parcels would contain tinned meats and fish, dried milk, coffee, cocoa, sugar, cheese, chocolate and soap, sometimes clothes and always cigarettes. The contents were frequently both pilfered and bartered. As food became ever scarcer, Barry tried to make sure that every child he could track down was supplied with, at least, dried milk. The Red Cross prisoner of war medical kits consisting of much needed supplies would become increasingly vital.

A certificate from the military district of Grasse gave Barry permission to visit British prisoners of war at the Fort de la Revère at La Turbie. La Turbie, with its arched passageways and steep staircases, is a medieval village around 600 metres above sea level and high above Monaco. The village's proudest possession is the great trophy monument to the Emperor Augustus, built by the Romans in 6 BC to celebrate his vanquishing of the troublesome tribes who populated the Alpes Maritimes at that time. The restoration of the trophy was financed by the American philanthropist Edward Tuck, who died in Monaco in 1938.

The Fort de la Revère was a dreary old fortress in a forested area above the village, built around 1883 and designed to cover enemy action from the east. Abandoned after World War I it found a new use in 1940 when the Vichy government opened it to intern Allied prisoners of war, initially RAF pilots and later soldiers and sailors. Barry and his Red Cross colleagues delivered British military outfits, shirts and underclothes. Food parcels were the most welcome of all. The internees were allowed out in guarded groups to shop in Nice. But, as instructed by Winston Churchill, they made repeated attempts to escape – sliding down a sewage shute onto the hillside was one option. Many made their way to Monte Carlo where they were sheltered in an empty apartment and fed by two elderly sisters, Eva and Susie Trenchard, who ran the Scottish tea shop in the town. After the war the sisters would be awarded a King's Commendation for bravery. The aim of most of the fugitives was to reach Marseilles and the escape lines which were being organised from that rough melting pot of a town.

In those summer months of the early 1940s, the sun beat down on the terraces and shrub land of the hill country as the cicadas throbbed out their metallic trill and, far below, the Mediterranean shimmered through its palette of blues from dawn to dusk. An atmosphere of bewildered suspicion hung over everything as heavily as did the heat. In Cannes, members of the French Service d'Ordre Légionnaire, the forerunner of the dreaded Milice (a French paramilitary organisation which held itself above the law) destroyed the statue of King Edward VII, a gesture which made the Cannoise uneasy, remembering how much fondness he had held for their town and how he and his fun-loving entourage had helped to swell its coffers.

As far as the local population of the Alpes Maritimes was concerned, there were those who felt a profound sense of relief that they would be governed by Marshal Pétain rather than the Communists, but the mass of people went about their daily business in a state of stunned apathy. The Italians had only been allowed, by the terms of the Italian-German agreement, to occupy the land won from the French during the

Italian assault of June 1940. This territory included Menton
and its immediate surroundings, plus the strip of villages and
pastureland that ran up through the Alps along the border.
The Italian command was installed in Nice and their military
scattered throughout the south from the Italian frontier to
the Rhone. But, outside their own designated strip, they were
not permitted to consider themselves occupiers, their role
being more of military police. On the railway that ran along
the coast, the trains went back and forth constantly, loaded
up with French arms, tanks and munitions to be taken
away to Italy as spoils of war. But the wholesale invasion of
Provence by its Italian neighbours had not taken place and
the region's inhabitants and their numerous refugee visitors,
both rich and poor, now had to face the prospect of life in
Vichy France, albeit under the eye of the Italians.

In an area deemed unoccupied, as long as it behaved itself,
the ageing and strongly Catholic Philippe Pétain expounded
his National Socialist ideals and guidance for social behaviour
under the New Order – the 'French state' better known as
Vichy France. The republican motto of *liberté, egalité, fraternité*
was replaced by the new state's *travail, famille, patrie*. Exercise,
games and youth camps were strongly encouraged in order
to promote clean and healthy living. Married women were
discouraged from working unless their husbands were unable
to provide for them and were urged to give up their jobs to
men. Mothers were expected to stay in the home, look after
their family and be discreet and biddable. They were to be
honoured as the bearers of the children who would carry
forward the future of the New Order. Schoolchildren were
taught the patriotic song 'Maréchal, Nous Voilâ', praising the
Marshal. Swimming costumes and shorts were banned away
from pools and beaches, along with trousers for women. It
was forbidden to serve spirits and cocktails before 8 p.m. and
a midnight curfew was decreed. In the puritanical spirit of
Vichy, the prefect of the Alpes Maritimes would order the

internment of around 2,000 prostitutes and homosexuals in a camp near Sisteron in the Alps.

Other rules followed swiftly, either from the German High Command or Marshal Pétain's own Vichy government. The persecution of the Jews began slowly, with the confiscating of businesses. There was to be no crossing, without permits, between the occupied and unoccupied zones; it was absolutely forbidden to aid escaped Allied military personnel in any way, under pain of imprisonment or worse. In the south, the police had orders to round up all escapees and send them to Fort St Jean at Marseilles. As a result, escape lines sprang up rapidly, run by those who knew, only too well, the possible consequences of their actions. The Italian Army, as enforcer, had the power to send anyone, if they stepped out of line, up to one of the high perched villages in the hills – and did so frequently. Eileen Gray, the Irish architect of the iconic villa E1027 at Roquebrune Cap Martin, who had moved to her new home Tempe à Pailla at Castellar above Menton, was interned in the Vaucluse as an enemy agent.

There was now only one way to learn what was going on in the world outside, and that was through one of the most precious and dangerous possessions of the wartime years, that other weapon – the radio. Despite the jamming of the airwaves by the Germans, it was possible to learn what was happening outside the prison that France had become. It was not long before the Vichy-controlled broadcasts and German controlled Radio Paris were seen to be no more than self-serving propaganda. Soon the children of those who hated the occupation and the New Order would chant within the safety of their homes '*Radio Paris ment, Radio Paris est Allemand*' ('Radio Paris lies, Radio Paris is German'). The punishment for listening to a clandestine radio was severe – and would become increasingly so. The broadcasts sent from the BBC (*Ici Londres! Les Français Parle aux Français*) by the Free French, were fragile links between France and England.

The south of France, in spite of its much-vaunted bounty of grapes, olives and citrus fruits, was not a productive agricultural area and the population quickly began to suffer from lack of food. January of 1940, even before the defeat, had already brought restrictions – the marching army had priority. Restaurants at that time were allowed to serve each client only one meat dish of no more than 100 grams, and that in exchange for coupons. Then came the order that no meat at all should be served on Mondays and Tuesdays and that butchers' shops should close on those days. Friday was then included, encompassing the traditional religious abstinence. Coffee, rice and soap began to become scarce and, as early as February, ration cards were introduced, graded according to age and trade. In March the patisseries, once filled with their delectable little works of art, were told to close three days a week and the sale of alcohol was forbidden on Monday, Tuesday and Wednesday. When Vichy rule began in July 1940, a new decree restricted the serving of sugar in hotels and restaurants and *le petit café, non sucré* became the order of the day. Olive oil, wine and citrus crops were compulsorily purchased throughout the south for shipment to Italy and Germany. The black market, which was to become a necessity, swung quickly into action.

Marshal Pétain's vice-premier was Pierre Laval, an ex-prime minister of France whose rough peasant appearance belied his business acumen. He was considered by many to be self-seeking and caring nothing for any political system. Extremely rich through acquisition of newspapers and radio stations, he had been chosen by *Time* magazine as 'Man of the Year' in 1931.[1] He would become 'the evil "shadow" over Vichy'.[2]

At that time there was no curfew in Vichy France as there was in the occupied north. In the south the French flag could be flown and the Marseillaise sung. For here, the Marshall had saved France.[3] Even American films could be shown. Correspondence with the outside world, suppressed during the Battle for France, was now allowed. The majority of the lively, elegant expatriates who had lit up the Riviera were gone. For Barry and Eric, almost all their friends would now be French.

The expatriate charities were disbanded. As far as the expatriates themselves were concerned there remained only a few of the mainly elderly, who had made the Riviera their home. The Aga Khan and the ex-Khedive of Egypt were still there in 1941 but soon left. Families of royal descent, such as the two branches of the Bourbons, stayed as did some exiled Russian princes and various widowed duchesses and countesses. The American Marie Clews of the Château of La Napoule, now a widow, refused to leave her home and the memory of her husband. As German officers took over the château she moved to the gatehouse for the duration of the war. Prince Jean-Louis de Faucigny-Lucinge, would note in his memoirs, *Un Gentilhomme Cosmopolite*:

> Some of these elderly ladies, almost without exception beautiful in their time, now took to bicycles and could be seen pedalling slowly through the streets of the town, veils floating in the breeze and frugal provisions in boxes on the back.[4]

Actors and singers such as Danielle Darrieux, Maurice Chevalier and Charles Trenet would be allowed to come and go as their services were required. Chevalier's mistress was Jewish and stayed quietly in their villa at Cannes La Bocca. Painters such as Henri Matisse and the artist-photographer Jacques-Henri Lartigue lived quietly in Nice and Monte Carlo respectively. The artist Pierre Bonnard remained in his villa Le Bosquet in Le Cannet, above Cannes. Marc Chagall, a Jew, found himself trapped near Marseilles and was spirited away to New York with the aid of the American-funded Emergency Rescue Committee in Marseilles run by Varian Fry. In spite of being forbidden to do so by the United States government, Fry enabled many Jewish artists and intellectuals to escape by various means, until he was ordered to return to America.

Barry and Eric would have been more in touch than others with events going on in the outside world through contact with the Red Cross. In spite of the fraught situation Barry was able to continue with his aid work along the Riviera as far as the beleaguered border town of Menton, now ceded to the Italians. Even the surprise attack on Pearl Harbor by the Japanese in December 1941 which caused the United States to enter the war on the side of the Allies did not prevent him, protected by his position with the Red Cross, in going about his work – that was until Operation Torch. On 8 November 1942 American and British forces invaded Vichy-governed French North Africa, and after military and political skirmishes brought the area under the control of the Allies. This resulted in the German Army in France sweeping aside the demarcation line, eliminating the concept of Unoccupied France and controlling the Free Zone through the Italian Army and themselves. Vichy virtually lost its power as a government and three days later Barry was arrested.

He was not alone. A train with unusual passengers left Vichy station at 4.15 p.m. on 11 November 1942, bearing around 127 Americans along with a sprinkling of nannies, maids and other servants. It was a train commissioned especially for 54 United States embassy staff, headed by their chargé d'affaires Somerville Pinkney Tuck, plus 24 others from the Marseilles consulate, 16 from the consulates of Lyon and Nice, 15 Red Cross workers and 18 journalists. Among the latter were Lansing Warren of the *New York Times* and Henry G. King of the United Press. The passengers were allowed to bring personal belongings, with few restrictions, which required an entire extra carriage, and the whole cargo was bound for Lourdes. They all thought they would be sent on to Lisbon to board ship and head for home. In fact they were to be bartered. The Germans demanded the Americans be exchanged with members of the Vichy Armistice regime in North Africa, together with the German consul. This demand was refused point blank by the United States government and the hapless group, after two months in small hotels at Lourdes, was dispatched to Baden Baden and internment. As Evelyn Waugh in *Officers and Gentlemen* wrote about a group of soldiers becoming prisoners of war, 'Thus began the ghastly series of concert parties.'[5]

Their internment camp, where they arrived on 16 January 1943 was the elegant Brenners Park Hotel in the Black Forest. From 1941 the hotel was controlled by the German Oetker family, of baking powder and shipping fame. In later years they would buy the Hôtel Eden Roc on Cap d'Antibes. The internees were far from uncomfortable. Almost every room had a private bathroom, there were suites, maids to service their rooms and waiters to serve dinner in the elegant dining room, where they were expected to dress appropriately. Although the food consisted of many potatoes and often tough meat, there was a good deal more in quantity than the ration of the average German civilian. The International Red Cross parcels played a large part in providing further comfort. One letter, from the American camp doctor Harold C. Stuart to his family, records that they have been allocated 75 German cigarettes per person, to last four weeks, and that 'The Red Cross package this time had three packets (for two weeks) so these together provide seven a day, which is not bad.'[6]

The fact that the internees were well-educated professional people meant that they were resourceful at keeping themselves occupied while being frustrated at their lack of freedom. The Red Cross personnel, particularly the nurses, longed to be back in the field 'sleeping on straw mattresses'.[7]

Among those interned was Thomas Kernan who had been, when the Nazis arrived in June 1940, director of French *Vogue* in Paris and a representative of Condé Nast publications in

Europe. After unsuccessfully trying to continue to publish
the magazine under German occupation, he left Paris for
America early in 1941. The Germans would take over *Vogue*,
copying it almost perfectly. Kernan's excellent book *France on
Berlin Time*, published in 1942, describes how the German
government subtly but thoroughly, through their fifth
column, prepared for the conquest of France throughout
the 1930s and now had in place an efficient machine for
supplying Germany with labour, capital, food, raw materials
and industrial products of all kinds, especially arms and
munitions. A stickler for punishment, Kernan returned to
France with the American Red Cross and was soon interned.
His many letters from Baden Baden to his sister give a
fascinating insight into months of uncertain, if comfortable,
internment. While in captivity he wrote a novel, *Now with the
Morning Star*, about a young German soldier.

The German authorities, keeping an eye on how well their
own consular staff were being treated in the United States,
reciprocated in kind. There was a certain amount of freedom.
The internees were allowed to swim in a local pool, play
tennis and go for walks in the forest, always accompanied
by a guard although there was little chance of fraternising
with the locals. Anyone who needed hospital treatment was
allowed to receive it in Frankfurt. They could keep dogs, but
not cats. Lectures, classes and clubs abounded. There were
nine children in the group and they did not escape lessons.
Constance Harvey, ex-vice consul at Lyon, wrote to a friend
that they had 'a regular university which gives courses in six
modern languages, music and drawing, philosophy, history,
literature and mathematics'.[8] She felt they were all living in
such an ivory tower 'that one seems hardly to be living in the
world at all'.[9] Morale was generally good but people did get
fits of the blues from time to time. Harold C. Stuart gave a
course on 'Anatomy and Physiology' and wrote to his family,
'we all find ourselves spreading out every little job to consume

as much time as possible'.[10] One Red Cross internee, Robert A. Jakoubek, hoped the US State Department would get the Red Cross personnel out first, 'as this joint is getting on my nerves more and more'.[11]

'My darling Mother', wrote Barry in July of 1943, 'There is so little to write about it is hard to know where to begin. Here, our life goes on exactly the same. We are all well and our morale is excellent, but naturally we are all bored to death despite our activities.' He goes on to say how lovely the gardens of the grand hotel are: 'It's no wonder! The amount it rains here!' He is designing the scenery and costumes for the plays they are putting on (they call themselves The Badenspielers) and houses for 'all the boys in the group', which he finds great fun. He delights in the concerts and choirs in the local church, 'which is very fine', particularly two pieces by Mozart, the Baden Mass ('it was magnificent') and the Trinity Mass. Many letters were received, through third parties, from French friends on the Riviera as well as news from Eric, now in England. Barry ends by writing: 'I can't imagine what it will be like to be able to go into a store and buy anything without a *bon* or a ticket. It won't seem real. And to be able to go to a petrol pump and fill up the car will probably only happen in Heaven' and 'Well, Mother darling, I'll say goodbye for the moment and God bless and keep you. Your own boy. Barry.'[12]

It is only comparatively recently that a pile of theatrical programmes was found in a bookcase at Le Trident. One cover shows a broken chain against the image of a rising sun and the title 'Official American Group. Formerly in Detention in Baden-Baden Germany'. The actors' performances included *Victoria Regina* by Laurence Housman, Oscar Wilde's *Lady Windermere's Fan*, and *The Wages of Sin, A Modern Melodrama*, written by a member of the cast. The illustration for the latter production depicts, on the front page, a small bird being entwined by an evil snake, forked tongue flickering.

The final page has the bird astride the inert snake, firmly pecking at it. Although the play was a domestic melodrama, the illustrations were meaningful. In spite of his extrovert personality and good looks, Barry tended to be involved with the stage settings rather than as an actor.

During these months there was much communication between the State Department and the Swiss legation, which handled both American and German interests. Bartering was the order of the day. The staff of the German consulate in Algiers and its Vichy counterparts had been interned at Staunton in Virginia, and other German officials at Ingleside in Texas. Negotiations to exchange the Germans in America and the Americans in Baden Baden went backwards and forwards at a snail's pace. What the group at Baden Baden, marooned in relative comfort and German courtesy, did not know was that at the beginning of 1944 when Germany began to feel threatened by defeat, there was a period during the negotiations when it was suggested that internees might begin to be 'treated roughly'. But this didn't happen, agreement was reached and on 19 February 1944 the internees bade farewell to their spa hotel, moved to France and were transported on a 'hell train', sealed in and with no food and little water, to Lisbon.

The M.V. *Gripsholm* of the Swedish American Line must have been one of the best loved ships ever to have crossed the Atlantic. Built in 1924 at Newcastle-Upon-Tyne in Britain by the Armstrong Whitworth company, she was the first motor ship running on diesel and used as a cruise ship and transatlantic liner. From May 1942 to April 1946 the *Gripsholm* was put under charter to the US government as an exchange and repatriation ship. Under the auspices of the International Red Cross she sailed the Atlantic and other seas fully lit with the word 'Diplomat' painted clearly on her sides. During this period she and her crew made 11 humanitarian voyages across war-torn seas. A post-war testimonial from the then secretary of state James F. Byrnes, writes of their dauntless spirit.

On 6 March 1944 around 600 passengers, gathered from various localities in Europe, were embarked on the *Gripsholm*, headed for the Jersey City dock. The voyage would take nine days. But America was not to welcome the huddled masses with open arms. In a flurry of memos across the desks of the FBI under the director, J. Edgar Hoover, there was anxiety as to who exactly might be on these ships. It appears suspects ranged from possible spies to German propagandists, to those simply trying to enter America illegally. Committees were in place to receive the ship when it docked on 15 March and much time was spent interrogating passengers.

For Barry there were no such problems and he was soon on his way to his mother in Pittsburgh. But he would not stay long.

⟶ 12 ⟵

Waiting for Melpomene – Eric

I think to be in the Resistance you had to be maladjusted.

Marcel Ophüls, *The Sorrow and the Pity*

In the summer of 1941 a Scottish pastor, Donald Caskie, had a shock when Eric Sawyer turned up at his Seamen's Mission in Marseilles and handed over the sum of 850,000 francs (around £5,000). The Mission was being used as a safe house for military personnel who were hoping to flee France by boat to Gibraltar or over the Pyrenees to Spain and onwards. It was from here the famous Pat escape line was first organised by Pat O'Leary (real name Albert Guérisse). There are various versions of Eric's visit to the Seamen's Mission, but Caskie described the encounter in his book *The Tartan Pimpernel*:

One morning, a dapper gentleman called to see me ... 'You need money, I know. I have brought you a little contribution' ... My visitor was a very charming person but I had become a wary clergyman. 'I insist sir, before I accept money I must know more of you'.

The blue eyes glittered in the dark, tanned face. His obvious amusement was slightly irritating. In one short sentence he calmed any remaining fears I had.[1]

Eric explained his work. It seems he had instructions from the British War Office 'under no circumstances to be repatriated to England as he, and others, were remaining on the Riviera under direct orders'.[2] He had therefore been busy raising funds from French branches of British concerns in France. This money, obtained from firms still operating in the country, was lent on an undertaking from the war office it would be repaid once the hostilities were over. Later this undertaking was extended to private individuals. Strangely, it seems the patron of this fund-raising was Bendor, the Duke of Westminster, ex-lover of that elegant collaborator Coco Chanel. Bendor had, like so many of the aristocracy, been vehemently pro-Nazi in the 1930s.

The end of 1942 saw the fortunes of war begin to swing in favour of the Allies and the German Army was defeated at El Alamein in November. But these events did not help France. Lack of fuel meant that increasingly there was no heating and no hot water. Overcoats were worn around the clock. Gas and power shortages made cooking increasingly difficult. Camping stoves, and in the country wood fires, heated small meals. As there was no petrol the rare unofficial cars, the *gazogènes*, were propelled by cumbersome charcoal-burning stoves perched on the back, and makeshift bicycle rickshaws appeared on the roads of towns and cities.

Queues outside shops often began as early as 4 a.m. when word got around that new supplies had come in – and such supplies did not last long. Milk was requisitioned and rice became non-existent. Horses were seized by order – the odd one concealed riskily among cows in their byres – and to slaughter an animal was illegal. The permitted squares of hard soap became the '*savon national*'. British submarines patrolled the Mediterranean (painted blue for that sea and green for the Atlantic) blocking supplies from North Africa. Those supplies that did get through were taken by the local authorities or seized by the occupiers. If there had been surplus foodstuffs left in the agricultural north there was no transport available to get them to the needy south, even if this had been permitted.

On 9 January 1942 Captain Peter Churchill of the SOE F (Special Operations Executive, F for French section), climbed down from the submarine P36, and into a canoe riding on the winter waters of the Mediterranean. P36 then dived almost immediately and sped away, leaving Churchill quite alone. He was heading for Miramar, around two sea miles distant from where he had been dropped. It was 7.15 p.m. and dark but Peter Churchill knew where he was going. This was the elegant small hotel St Christophe – a kilometre along the coast from Le Trident – where he had enjoyed several pleasurable holidays in the past. Finding the iron ladder which he had climbed so often after diving, he grappled his way onto the flat rock above. After slashing and returning the deflated canoe to the sea he set off on foot in the direction of Cannes, carrying his only luggage, an attaché case which held his pyjamas – and a large amount of French francs. At Théoule he decided to rest, creeping into a large garden and sheltering under some trees. It began to get colder and wrapping himself in his raincoat helped not at all. By 4.00 a.m. he gave up and trudged towards Cannes in what became a snowstorm. By the time he took the road through the industrial area of La Bocca the snow was six inches deep and he was drenched. At 9.00 a.m. he reached Cannes, passing the already endless queues of people outside the food shops. He then caught a bus to Antibes to make contact with 'Carte', one of the few Resistant networks of that time. The Resistance on the Riviera was finally creeping into action. Eugenie Rocca-Serra, who served on one of the escape lines out of France, would write, particularly of Cannes, 'The situation ... was very difficult for anyone wishing to do clandestine work. People talked too much of a natural vanity which made them boast of any operation they undertook.'[3]

There is little doubt that Peter Churchill was in contact with Eric Sawyer, as on Eric's army record it is noted that he worked for the SOE from 1940 to 1943. And during 1942 the feluccas *Seawolf* and *Seadog*, captained by two intrepid Polish seamen, scuttled back and forth along the coast from Gibraltar making clandestine pick-ups and drop-offs in the area of Le Trident and on to Antibes. To the west of Miramar, Germaine Sablon, actress and singer, sister of the more famous crooner Jean Sablon, was living quietly in her seaside house at Agay, and working with the Resistance. Her bay, too, was used to deposit stores and pick up agents by felucca. She shared her house with two other Resistants: her lover, the journalist and writer Joseph Kessel, a future member of the Académie Française, and Maurice Druon, Kessel's nephew, a prize winning novelist. Both men were Jewish and all three were planning their escape via Switzerland and the Pyrenees. In 1943, once in London and working with the Free French, Kessel and Druon wrote the lyrics for what would become the hymn of the Resistance – 'Le Chant des Partisans'. This was set to the haunting music of a Russian song by the singer Anna Marly:

Ami, entends-tu le vol noir du corbeau sur nos plaines?
Ami, entends-tu les cris sourds du pays qu'on enchaîne?

Friend, can you hear the dark flight of the crows over our
    plains?
Friend, do you hear the dulled cries of the country in chains?[4]

The haunting song became so popular it was even suggested it should replace the 'Marseillaise', which had been banned in the Occupied Zone and severely tweaked in Vichy France.

Eric, in hiding, worked hard at making contact with those who were already involved with the Free French or the SOE, or simply determined to join De Gaulle in London. On its sparsely inhabited coastline Le Trident was supposed to be deserted, apart from the Italian couple who acted as guardians. If any unwelcome attention was given to the house, Eric would descend his rocky mountainside and hide in a cave by one of the small beaches. He was incensed when a group of Italians moved into a building just around the point from Le Trident, declared it a hospital and mounted a gun emplacement pointing out to sea. He was now in greater danger.

Girard de Charbonnières was familiar with the muse Melpomene. Thirty-five and an ex-diplomat, who had been living alone in his family villa on Cap Ferrat, on 1 December 1942 he was walking nervously up and down the Croisette between the Carlton and Martinez Hotels. It was almost 8.45 p.m. and dark. From time to time he glanced at his watch. Apart from a solitary bus propelled by its *gazogène* generator, the Croisette was almost deserted. De Charbonnières had been told to put his belongings in a small case and wait for a car that would stop for no longer than a second. If he was not opposite the Martinez at the appointed time the car would not wait. He had been accepted as part of the Melpomene escape group and had spent the past few weeks being driven almost mad by Melpomene and her coded messages from the BBC.

Melpomene is the name for a Greek muse and perhaps a strange choice for BBC coded messages about specific felucca pickups from the Riviera coast. Although initially the muse of singing, she was subsequently proclaimed the muse of tragedy, often seen holding a distraught mask in one hand and a knife or club in the other. But she was undoubtedly beautiful and had the power to invoke lyrical phases – being, in short, very theatrical.

The messages were being sent from the SOE through the BBC programme *Ici Londres*, in cooperation with the BCRA, de Gaulle's Bureau Central de Renseignements et d'Action, his own special operational force. A large radio in a room on the fourth floor of the Carlton Hotel was operated by

'Denis', Jacques Robert. Jacques Robert was also known as 'Rewez', chief of the local Phatrie Resistance network and a force to be reckoned with. He was one of the few to become quickly involved in the embryo Resistance. By the time he was installed in front of his radio in the Carlton he was being keenly hunted by the Gestapo who, although they did not yet have their tracking vans on the Riviera, searched avidly for clandestine radios and their operators. The chief concierge at the Carlton was a member of the Resistance, working under the noses of the Vichy police and those shadowy members of the Gestapo who now haunted the coast.

Melpomene's messages were unfortunately confusing, due to her endless supply of perfumes coupled with her choice of exercise. The codes, in French, were given out as follows: the listeners must note the first letter of the perfume which Melpomene would be wearing; if she used lavender, the initial l was the twelfth letter of the alphabet and to this one must add seven days, i.e. 19 days from the day the message had been received; that would be when they hoped to send the felucca; but if Melpomene was 'to walk on the green lawn', it meant the felucca was actually en route to arrive on the promised day.

For de Charbonnières, over the following weeks the muse never ceased to douse herself with lily of the valley, fern, rose, thyme and geranium without ever walking on any kind of lawn. Then suddenly came the message: *Melpomene se promène sur le gazon vert* – the day to escape had arrived. Which is why he found himself in the dark on the pavement opposite the Martinez, being hauled into a solitary car which had screeched to a halt beside the kerb. The five men inside greeted him amiably as he noted, with horror, light glinting on two machine guns. Much as he longed to leave France, he began to regret the escapade he had become part of. The car sped down the Croisette, turned left and took the road through La Bocca to Mandelieu. At La Napoule they reached the Corniche d'Or where they slowed down. By a miracle they had not been followed.

So began one of several flirtations with Melpomene. De Charbonnières in his book *Mon Chemin Vers De Gaulle* (*My Path Towards De Gaulle*) described his arrival at Le Trident. A sharp turn onto a steep path on the sea side where, after two narrow bends, the car stopped and everyone clambered out. 'Careful', said someone, 'Watch the steps'. Descending the 30 twisting stone steps in the dark they arrived at the studded double front door. The leader of the group fetched keys and they all trooped into the house, rather startled to find themselves immediately confronted by a large kit bag upon which were clearly inscribed the words, 'Colonel Eric Sawyer Intelligence Service'. Taken into a large room, lit by many lamps, they found a group of men. Here comfortable sofas and armchairs were upholstered in white material, matching the curtains which were drawn over large windows looking to the sea beyond. They had arrived at the villa, which was now being used as a prospective jumping-off point by the Phatrie Resistance group. It was excellent for its purpose. The agent handling the property had been approached and the following day Eric appeared. He agreed to let the group use the house as an escape base, provided he and two of his friends, Tom Kenny from Marseilles and Frederick Price from Cannes, could be of the party.

The leader of the group of around ten men was Antoine Masurel, young and blond. He was the second in command of the Phatrie network in the south and a member of the Forces Françaises Combattantes (the Fighting French Forces), a clandestine military organisation attached to the Forces Françaises Libres (the Free French Forces), the government in exile led by de Gaulle in London. Masurel's family had bought a plot almost next door to Le Trident, upon which Barry had built a small pavilion. Those in the sitting room of Le Trident on that December night were almost all hunted and desperate to leave. De Charbonnières, determined to join De Gaulle in London, would write that he felt like an intruder, not being a Resistant like the others, for apart from Masurel who had introduced himself, he knew none of them. Eric himself was well known on the Riviera, there was René Massigli, ex-French ambassador to Turkey who had been summoned to London by De Gaulle, André Manuel, Massigli's minder, who had a high position in the Free French, Frederick Price who was generous in his monetary support for the Resistance and for whom Barry had built the grand Mas de Terrafial in Cannes and who would become one of the founders of Unilever, and the Canadian Tom Kenny, now married to Suzanne, the pretty 17-year-old daughter of the owner of the Martinez Hotel on the Croisette.

The men trooped into a neighbouring room where, laid out on a table, were a line of electric torches along with pieces of red muslin. These were, explained Masurel, intended to change their flashes from white to red in order to signal to the felucca. The operation was under the orders of the British Secret Intelligence Service (SIS). In groups of three the men took it in turns to stand on the edge of the terrace in the cold, dark night and signal into the blackness over the vast expanse of sea. On that particular night it had been arranged that the felucca *Seawolf* would ferry the party from the rocks below to Gibraltar. These feluccas were almost always ferried by two brave and tough sailors from Poland. The tension mounted as the time for the arrival of the felucca was imminent but, as the hours passed and many glasses of whisky were drunk, hopes sank. While told not to talk too loudly in this deserted place, de Charbonnières was aghast to learn of the Italians just out of sight just around the point, while at Le Trident a group of men were flashing lights out to sea and expecting lights to be flashed back from the deep.

'*Toujours rien*' was the report as the signalling groups returned in twos and threes from the terrace, and by 6 a.m.

tired, unshaven and disillusioned men were draped on chairs
and sofas contemplating what to do next. Then, one by
one, they disappeared into the dawn. As his papers were in
order, a cold and unimpressed de Charbonnières climbed the
mountain to the Corniche road where he caught the early bus
for Cannes.

There would be another failed attempt four days later,
and yet another in January 1943. Nothing seemed to lure
Melpomene to pause in the seas under Le Trident and embark
her precious cargo. Various reasons given by the captains
were: bad weather, shore signals unseen and, on the final
occasion, fear of what were thought to be bright lights and
enemy machine gun fire but which were, in fact, an Italian
division racing along the Corniche d'Or, headlights lit, and
changing gear as they negotiated the bends. These failures are
recorded in Brooks Richards *Secret Flotillas*, which lists 'failed'
beside every mention of poor Melpomene. And *Seawolf* and
its companion boat *Tarana* had spent many wasted hours.

René Massigli, after the last attempt in January and still
on the run, was eventually scooped up by a Lysander near
Lyon and flown to a bumpy landing in Cornwall, before
being deposited at Tempsford Airport in Bedfordshire in
South East England. Eric, Tom Kenny, de Charbonnières
and Suzanne Kenny, carrying her baby Patrick, all escaped
separately in hazardous winter journeys over the Pyrenees
and on to an uncertain fate in Spain. Jacques Robert and
others of the Le Trident group would return in later years and
sign their names in the visitors' book. Massigli, now a French
ambassador, sent his card, 'with my thanks and souvenirs of
Melpomene'. Gracious, he seemed to bear no grudge for her
failures.

As for Melpomene herself, she had been (as behove her
persona as tragic muse) such a part of the high hopes and
deep disappointments on those chilly winter nights of 1942
and 1943 that Eric and Barry would have her name and one

of her messages carved into a plaque by the front door of Le Trident. Here she will always, '*Promène Sur le Gazon Vert et se Parfumait a l'Heliotrope. Decembre 1942. Janvier 1943.*'

No one knows exactly what route Eric took over the Pyrenees, for he would not speak of the war years, but once back in London in March 1943 he wrote from St James's, his London club, to Lord Selbourne, in charge of the SOE. He pleaded for help in rescuing people from the Riviera coast, giving his opinion that feluccas were no longer practicable as there were many enemy patrols. Passage over the Pyrenees was now only possible by the high passes, as the easier routes were closely guarded, and the highest passes could only be undertaken by those who were physically very fit. He gave his credentials for his suggestions:

1. As owner of the property at Theoule near Cannes from which three abortive attempts were made this winter to take parties off by boat, at all of which operations I assisted.

2. As having myself successfully escaped over the Pyrenees in January of this year.

3. My intimate knowledge of conditions in the south of France during the war and during enemy occupation.

4. If individuals are considered worth getting out they should be given the maximum of security. Surface craft do not provide this, even under the most favourable conditions. The only practicable operation by sea, therefore, appears to me to be by SUBMARINE ... Essential food supplies could be brought in which are urgently needed by those in hiding, who have no food cards or means of procuring supplies.

[And:] ... if you see any way in which I can be of further service in the way of rescuing our friends in France, I am entirely at your disposal.[5]

The letter seems to have been batted around the offices of the SOE. His suggestions were taken seriously and 'strenuous efforts' were made to persuade the Admiralty to allow SOE to use a submarine for this purpose.[6] But the general conclusion was that submarines were in very short supply and none could be spared. Suddenly, at the end of one of the memos the writer (all were signed simply with initials) added: 'I think I ought to mention that we have already had some dealings with Colonel Sawyer and I am not at all satisfied as to his bona fides.'[7] The SOE were consistently suspicious of those who escaped from occupied countries and made their way to England. Many were interned until they proved they could be trusted. Eric had escaped this fate. A reply to this note pointed out that there were now people in London who could vouch for Eric's Resistance activities in the war. It was decided he should be trained as a 'facilitator' but it seems he demurred and, now 53, joined the British Army once again.

In July of 1943, American forces captured Palermo in Sicily. Mussolini was suddenly arrested by his own people and Marshal Pietro Badoglio, known for his cruelty during the Italian occupation of Ethiopia and Libya, took over. Badoglio pronounced his intention to carry on with the war, but at the same time began negotiations with the Allies. This dithering policy boded ill for Italy and the Italians. In September, Mussolini was rescued by the Germans and re-established a fascist government at Lake Garda in northern Italy, thereby creating two Italys. On 1 October the Allies entered Naples in the south and on 13 October the Badoglio government declared that Italy was at war with Germany. In the south of France there was a mass rush eastwards towards the border by retreating Italian troops, jettisoning their arms, munitions and uniforms en route and pursued by the Germans, who had moved swiftly down and through the south. The Vichy regime became impotent and the Nazis took control of the whole of France. The Gestapo now had open season in the south and so began the *rafles*, the terrible round ups, of Jews both French and foreign. In Nice the Hotel Excelsior was the notorious headquarters of the Gestapo where around 3,000 Jews, including children, were gathered from the hills and coast of the Alpes Maritimes before being sent by train to Drancy transit camp near Paris, and onwards.

Le Trident was taken over by Russian slave troops placed there to defend that part of the coast. Badly treated and expendable, these were wild and fierce men with little to lose, and the villa suffered accordingly.

Eric served during the war in North Africa and Italy as a staff officer in Civil Affairs, before joining the French section of SHAEF, the Supreme Headquarters Allied Expeditionary Force set up to plan the invasion of Europe. Before leaving Le Trident he had written in the visitors' book:

x x x x x x x x
END OF AN EPOCH
x x x x
Exeunt Eric & Barry

La Domaine du Sault — Isabel Pell

Miss Pell, You are a Fairy
> Victor Werny, discussion, September 2010

In Puget Théniers, a perched village in the Alpes Maritimes, Isabel Townsend Pell swung in a kilt down the cobbled main street. Tall and fit, with a white streak in her brown fringe, she was a striking figure and this pleased her. The fact that the kilt did not belong to her, was in a Gordon tartan and Isabel had no Scottish ancestry, would not have bothered her in the slightest.

The kilt in question was the property of Dorothy (Dickie) Fellowes-Gordon, an attractive, cool-mannered socialite descended from a prominent Scottish family, the Knockespochs of Aberdeenshire. Blessed with a lovely singing voice, she preferred nevertheless to live a life unhindered by practice and hard work. With her elegance and insouciant air, she was much admired. In the early 1930s she moved into an old mill house, La Domaine du Sault, on a hilltop in the twelfth-century village of Auribeau sur Siagne in the countryside above Cannes. She had bought the house from Janet Aitken, the daughter of Lord Beaverbrook, the newspaper proprietor and politician, and in 1938 she asked Barry to build an elegant extension of salon and dining room, giving on to a wide terrace. Although this was a fairly modest home, it was set in 32 acres, which included a waterfall, jasmine terraces and wonderful views. Here, in her country home, Dickie was a contented smallholder, growing vegetables and raising hens. She shared this house, and various other abodes, with 'the hostess with the mostest' Elsa Maxwell who, in those pre- and post-war years, was the party-giver of Europe. Elsa's fiefdoms ranged from California to New York and from Venice to the Riviera – with particular emphasis on Monaco. Plump, far from beautiful and with the air of an energetic peasant, she was clever and talented. Pianist, song writer, author, journalist, her greatest talent was her ability to entice and gather together the beau monde of the day and give them each other, combined with fun. Having no funds of her own, she was able to organise gatherings whose cost was paid for by others. She was a supreme networker. Cole Porter wrote a song for her and Noel Coward, who felt he owed her much, immortalised her in 'I've Been To A Marvellous Party'. She became the leader of café society, typically introducing the actress Rita Hayworth to the handsome playboy Aly Khan, which resulted in a troubled marriage. Introductions were her thing. Elsa desired women guests to be beautiful and beautifully dressed and she expected 'vivacity'.[1] In 1927 she was employed by Prince Pierre of Monaco, Prince Rainier's father, to help with the promotion of the principality as a summer resort. She would claim the tennis courts, Olympic-sized swimming pool (plus a fatally flawed rubber beach) and much else as her own ideas. The two women were friends of the couturier Jean Patou and it was Elsa who professed that it was she and Dickie who dreamed up the name Joy for the, then, most expensive perfume in the world, created during the Great Depression.

Elsa and Dickie seemed mismatched and their relationship was enigmatic. They had met in 1912, Elsa being the elder by eight years. She, who would maintain 'I married the world', professed to have no experience of, or desire for, sex although she developed a fervent crush on the opera singer Maria Callas.[2] Dickie had various heterosexual love affairs, but nevertheless they would be on-and-off companions for over 50 years. Elsa always felt Le Sault was her Provençal home but when in 1939 Isabel Pell – whom Dickie had met in New York – joined the ménage it seems Elsa, in a fit of temper, left the house abruptly, eventually sailing for New York. Dickie followed at the beginning of 1940 leaving Isabel, together with the latter's new companion, a French aristocrat, in charge of her home.

From New York's upper crust, in spite of a less than happy childhood Isabel Pell brimmed with confidence. Through her father she was descended from John Pell who, from 1670, held the title of Lord of the Manor of Pelham, Westchester County, New York. Pelham lands included the borough of the Bronx and the southern part of Long Island Sound. Her uncle, Stephen H.P. Pell, had been awarded the Legion d'Honneur and the Croix de Guerre with Star and Palm for his service in the French Army in World War I. In 1909 he restored the historic Fort Ticonderoga on Lake Camplain in northern New York. Isabel's socialite father, S. Osgood Pell, a real-estate broker, had married her beautiful mother, Isabel Townsend, in 1899. By the time she was 19 this Isabel had given birth to her daughter, Isabel Jr, and had divorced her husband for his infidelities – a brave move in those days. From then on Isabel's father took little or no interest in his small daughter, apart from granting her an allowance of $150 a month and paying her tuition fees. Isabel felt this estrangement keenly and her childhood letters, begging for both love and money, show how this rejection must have affected her life generally. The rejection came to an abrupt end when, in a terrible accident, Osgood Pell's Lincoln car was hit sideways by a speeding train on a crossing near Long Beach, New York. Pell, his chauffeur and one other passenger were killed.

Fortunately for Isabel, Stephen Pell had no daughter of his own and became a surrogate father, giving her the support and affection she had not had from her own. She attended Holton-Arms School in Washington DC, where she was known simply as Pell. Sporty, independent and handsome, many of the girls had crushes on her. Coming out as a New York debutante in 1920 she did all the right things, such as dancing at the Blue Bird Ball at the Waldorf Astoria and becoming involved with Junior League activities. She had grown into a glamorous cigarette-smoking woman, with her bobbed, honey-coloured hair, elegant clothes and always wearing the new Tabac Blond perfume by Caron, which was described as '*androgyne*' and 'a feminine fragrance with notes of tobacco and leather'.[3] Quickly growing bored with the social round Isabel had already raised eyebrows by taking a job in a dress shop and then landing the part of a maid in *Fool's Errant* at Maxine Elliott's theatre. A theatrical career which lasted five minutes.

In February 1924 her uncle gave a dinner at the Ritz-Carlton to announce the engagement between Isabel and the suitable Lorenzo Thomson of Madison Avenue. The wedding date was fixed for June. By April the engagement was amicably broken off – Isabel had discovered what she needed and that was not a husband. She preferred women and made no secret of the fact. Honor Moore, during her research for *The White Blackbird*, the biography of her grandmother the artist Margarett Sargent, came across people who, while being impressed by Isabel with her elegant clothes and style, also felt she was 'cruel' and 'a terrible liar'.[4] But Mercedes de Acosta – playwright, novelist and lover of many beautiful women in the arts and Hollywood – later wrote that Isabel was kind and a lovable person and this seems to have been how many people saw her. But it is not in doubt that she stretched the truth to its limits when it suited her.

With her extrovert, maverick character Isabel now lived as she pleased and with whom she pleased, played golf, rode and drove her stunning Duesenberg J convertibles on the roads of the East Coast. That was until she indulged in a too public affair with a soprano at the Metropolitan Opera and at last realised she had gone too far in a society that was intolerant of such behaviour. Her uncle may have had a quiet word with her or perhaps Isabel felt she should move to pastures new, for in the 1930s she left for Paris together with a generous allowance to encourage her to stay abroad.

Geoffrey Jones, an American soldier with whom she would work in later years, felt Isabel was:

> One of those strange people who came out of the flapper era. She might have been lifted intact from a page written by F. Scott Fitzgerald. She was quite tall, built huskily, but was rather attractive-looking, wore her hair in a flapper cut … Quite pleasant, with an enormous zesty laugh. Never tried to hide her way of life, but she certainly had complete acceptance in Europe. In America we'd consider that she should be severely ignored … but in France she was only regarded as, well, eccentric.[5]

It was in Paris that Isabel met unhappily married Claire Charles-Roux, Marquise de Forbin la Barben. Claire, though shy and delicate-looking, was an expert rider and champion skier. Her father had been lieutenant-colonel of a cavalry unit in the Algerian Light Infantry and an aide to General Lyautey in Morocco. Claire was born there and had learnt to ride bareback on Arabian ponies in the desert. Her brave and decorated father died from his wounds during World War I when Claire was 10 years old. The Charles-Roux family, part of the influential Greek diaspora, were originally rich soap manufacturers in Marseilles, who later moved into banking and shipping. Her brother Jules Henri François was a French ambassador and later aide-de-camp to General de Gaulle in London and Algiers.

The man Claire married, under pressure from her family, was Antoine de Forbin de Barben, a Provençal aristocrat from an ancient family who had been arms dealers and successful merchants in the fourteenth century, before becoming involved with the royal courts of Provence. Their home was in Avignon, where their splendid *hôtel*, or town house, still stands. In Aix-en-Provence there is a Place de Forbin de Barben, and near Salon de Provence is their ornate château. But the elegant luxury of the de Barben homes held no attraction for Claire. It seems that, as they both preferred their own sex, this was almost certainly a *mariage blanc*, i.e. a marriage of convenience. Claire would say they had led very independent lives since they married and had established a 'gentleman's agreement', which grew sour as time went on.

It was 1939, the Phoney War, and Isabel and Claire became involved, along with Dickie Fellowes-Gordon, with the committee meetings and charitable organisations which had sprung up along the coast. A committee member in Cannes described Isabel as, 'An obvious American, beautifully clothed by Chanel and Molyneux, very efficient and self-confident' – but with a tendency to giggle at meetings.[6] But Isabel was greatly stimulated by the period of history she was passing through and she entered into it with gusto. In Cannes she became vice-president of an aid organisation dedicated to raising funds for the *chasseurs alpins*, those admired sturdy soldiers who, in their dark blue uniforms and floppy berets, travelled the mountain roads with their rapid shuffling walk. Dickie was on the committee, the president was Prince Jean-Louis de Faucigny-Lucinge, whose company owned the Carlton Hotel (and who, having no sympathy for the Vichy regime, would have to watch his step as time went by). Others were the Englishman Captain Grant Milne, who would be shot by a German patrol on the bridge into Vence and Mrs Herman Rogers, to whom Wallis Simpson ran as the press hounded her after the abdication of King Edward VIII. Here she had found refuge in the Rogers' Villa Lou Viei in Cannes, which had been extended and remodelled by Barry, perhaps in anticipation of receiving these eminent guests.

When the United States entered the war in December 1941 and thus became an enemy, Isabel, living as she did in the hills rather than on the coast, was initially left alone. As for Claire, the villagers of Auribeau remembered that she was discreet and little was known about her. From around that time, until the Liberation, it is not known exactly where Claire went or what she did. Her brother was already working for the Free French in London and at some point Claire joined one of the Maquis Resistance groups – a challenging decision for a woman of her background, as many were Communist.

Isabel concerned herself with the welfare of the Auribeau village children, in 1942 opening her house for diphtheria vaccinations and generally acting as lady bountiful, supplying the small school and those in need. She was probably able to obtain funds through the Swiss legation and made sure she had an adequate supply, for these would soon be needed. Alongside her philanthropy, Isabel made no secret of her disdain for the whole concept of Vichy France and its puppet relationship with the occupying Germans in the north. Her rather isolated Le Sault became a centre for the diffusion of propaganda and a meeting place for those unsympathetic with the Vichy New Order. The Italians (apart from their secret service the Ovra) were generally fairly benign. Those who became a nuisance were rarely sent to prison camps (that was Vichy's job) but were told to remove themselves high into the hills, report to the local Italian headquarters several times a day, and not be disruptive. Later in 1942 Isabel fell into this category and for her the chosen village was Puget Théniers.

Puget Théniers is an ancient feudal settlement situated on the Var River, 60 kilometres north-west of Nice, far enough away to keep Isabel out of trouble – or so the Italians thought. Surrounded by granite hillsides and deep gorges, with the ruins of a twelfth-century château and narrow streets lined with medieval houses, it was then the archetypal Provençal mountain village. Isabel, whose home was now an attic room in an old house, soon made herself known and took advantage of her time away from the coast. Surprisingly, she seemed to have been given considerable freedom. In the surrounding hillsides, where it was easy to hide, she heard of the small Resistance groups which were now beginning to form and, loose cannon that she was, determined to become involved. These numbers swelled greatly, in February 1943, by the order of Service de Travail Obligatoire which swung into action throughout the whole of France. What had been formerly a campaign promising good conditions and compensation for those willing to work in Germany now became, in the face of increasing unwillingness to take up the offer, deportation preceded by terrifying roundups. This threat was now so great that to join the Resistance, although a tough and comfortless life, was infinitely preferable to the risk of being sent to Germany. They lived, like the outlaws they were, in the forests and scrubland of the hills. Insufficiently clothed, often cold and hungry, they relied on friendly farms and villages for food and occasional shelter, applying pressure if supplies were not forthcoming. Allied agents got money and arms to them when and where they could.

Urging disaffected young men of the area to join the Maquis, Isabel became a focus of the local embryo Maquisards of Puget Théniers, involved in their plans and funding them to the best of her ability. Carrying messages between partisans, she loved nothing more than to join them around their camp fires in the woods, which must have fed her thirst for adventure. But she did not neglect the children of Puget Théniers and there are those today who still remember her vividly. Her generosity earned her a specially composed song:

> Miss Pell, vous êtes une fée
> Et des milles difficultés
> Pour nos chèrs enfants de Puget
> Vous avez su triompher

Miss Pell, you are a fairy and over the thousand problems of our dear children of Puget, you have triumphed.[7]

In September 1943, the Germans descended into the Free Zone and, in the brief confusion that reigned, those interned in the hills simply walked out of confinement. For some it was a release but for the Jews of the south it was nothing less than terrifying.

Isabel returned to Auribeau, where she was quickly put under house arrest and, as the German Army began to mine the beaches and build blockhouses on the coast, she simply continued whatever work she was able to do with the Resistance. She kept contact with all that was going on in Puget Théniers, sent and received messages from their Maquis group and hid fugitives in her cellar along with guns and ammunition. Members of the local Resistance came and went. In April of 1944 a detachment of the German Army circled Puget Théniers and took away as prisoners all men between the ages of 16 and 50, of which three were executed. Was she indirectly responsible for this? There were those who thought she was. A frantic message was sent to Isabel that all contact with Puget Théniers must stop immediately. She was now in real danger and kept a low profile, sleeping away from the house at night. At 7 a.m. one day in July a group of armed Gestapo agents broke into Le Sault, fired questions at her and searched the house. Surprisingly, they failed to find the stash of arms, spare clothes and papers hidden in her cellar. With her record it is extraordinary she wasn't arrested and put into a prison camp. As rumours of the impending Allied landings took place she took to the hills and lived for ten days with the newly formed Auribeau Maquis. When the Gestapo visited the house a second time they found it empty.

Isabel now became determinedly involved in that most exciting and longed for event - the Liberation of August 1944. With Claire now back in Auribeau, Isabel sent a note offering her services to Major General Robert Frederick, commander of the liberating 1st Airborne Task Force (the Devils' Brigade) and now in charge of the Civil Affairs Division based in Nice. It was vital that newly liberated areas should be placed under civil control during the period of military occupation and until restored governments were deemed ready to take over. Now the two women came into their own. In Nice, Isabel worked closely with the enigmatic but much respected Frederick. She proved herself invaluable in many ways, knowing the area and having a good sense of who was really in need and who could do without - 'picking out the real people from among the fakes' - and driving trucks filled with supplies around the countryside.[8] Frederick recorded that she wanted a uniform but, as they had none to give her, she had to do without (she cobbled one together for herself). She had also claimed she spoke excellent French but, in spite of the years she had spent in the country, it was found her French was 'atrocious'.

Captain Rupert Graves of Civil Affairs, who came to know her well, felt:

That there are some people who seem peculiarly out of step during uneventful times but whose lives achieve sharp meaning during extraordinary periods. Isabel Pell was one of these.[9]

As for Claire, she was commended in an official despatch for her bravery during Operation Dragoon. While still with the Maquis she was told nine American paratroopers and twelve German prisoners were lost in the mimosa hills of Tanneron above Mandelieu. Taking a guide with her she went into the area, where there was still a heavy German contingent, eventually finding the paratroopers and guiding them safely back to their unit. She was assigned to Captain Geoffrey Jones in his branch of Civil Affairs in Grasse, covering that area in the same capacity as General Frederick in Nice. Geoffrey Jones would say that he admired, even loved, Claire. His Grasse headquarters were manned by a group of attractive French women volunteers, all of whom had interesting backgrounds. Being volunteers they were not paid, but were fed. However, those French who worked with the Americans to try to bring equilibrium and much needed supplies to the liberated areas were not always looked upon with favour by their compatriots.

In November 1944, the Liberation Committee of Puget Théniers made Isabel, in her presence, an honoured citizen in an impressive ceremony attended by the townspeople, ex-Resistants and officers of the American Army. A small street in the town was named after her and is still Avenue Isabel Pell. The accompanying plaque describes her as 'Citizen of the USA. The Spirit of the Resistance at Puget Théniers'. Although there were elements in the official Free French groups who seemed resentful and wary of the role she had played during the war, and there was muttering in certain quarters when her name was mentioned, she was untouchable, being loved and acclaimed by so many.

Through the auspices of the Red Cross, Isabel wrote to Ruth Cowan in America:

Tell Dickie [Fellowes-Gordon] the house has suffered comparatively little damage; but the beautiful woods, except just in front of the house, was [sic] burnt to the ground by the Boches, who are not human beings, but beasts of the lowest type. I succeeded in saving Dickie's silver and all of her furniture and most of the broken windows are fixed. I escaped being shot at by a day.

Tell her, her house was a very famous centre for the resistance and today stands proudly as a monument to the great work of the Maquis. Tell her the love I have for France is very great and I thank her for leaving her place in my care during the last five years ... Heine my dog is thin but has come through it all.[10]

At the end of the war Mercedes de Acosta visited Isabel at Le Sault in Auribeau. She was given a room with a view of the distant Mediterranean. In her autobiography *Here Lies the Heart*, she wrote of her reception: 'Isabel led me to a lovely tiled floor room where the shutters were closed just enough to allow the sunlight to play on the floor and to let in that wonderful heat of the Midi during the summer months.'[11] Here Mercedes met Claire, writing of how extremely thin and ill she looked when she first saw her, but later, 'I noticed then how really beautiful Claire was ... I noticed the formation of her small skull, the delicate modelling of her brow, the exquisite chiselling of her nose.'[12] Mercedes compared her to a fresco she had seen in Pompeii and quickly scooped her up and took her to America. Here, she was cosseted by Mercedes and various Hollywood stars, before eventually returning to Europe and dying in Switzerland in 1992 aged 84. Her husband had died childless in 1987 and his line of de Forbin de Barben came to an end.

Around 1946 Dickie and Elsa returned, bringing medical supplies, to claim back the house in Auribeau. During the first Cannes Film Festival in that year, Elsa would give rustic supper parties in the garden to such personalities as Jack Warner, Darryl Zanuck, Tyrone Power and Gene Tierney. One of these included the Windsors, the Duke looking incredibly bored. Isabel returned to the United States. She had had a 'good war' and after the intense excitement of working with the Resistance, coupled with the eulogies bestowed upon her by the inhabitants of Puget Théniers, returning home must have seemed very tame. Not only did she become just another American but her sexuality, accepted in France, was out of step with the post-war purity of America. It may have been for this reason that she embarked on a rather reckless campaign of self-promotion. She organised syndicated articles in which she called herself 'Fredericka' of the French underground, one of her stories embellished with a dramatic drawing of an energetic young woman sporting a French beret, pointing towards a burning building and flanked by rather troubled looking American soldiers. A wounded victim lies in the foreground. She had taken for herself Claire's courageous escapade, when the latter climbed through the woods to reach a group of lost American soldiers and led them to their unit. The flaming building and the body were added for effect. Extraordinary and exaggerated anecdotes came thick and fast. On old letter heading of the Franco-American Service of 1939, of which she had been president, she listed virtually all of the Cannes aid programmes as if she had been mainly responsible for their existence. Each entry concludes 'Accomplished'. It was simply not the case.

But she had no need to exaggerate in this fashion, for she had been courageous, efficient and more than done her bit for France. She must have felt desperate to impress her fellow Americans with thrilling tales of her war, at a time when so many others had their own stories to tell. But the unease did not last long, for in June 1952 Isabel died of a heart attack, toppling from her chair in a New York restaurant. She was 52.

Dickie Fellowes-Gordon sold Le Sault in 1958 and left the Riviera. No longer would the stars of Hollywood gather around a mill wheel on rickety kitchen chairs. Probably only someone like Elsa could have tempted them to do so.

$\twoheadrightarrow$ 14 $\twoheadleftarrow$

The Champagne Campaign

The happy faces of the French population were not a uniform expression of deep gratitude.

Robert H. Adleman and Colonel George Walton,
The Champagne Campaign

After being repatriated to the States from his internment at Baden Baden, Barry had stayed only four months before making his way to Italy and joining the American troops destined to liberate the south of France. He landed with them on the south coast of the Var in August 1944 and one can only imagine his joy and relief at being back at what would always be his home.

Under the command of US General Alexander Patch in the misty dawn of 15 August, a group of parachutists of the 1st Airborne Task Force, together with French paratroopers and the 2nd British Independent Parachute Brigade, landed on a plateau in the Massif des Maures in the Var and began the Liberation. The units had been drafted from the battle fields of Italy, and now they were to set up and co-ordinate the actions of the different Resistance groups and provide badly needed equipment and trained men to aid in sabotage activities in preparation for the imminent Allied landings. A component of the 1st Airborne Task Force would become the tough, even rather wild, Canadian/American 1st Special Service Force – the Devil's Brigade – led by the equally tough and highly respected General Robert Frederick, whom Isabel Pell came to know well. This brigade, drawn from men from widely diverse backgrounds, was considered 'ferocious' with their actions often seeming on the verge of being suicidal.[1] So began Operation Dragoon, so called because Churchill had been against the plan from the outset, only grudgingly giving in to the determination of General Eisenhower, the supreme commander. Churchill felt he had been 'dragooned' into the plan having favoured using the troops to invade the oil-producing countries of the Balkans.

In the south the Resistance movement had taken time to reach the vigour of its counterpart in the occupied north. It was slower in getting started despite the influx of, mainly Communist, Spanish Maquis (the remnants of the defeated Spanish Republican Army). But towards the end of the war, the southern Resistance grew rapidly in numbers. When, in June 1941, Russia entered the war on the side of the Allies, many members of the French Communist Party formed groups of what became the Francs-Tireurs. At the end of 1943 when the Germans invaded the south, members of the French Armistice Army (those members of the French forces allowed to exist but confined to barracks by the Germans) formed their own military Resistance, Les Groupes d'Armée. These professional soldiers despised the unstructured Maquis as much as they were disliked in return. Each of these groups were prepared to fight for recognition, even power, once Europe was at peace.

The parachute landings in the Var were followed by over 400 gliders, carrying men and equipment, which were instructed to land in the area of the Argens Valley near the village of Le Muy. Many of these lightweight machines missed their landing spots, only to crash among the vines and trees surrounding the plateaux, or on the many poles erected by the Germans in order to thwart such an invasion. The troops were detailed to protect the right flank of the American 7th Army as it landed on the southern coast and made its way up through France. It was essential to control Le Muy, about 24 kilometres inland from the town of Fréjus, for from here a spider's web of roads led in all directions and to block these effectively would be to block the movements of the German Army.

On that summer morning, landing craft of the 7th Army raced on to the beaches of Cavalaire-sur-Mer (now called the Plage du Débarquement), Pampelonne (near St Tropez), St Raphael, St Maxime, Dramont and Antheor to the west of Le Trident. On the same day US Forces, with a small British contingent, landed on the coast east of Toulon. With them was General Jean de Lattre de Tassigny and his Free French troops. This brilliant and respected soldier would lead the French 1st Army as, with two United States battalions under his command, it liberated Toulon and Marseilles. Around 60,000 prisoners were taken, at the cost of nearly 6,000 Allied casualties. The Free French then continued northwards fighting their way through to Alsace and across the Rhine to Berlin.

As the coastal towns and hill villages to the west were liberated rapidly, the towns to the east took longer. At Theoule, to the east of Le Trident, there was much exchange of artillery on the ground and bombardment from Allied ships ranged along the coast. Theoule was the first town to be liberated on the Alpes Maritimes coast and the most severely damaged.

The Allies had swiftly made their presence felt by land, sea and air. During bombardment from Allied planes and shelling from their ships at sea, dedicated to taking out the batteries and enemy gun emplacements in the hills above the coastal towns, swastikas were pulled down from public buildings and the French *tricolore* raised in their place. During this time an Allied bomb landed on a crowded Nice railway station killing many, while others lost their lives when a railway bridge near the town was destroyed, along with the train travelling across it. Although accepted fatalistically by the population, the Allied attacks were terrifying.

In one month, with the help of Resistance groups, the Allied Army swept north and west to Avignon and up the Rhone valley through the centre of France. The unexpected rapidity of the advance was due to an enfeebled German Army, whose more professional troops had been sent to the north, and the courageous fighting and sabotage carried out by the local Resistance which had come into its own. At the beginning of 1944, endeavouring to avoid a *guerre Franco-Française* (war among the French themselves), General de Gaulle had brought the majority of the groups together as the Forces Françaises de l'Intérieur (the FFI, which included the Free French abroad), enabling him to speak in the name of France as the Liberation approached. It was the FFI's evocative Croix de Lorraine armbands that would flash through the streets of Paris in 1944 as they fought for their city.

The Hollywood star Douglas Fairbanks Jr usually commanded beach-jump units which had the dangerous mission of running up onto beaches and enacting fake raids throughout the Mediterranean and particularly in Italy. On the Riviera in 1944 his unit, composed of two gunboats, four torpedo boats plus other vessels, cruised the beaches between Cannes and Nice to distract the Germans from the other, genuine, landings. For Fairbank's wartime service he was decorated for valour by the American, British and French governments.

Although Cannes was not heavily defended, a company of the Devil's Brigade suffered heavy casualties as it approached, being pinned down by enemy troops equipped with heavy guns, dug in on the east bank of the Siagne River. But on 25 August, the day Paris was liberated, so was Cannes. Tears, kisses, flowers and wine flowed. The liberation of Nice was trickier and the town was not freed until 30 August. From there, the Devil's Brigade fought their way eastwards towards the Italian border. The border was long, the terrain tough and the fighting often bitter. The Brigade lost many of its men, killed or wounded. There are memorial plaques to the Devil's Brigade along the coast and in the hill towns. In Draguignan in the Var there is a beautifully tended American cemetery where those who did not survive the liberation of the south of France lie, far from home. Two thousand two hundred Americans were killed with 2,300 wounded, missing or captured. Of the French forces 4,700 lost their lives. History has not bestowed on Operation Dragoon the recognition it deserves.

Tragically, freedom was mixed with horror, with the discovery of savage reprisals as the Gestapo took their revenge. On the same day the German troops withdrew, eight prisoners at the Gestapo Headquarters at the Villa Montfleury in Cannes, Resistants from the local area, were grouped together and shot. It was the Gestapo's final gesture to the people of the town. This was a repetition of the massacre of a group of Resistants held at Nice, who had been taken out into the countryside and shot on the day news of the Allied landings reached the Gestapo in that town. Among them was 35-year-old Hélène Vagliano from Cannes. Brought up at a boarding school in Ascot, England, of Franco-Greek extraction, her bravery in refusing to name her fellow Resistants under repeated torture made Hélène a martyr of the Resistance. A street in Cannes bears her name.

Now General Frederick found himself confronting a pile of paperwork in Nice. He had been told to set up a Civil Affairs operation in that town and in Grasse to administer the activities of all the people of all the nations who had gathered along the Riviera. One of the remits of the US Civil Affairs was, like the Red Cross, to supply food to an almost starving population and they were responsible for the distribution of meagre rations. All foodstuffs were measured out in grams per person. One report of 1945 stated: 'the food problem is again very acute and the needs of this area are not being met'.[2] For the local people there were still serious shortages. In fact *les rutabagas* (swedes) had become a staple diet. Bread was scarce, black and badly made from, among other things, the fruit of the carob tree and was sometimes so vile it brought people out in boils. 'Coffee' of grilled barley and acorns was almost undrinkable. Those who were ill or old, or too poor or proud to buy from the lively black market (the BOF – *beurre, oeufs, fromage*), often died quietly of malnutrition in their homes. Children, their tummies swelling from lack of a balanced diet, frequently succumbed to tuberculosis and rickets. In spite of efforts to eradicate the black market, it continued to flourish.

The military division of the Civil Affairs was given the power to re-establish national courts and to allow the Allies to requisition lands, buildings, transportation and supplies. In return, military personnel were expected to respect local laws. After much negotiation with the newly formed French National Committee, the liberated areas were to pass under French political authority as soon as deemed possible. In the south the Allies were instructed to have no dealings with the remains of the Vichy regime except for the purpose of liquidating it. Everyone disliked the Civil Affairs situation, both the Allies and the French. And in the midst of all that was going on was the wave of retributions, trials and punishments, legal and otherwise, now rampant among the population. The Americans were instructed not to become too involved with these reprisals. American soldiers who happened to observe one of the lamentable rituals of head shaving of prostitutes had to bite their tongues.

The United States Riviera Recreational Area (USRRA) consisting of Nice, Cannes and the Riviera coast (excluding Monte Carlo which, although neutral, had not acquitted itself well during the war) became a playground for hundreds of battle-weary troops. The US government had requisitioned, for enlisted men, 67 hotels for the purpose, including the Negresco Palace. In a friendly booklet entitled *Welcome to the Riviera* the authorities gave a history of the area as well as advice and lists of nightclubs reserved exclusively for military personnel and their guests. Enjoying service that few had experienced in their lifetimes, they were allowed this paradise for one week, before returning to their units. So the liberation of the Riviera became known as The Champagne Campaign. At one point these military visitors were said to number around 60,000. Cannes got the officers.

The Nice edition of the journal *Espoir*, in an article translated by a Civil Affairs employee, wondered at the fact that so many girls in Nice could speak English.

> These employees throng the Negresco and the Ruhl ... where one can see them chatting agreeably with the 'restees'. The same girls stroll in the streets with the army badges in their buttonholes, worn as proudly as if it was the *Croix de Guerre* or *Croix de Lorraine*, munching the indispensable chewing-gum. And yet it is so inelegant, a woman who chews gum![3]

The hard-fighting Devil's Brigade submitted to no discipline other than that from their own General Frederick, and their rowdy and destructive behaviour in the towns when on leave caused some café and restaurant owners to declare they missed the German troops, from whom no such vandalism would have been tolerated by their officers.

Now there was another entry in Le Trident's visitors' book:

LIBERATION:
By Canadian Airborne
16 August 1944

The villa was actually liberated by the American/Canadian Devil's Brigade. There was no Canadian Airborne force. The

Italian housekeepers, having been powerless to protect it, the house was in a sorry state, having also been used by Italian troops for six months in 1943. A mirror bearing a bullet hole is still in the possession of Eric's family.

With Eric still engaged in the British Army, Barry returned to Le Trident and began to put some sort of order into the house. Following hard on the heels of the armies who had flooded into the south of France were charities from the USA, Britain and elsewhere. Now with the rank of captain, Barry began working with the Civilian War Relief of the American Red Cross, based at the Carlton Hotel in Cannes, supervising the supply of food, garments, and medical supplies. He would do this until November 1946, constantly on the move between towns and villages along the coast. So respected was he for his work in that year the town of Menton, next to the Italian border, made Barry an Honorary Citizen. This was 'In recognition of his compassion, for all he had done in the region, for the soldiers, the wounded, the homeless, the deported, prisoners and children.'[4] It was only very recently that this citation came to light for, typically, he did not speak of the war or his part in it.

The war correspondent and journalist Ruth Cowan found herself on the Riviera in 1945. It is the excellent Miss Cowan one must thank for news of those expatriates who had stayed on and become involved in the war, for she quickly found and became friends with many, and all seemed to be friends of Barry and Eric's. On her return to America Ruth wrote a vast amount of letters, as she was able to receive correspondence from France through the Red Cross and relay news back and forth between the States and the Riviera. The letters were full of praise for Barry and show a significant insight into his character.

Baron Hubert Lejeune (a close friend of the couturier Elsa Schiaparelli) wrote to Ruth from the elegant Forest Hills Hotel in New Hampshire in 1945, very happy to have news of his friends on the Riviera: 'As for Barry he is such a <u>wonderful</u>

person, cheerful and so human, and he can do such a lot ... because he knows and understands all those "Midi" people so well and they trust him.'[5]

A supervisor of Foreign Operations at the Red Cross also wrote to Ruth that she had received a letter from Barry:

> I hope you had an opportunity to enjoy him as much in France as we did in Washington. He is a most unusual person, so gracious and generous, and we were heartbroken to let him go back to France. That was, however, complete selfishness on our part because, as you know, Barry loves France very, very much and I do not believe could ever be happy anywhere else.[6]

Barry wrote to Ruth Cowan in July 1945:

> My house is getting along quite quickly, most of the big work is finished and I hope when Eric arrives that he will be able to live there. In case you do not know, a simple mattress costs $250. So we are not to have very many beds. The Coast is swarming with Americans on leave. So the nights are hideous with songs. Why do Americans always sing when they get drunk, and why do they choose my corner of the Carlton to sing at? At any rate, it is all very gay and lots of fun. Bless you and love, Barry.[7]

And in another letter: 'France is as wonderful as ever and I love it more than ever.'[8] For Barry the glass was always half full. And in the visitors' book:

1945

Restoration of Le Trident

1st Oct – Eric returns to live

with Peter III (Peter Toy, Prince of Monaco)

Peter was another small white dog.

15

The Hotel Martinez

In the turmoil of charges and retributions suffered after the Liberation, the great Hotel Martinez on the Croisette in Cannes stands, in its Art Deco splendour, as both victim and accuser. With its grand entrance hall supported by columns, its reception rooms fanning out from the centre, its 500 luxurious suites and bedrooms with furnishings from the London firm of Waring and Gillow, in 1929 it became the third, and most luxurious, of the three palaces of the Croisette, and much favoured by the beau monde. But for several decades after the Liberation of 1944 for those in the know, the Martinez was not the place at which to be seen – 'one did not go there'.

During the war the hotel was occupied by refugees from the border with Italy, the Italian Army and, from November 1942, the German Army. Upon the liberation of the south in 1944 the American Army moved in and there was much celebrating.

In 1941 the Canadian Tom Kenny from Marseilles, a good friend of Eric Sawyer, had married Suzanne Martinez, the pretty young daughter of Emmanuel Martinez. Martinez had no children with his wife and Suzanne, who he always recognised, was a love-child who had been adopted by Emmanuel's rich lover Emma Digard, who became Suzanne's 'step-mother'. At this time the Resistance group Phatrie would meet in the hotel in a rather relaxed manner. André Manuel, attached to de Gaulles's Bureau Central de Renseignements et d'Action, visited these groups at the hotel on several occasions and felt that 'everyone would have known we were Resistants'. Traced to Cannes through his links with the escape lines in Marseilles, in 1941 Tom Kenny was arrested on the terrace of the hotel but eventually released with little evidence against him and reunited with Suzanne. They settled into suite 305 at the Martinez, where Tom began making contact with local Resistants, including Eric. Suzanne remembers the couple would visit Le Trident for lunch with Barry and Eric each month and, once their son Patrick was born, were provided with condensed milk from the American Red Cross stores and a layette for the baby.

When in November 1942 the German Army took over the south of France, it became vital for many Resistants to escape. In February 1943 Suzanne, carrying her two-months-old baby Patrick, undertook her own treacherous journey over the freezing Pyrenees in the footsteps of Eric and her husband Tom Kenny, who had both escaped in January after the failure of the third Melpomene venture. All three Kennys were reunited in England. Tom would join the RAF and work in RAF intelligence for the duration of the war. In 1943 he was awarded the George Medal, which rewards acts of bravery.

Emmanuel Martinez, from an old Spanish family, was born in Palermo in 1882. His father was Baron Giuseppe Martinez. Having learned the trade in London and Paris, he was put in charge of several large hotels before moving to the south and becoming general manager of the Carlton at Cannes and then five *palaces* in Nice. Based on his now vast experience, he was commissioned by a group of financiers to build the great *palace* in Cannes which would bear his name. But existing financial problems were soon made worse by the stock market crash and the subsequent depression which affected all the hotels along the Riviera. Even the increasing numbers of guests as the 1930s wore on did not improve the situation.

Desperate for funds, Emmanuel Martinez made a disastrous arrangement. Through his accountant, Marius Bertagna, he was introduced to a Russian called Michel Szkolnikoff, a high-profile collaborator. Szkolnikoff, who wished to buy the Martinez, had been given a German passport and allowed free passage throughout the country, selling textiles and other goods to the Germans and acquiring real estate in the large towns of France both for the Germans and himself. Through this, and a thriving black market operation, he added to his riches. Marius Bertagna was, unbeknown to Martinez, also administrator for one of Szkolnikoff's companies in Monaco. There was much sleight of hand and exchanging of documents but no money changed hands and no shares were sold. Upon Liberation, Szkolnikoff fled to Spain where, a year later, in 1945, he died during a kidnapping attempt. Bertagna then denounced Martinez, stating he had sold the hotel to Szkolnikoff. The French state did not hesitate. They confiscated the hotel immediately, proclaiming Emmanuel Martinez a criminal collaborator and that he had sold his personal shares to Szkolnikoff. The hotel was put into the hands of the Administration des Domains, an organisation which managed state-owned real estate. Bertagna was put in charge of the running of the hotel.

In the face of repeated death threats Martinez escaped first to Italy and then to England, to live with his daughter and Tom Kenny. He would not be allowed to enter his hotel again. In December 1944, in his absence, he was sentenced to 20 years in prison as a collaborator. But in 1949, hearing testimony from around 30 Resistants, Allied personnel and Jews, Martinez had hidden or helped to escape, the High Court in Lyon acquitted him of all charges of collaboration and restored his good name. This didn't help him at all, for there were those in Cannes whom it suited to perpetuate the slander. As the courts were unable to establish who owned the hotel at the Liberation, they were powerless to restore the business to its creator. The state then deemed Martinez liable, as Szkolnikoff was missing, to pay a total fine of almost four billion francs (1945), an impossible sum to raise. It continued to accuse Martinez of having, by selling shares in the hotel, done business with one of the worst collaborators of the war. Martinez always maintained his innocence, affirming he had not, in fact, sold to Szkolnikoff. But having lost everything, he returned to Italy where he died, ruined, in Genoa in 1973 aged 91. A year later, in 1974, the Cour de cassation, the High Court of France, upheld his plea and ruled that Martinez had never sold his hotel during the war. But Emmanuel Martinez would never know he had been vindicated.

The hotel, now unpopular as a result of the rumours which surrounded it, was run in a desultory fashion by Les Domaines until the early 1980s, when it was sold at a fraction of its value to the Taittinger family who upgraded the building to become, once more, one of the most important hotels on the Riviera. It is now owned by a Qatari company.

From the end of the war to the present day, the Martinez family have striven to regain control of the hotel and to gain compensation for the supposed inefficiency of Les Domaines. Suzanne Martinez, a vivacious lady in her 90s, now wants, as much as anything else, to see her father's good name and the honour of the Martinez family to be restored. She feels if the portrait of Emmanuel Martinez, the creator of this great hotel, was once again displayed in the hall of the Martinez, that would be one of the greatest rewards of all.

All Change

Most of the new visitors, however, had little money and were scorned.

Mary Blume, *Côte d'Azur*

Barry's clients began slowly to return, although many were discouraged by the currency restrictions for travellers and the soaring cost of living (cheques were often cashed with local businesses, circumventing the exchange controls). As no one was building houses, commissions had to be picked up when and where they could. One of the first, in partnership with the Cannes architect Marc Rainaut, was to rebuild the bombed marshalling yards at the train depot at La Bocca, a suburb of Cannes. The 'hispano-mauresque' Palm Beach Summer Casino at the eastern end of the Croisette had been turned into a blockhouse by the occupying German Army and then ravaged by an Allied bombardment in July 1944. Barry and Eric were two of six architects who worked on the restoration. The Casino did not fully open its doors until 1951, when its great swimming pool was restored.

The Riviera did not return to what it had been. It would never be the same again. The years between the wars were a time capsule which would enter into history, a period to be chronicled in novels and biographies, and the enchanting songs and music of the era. The constant socialising of the owners of the great villas along the coast, the atmosphere described by Edward VII as being 'one great garden party' had changed and would eventually fade away.[1] Some of those who had entertained, dined and danced in the old days had become ill, died or simply put their houses up for sale. Several great villas would be turned into expensive apartments, others pulled down to make way for modern blocks.

During the war the coast had been transformed by the German Army with blockhouses, miles of barbed wire and other defences. Barry and Eric's beloved Cannes had also suffered. Great slabs of concrete were piled along the edge of the Croisette. A stockpile of 2,000 kilos of melinite had exploded during the Liberation, badly damaging the quays of the old port which had been heavily mined. Mines were everywhere, even in the drains of the Croisette. Large numbers of prisoners of war were brought in to clear them, but the mines were often detonated as they were discovered. There were many casualties. The town had also suffered Allied bombardments from ships out at sea as they fired high in order to knock out the gun emplacements in the hills above. They did not always fire high enough.

The world was in a state of flux. VE Day had come and gone in May of 1945 but President Roosevelt did not live to see it, for he had died in April and the new president of the United States was Harry S. Truman. The French Provisional Government, formed in June 1944 and initially governed by de Gaulle, would introduce social security, labour laws and votes for women. This lasted until 1946, then made way for the crisis-ridden Fourth Republic, which would see twenty different governments come and go over the next ten years. In Britain in July 1945 Winston Churchill, the hero of the war who had inspired the Allies with his oratory, was voted out of power when Labour, under the quiet and confident Clement Atlee, gained a landslide victory over the Conservatives. The people of Britain were desperate for social change. In one of Churchill's election speeches he proclaimed: 'And let us make sure that the cottage home to which the warrior will return is blessed with modest but solid prosperity', which was not how people now wished to think of themselves. Nevertheless, he would return to govern. In June 1945 the Allies divided up Germany and the United Nations Charter was signed in San Francisco. It was impossible then to foresee how fundamentally Germany would change, face up to, and strive to redeem the actions of the Third Reich.

In 1946, in a France suffering badly from the effects of war and occupation and in the grip of political turmoil, nothing functioned as it should. The Communist Party, once banned, was now flexing its muscles with a vengeance, having gained ground as part of the Resistance. Many towns and villages would vote for Communist mayors. Russia was sliding its fingers into Eastern Europe and beginning to be seen for the threat it would become, and talk of a resumption of the war was everywhere. Prices were unrealistically high and the food shortage still grave. Only the food parcels from abroad, with their tinned fruit, meat and fish, could be depended upon. There was little or no fuel. The dire lack of transport continued, for there was still little petrol for the few cars or lorries, and the German Army had destroyed most of the locomotives. Insufferably crowded buses and trains were for the brave or the desperate.

In spite of these hardships, things were stirring down on the coast. In April 1946 the Duke and Duchess of Windsor returned to their rented Château de la Croë on the Cap d'Antibes, visited Barry and Eric in Le Trident and signed the visitors' book, thanking Barry for the bouquet of flowers he had left to welcome them. Several years later, tired of life on the Riviera, the Windsors would abandon La Croë and settle near Paris. In Cannes, in July of that year the Palm Beach Casino, restored and without its accompanying blockhouses, staged its first entertainment since the Liberation. On 19 September a Battle of Flowers on the Croisette, followed by a magnificent firework display, heralded the delayed opening of the first Cannes Film Festival held in the belle époque Municipal Casino. Here the great hall was equipped as a cinema and the artist Jean-Gabriel Domergue created sumptuous decorations for the festival receptions. Among almost 45 main entries, which suffered power cuts and films fitted the wrong way round on projectors, Cary Grant starred in Alfred Hitchcock's *Notorious*, Rita Hayworth in *Gilda*, and Michele Morgan in *La Symphonie Pastorale*. David Lean's *Brief Encounter* was awarded the Grand Prix as was Roberto Rossellini's *Rome, Open City*. *La Bataille du Rail*, a film on railway workers in the Resistance directed by Réne Clément, won the Jury Prize. The less successful festival of 1947 was held in a brand new Art Deco Palais des Festivals on the Croisette, built on the site of the once sought-after Cercle Nautique, the exclusive sailing-club of Cannes. There was no festival in 1948 or 1950 due to lack of funds. In 1949 and 1951 the festivals were overwhelmingly French. On these early gatherings the stars walked up a blue carpet, until the wife of the Mayor of Cannes decided that red would be more flattering to evening gowns. In 1952 the festival changed its date to May and has run yearly ever since.

Perhaps to celebrate Liberation, from September 1946 to May 1947 Barry and Eric went on a whistle stop tour of the United States and Mexico. Starting from and finishing in Paris, sailing on the SS *Washington*, they visited 26 towns and cities from the east coast to the west.

To the British who were slowly returning, it was of great significance that the bust of Edward VII, which had been destroyed by the Germans, was reinstated in Cannes by the Cannois themselves – a small gesture towards the *entente cordiale* he had so vigorously endorsed.

There were other, more fundamental, changes happening on the coast. Rather than simply servicing expatriates the

French themselves now began to take over. Why be a servant, working long hours, cleaning, serving meals and chauffeuring for the rich on low wages, when one could work in the emerging small factories and garages and thus feel more independent? Everyone agreed that tourism would always be vital for the economy, and here it was the French who, as with the film festival, would do the organising. From now on the Riviera, although always dependent on others, would be theirs. It became more courteous, in certain situations, to use the term Côte d'Azur rather than Riviera. Although in 1947 prices were still sky-high after devaluation of the franc, the three-year Marshall Plan, the much-needed American aid programme for Europe, was launched in June 1948 and began to make a difference.

Barry, Eric and Eric Dunstan, now resettled in their homes, were again holding various posts on the committee of the Sunny Bank Anglo-American Hospital in Cannes. In 1945 Barry wrote a letter of gratitude to Margaret Williams, the matron of the hospital she had kept open during the war,

> In 1940, when the official representatives [Major Dodds, Consul-General at Nice, and others] left in a panic, your example of staying at your post has comforted every English and American person that I know, and showed the French what England is made of.
>
> I need say nothing of these dreary five years that you have taken care of those very difficult old people. You know what I feel about it and, as an American, I would like to have you know that none of us will ever forget it. ... I am very proud to have known you and to have been associated with you.[2]

In 1951 commissions began to build up once again. Barry designed a small villa for his neighbour at Miramar, Jean Masurel. Jean was the brother of the respected Resistant

Antoine Masurel, who had spent three cold nights at Le Trident in the winter of 1942–3, having tried to organise the feluccas which never arrived. Various extensions were undertaken for other villas, but what would put the practice back on its feet were the commissions for work on 'cottages' at the Château de la Garoupe – where else, but on the Cap d'Antibes.

The great houses were often rented out and in July 1935 Wallis Simpson had written to her aunt in America that the Prince of Wales was looking for a villa for them both to spend some clandestine time together in the summer. 'Provided he can get the Château de la Garoupe which has its own sand beach and also rock bathing and he would not have to see the awful people that haunt those shores.'[3] If she had not married the Duke, she may well have been of their number. In the end they took Lord Cholmondeley's Le Roc, which Barry had built for him at Golfe Juan.

The MacLaren/Norman family were the respected doyens of that part of the Riviera. They were a much travelled, liberal family involved in politics and good works and admired for their achievements and sociability. In 1877 Sir Charles MacLaren, the 1st Baron Aberconway, a British lawyer and politician, had married Laura Pochin, the daughter of Henry Pochin, an industrial chemist who was director of the Tredegar Iron and Coal Company. Laura would inherit the family's Bodnant Estate in the Conwy Valley in Wales, with its important gardens.

In 1907 Charles MacLaren had commissioned a large, long house of simple design from the English artist and architect Ernest George, to be built on La Garoupe, four wild acres at the tip of the Cap d'Antibes. He called the house the Château de la Garoupe, and the magnificent park which would surround it became one of the loveliest gardens on the Riviera. It was on the small Garoupe beach in the 1920s that the Murphys entertained their friends and established the vogue for sunbathing. Of the MacLaren's four children, it was their daughter Fay who would inherit La Garoupe. In the same year her father had bought the land on Cap d'Antibes, Fay married Sir Henry Norman, a Liberal politician, journalist and traveller. They had three children, and in 1922 purchased Ramster Hall at Chiddingfold in Surrey. Again, this would have an important garden.

Following in the footsteps of her mother Laura, Fay became involved in women's rights and causes, in 1916 travelling from her London house to her office on one of the first motorised scooters, a birthday present from her husband. During World War I she ran a hospital in France, for which she was awarded the French Mons Star and the British CBE. Later she became a founding member and trustee of the Imperial War Museum.

Fay Norman's husband had died in 1939 and she then gave land on the Garoupe estate to her children and asked Barry, whom she knew well, to build or remodel four 'cottages' in the Provençal style. These would be, by any standards, attractive and comfortable houses. In 1940 Le Clos, an old farm house, was remodelled for her second son Antony Norman before the war put a stop to all building. In 1950 work began once more with the construction of La Folie, a new house, for Fay's elder son Willoughby, and the remodelling of Le Clocher, incorporating the old bell tower. This was followed by La Tourelle, built on to an existing pentagonal summer house. These estate houses are all now owned separately and surrounded by high walls and solid gates.

On Fay's death the château itself was left to Antony, who would continue to maintain the splendid gardens, which were very popular with visitors. He kept a 'Red Book' in which every plant and flower in the garden were listed. And in the 1950s the musicians Lerner and Lowe rented the château and wrote there the music for the film *Camelot*. In 1996 the family sold the house and gardens, as well as the villa Le Clocher, to the Russian oligarch Boris Berezovsky who, after losing a High Court case in London, was found dead in his Surrey home. Berezovsky was embroiled in a history of money laundering and the French state has now impounded the main house and surrounding land. Closed to the world, with its wonderful gardens now unkempt and overgrown the Château de la Garoupe is, like Villa Le Roc, at Golfe Juan, in a sad state.

Barry was then asked by the English arms manufacturer, Anthony Edgar Somers, to remodel elements of the Villa Hier on the Cap d'Antibes. He added two staircases and a grand pool terrace flanked by a pavilion and loggia. In the centre of the terrace an octagonal basin containing an urn supported by dolphins, stood on a black-and-white pavement modelled on that of the Alhambra Palace. In 1988 this luxurious house would be the setting for the film *Dirty Rotten Scoundrels* starring Michael Caine and Steve Martin. He also remodelled Villa La Barbacane, on the Antibes ramparts, for the lawyer Dr Weisbrod, a house that is still admired today. The Villa La Gaiole, at Vallauris, was also remodelled for the dilettante racing driver Eric Loder, whose third marriage was to the Canadian Eleanor Curran of the fabulous jewels. These included the famous Deepdene (Canary) Diamond. Another was a pavilion for the Villa Le Paradou at Miramar, which Barry designed for Agnès Segard from a rich northern industrial family who had sought relative peace in the south during the war. But commissions were rather thin on the ground.

The tourist boards worked hard to tempt ever more visitors and Hollywood gave a helping hand with two films. *On the Riviera* of 1951 with Danny Kaye and Gene Tierney was a colourful musical comedy which tempted Americans back to the beauty and glamour of the coast. The other was *Monte Carlo Story*, a sober romance starring Marlene Dietrich and Vittorio De Sica, beautifully shot on location in Monaco. For among the increasing mass of building along the coast and the ever burgeoning campsites there was still glamour. For the young there were new attractions. St Tropez was the place to party and lie naked on the beaches inspired by Bridget Bardot, star of the film *Et Dieu Créa la Femme*. And it would be only a few years before the first charter flights began to land at Nice airport. The English, now joined by Dutch, Belgians, Scandinavians and the occasional American, began to buy modest farmhouses in the hills among the olive terraces and flowers, often becoming involved in the local communities. Here the charm and beauty, which was falling prey to urbanism on many parts of the coast, could still be found in abundance. On the sought-after areas by the sea, such as the Cap d'Antibes, many of the important houses were now bought by the rich of the world, who locked their gates and tended not to socialise with their neighbours.

With Maxine Elliott no longer at the Château de l'Horizon, Winston Churchill was now cosseted, in great luxury, by Wendy Reves whose husband, Emery, was Churchill's publisher. In 1954 the Reves had bought Chanel's villa, La Pausa, at Roquebrune Cap Martin, and from 1956 to 1959 he spent a great deal of time there. This convenient idyll was brought to an end by Clementine Churchill's dislike of Wendy and, almost certainly, by Winston's habit of outstaying his welcome. He was asked, sorrowfully, not to return. Wendy was not Maxine and La Pausa was not the Château de l'Horizon.

At the beginning of the 1950s Barry began to feel unwell. Always a heavy smoker (as was Eric) he succumbed to what is thought to have been peripheral arterial disease, a narrowing of the arteries which affects the blood flow – often caused by smoking. In this case it was Barry's right leg which was affected and in 1954 it was amputated in a local hospital. Once he had recuperated, the couple took stock. Although crutches, a wheelchair and a prosthesis now became part of their lives, the biggest problem was the steep flight of steps from Le Trident to the lane above. The solution was 'the ski run'. A path was built which ran in wide curves from the front door to the gate and up this Eric, with devotion but perhaps the odd expletive, would push Barry, in his wheelchair, over the following years. There was no question of not continuing to enjoy the delights of the coast, diminished though these may have been, for this was their social oxygen.

If a couple of Hollywood films were not sufficient to reawaken a longing for the Riviera in American breasts, then another event ensured the south of France could no longer be ignored on the other side of the Atlantic. Again Hollywood played its part. In 1956 a beautiful blond film star became engaged to a plump young man who was searching for a wife and of whom few people had heard. Barry and Eric must have been gratified to have received their invitations to the wedding of Prince Rainier III of Monaco to Grace Kelly, for what could confirm one's position in Riviera society more firmly? Dress for the ceremony was required to be either, 'uniform or formal dress with decorations'.[4] Barry and Eric, always perfectly groomed, would have taken this request seriously. Grace Kelly, already famous at 26, had attended the 1955 Cannes Film Festival to promote her film *The Country Girl*, in which she starred with Bing Crosby. A photo opportunity with Prince Rainier at his palace was followed by the Prince's trip to the United States later in the year, resulting in their engagement. And after several days of chaos and bun fights among international journalists in Monaco, their wedding ceremony proceeded calmly and elegantly. Grace Kelly became Her Serene Highness Princess Grace and, with a beauty which never faded, settled down loyally to a life which must soon have shown itself to be restricted and far from the excitement and companionship of her previous profession. Alas, it would not be a very long life. Twenty-six years later she would die as the result of a disastrous car accident as she drove back from the family's French villa to Monaco.

In 1958 General de Gaulle returned to power, perpetuating his healing myth that France had been liberated by its own people and had no need to feel over-grateful to the Allies. He founded the Fifth Republic and brought stabilisation to French politics. But the devastating Algerian War of Independence was still raging and only came to an end when de Gaulle granted the country independence in 1962. This resulted in the influx of around 900,000 French colonialists from Algeria, the *pied-noirs*, so called as many had originally gone to Algeria to work the land and to farm. Thousands of these, with their distinctive accents, settled on the south coast as it was warm and nearest to their lost country, thus adding to the face of change on the south coast.

Of Barry's final, unexecuted, plans one was for the enlargement of a villa on the corner of the Chemin d'Olivette on the Cap d'Antibes. It had been destined for the Riviera retreat of Maître Suzanne Blum, who would eventually rigidly control the life of the widowed and ailing Duchess of Windsor in the latter's home near Paris. Hugo Vickers in his biography *Behind Closed Doors* would describe the relationship between Maître Blum and the Duchess as 'one of the most sinister ... ever formed between lawyer and client'.[5]

Barry worked up to the end, dying at 60 in February of 1960 in the house he had built 35 years before among the red rocks of the Esterel. He was buried in the small cemetery above the town of Theoule. *The Times* of London printed a short nine-line obituary. Eric, left alone, could not know that he would live at Le Trident, without Barry, for another 25 long years.

There is a portrait of Eric, at 75, by the American artist Elmer W. Greene, who had been a guest at Le Trident. It is dated 1964, the year that Greene died. There is sadness in the eyes and the set of Eric's mouth. But, still looked after by Pierre and Gascienne Pocciola, Eric continued to be involved in the expatriate community and, as always, the Sunny Bank Hospital. Nor did the social round slacken and, no longer in the great Chevrolet but now in a small

Vauxhall Viva, he ventured forth for lunches and dinners along the coast, as energetically as he had done when Barry was alive. He played bridge whenever and wherever he could. Eric Dunstan, 'the man with the golden voice' of Le Moulin in the hills, now at the Ferme d'Orangers on the Cap d'Antibes, saw him frequently. He exchanged letters with Noel Coward and was invited to Coward's Swiss home Les Avants, although there is no indication he took up the offer. Many visitors flitted in and out of Le Trident over the following years, including the ballet dancers Anton Dolin and John Gilpin. Young men, often sent by other young men, enjoyed sitting on the terrace, drinking strong vodka cocktails and listening to Eric's stories of the past, while watching him feeding pigeons' eggs from the roof to his dog, one of the many Peters. Eric himself would never forgo his two Martinis before meals and, as always, was surrounded by the aroma of his untipped Balto cigarettes. And members of his family came and went.

An arrangement between Eric's nephew, Ralph Merton, and Eric was drawn up to ensure that Ralph would inherit Le Trident on Eric's death. However, if Eric ran out of funds, Ralph would then support him financially. Eric would live to 96 years of age.

Throughout his life Eric had been stoic and this characteristic did not fail him in old age. One evening, in his late 80s, driving back to Le Trident along the Corniche d'Or, his Vauxhall hit the side of the road and came to a standstill. The occupants of the car behind immediately scrambled out and rushed to help. Eric, though shaken, insisted he was unharmed and, above all, did not want to go to hospital. However, he agreed reluctantly to be driven home and escorted into Le Trident. So concerned were the good Samaritans for this aged gentleman they begged him to, at least, telephone his doctor. This, after searching for the number, Eric grudgingly agreed to do, only to discover his doctor had been dead for ten years and later, to find he had broken three ribs.

As Barry had died in his bed at Le Trident so, in March 1985, did Eric. The house, which had been so much part of their lives, continued to be a much-loved holiday home for Eric's extended family.

The couple's life on the French Riviera had left a legacy of elegant and comfortable homes and helped to open the coast to the acceptance of Modernism; Barry and Eric had passed through the delightful silliness of the 1920s, the sober years of the 1930s and, fearlessly, the darkness of the early 1940s. They loved people, and wore their deep attachment to France lightly and always with humour and style.

The family, when they visited Le Trident for their holidays, did not have to go far to pay their tributes, for Barry and Eric now lie together in a large, but simple, grave in the Theoule cemetery, high above the Mediterranean. Upon it is carved their names and, in the centre, a trident.

Notes

Chapter 1 – Le Trident

1. Laurence Binyon, *For Dauntless France: An Account of Britain's Aid to the French Wounded and Victims of the War* (Hodder & Stoughton, 1918).
2. Ibid.
3. Beverley Nichols, *The Sweet and Twenties* (Weidenfeld & Nicolson, 1958).
4. Letter from Barry Dierks to his mother, official American group in detention, 12 July 1943. Ruth Cowan Papers (MC417, Folder 131–134), Schlesinger Library, Radcliffe Institute, Harvard University.
5. Alumni Relations, *Thistle Yearbook 1921*. Carnegie Mellon University.
6. Alfred Allan Lewis, *Ladies and Not-So-Gentle Women* (Viking, 2000).
7. Philip Hoare, *Noel Coward: A Biography* (Simon & Schuster, 1995).
8. Noel Coward, *Semi-Monde* (Methuen, 1999).
9. Beverley Nichols, *Twilight: First and Probably Last Poems* (Bachman & Turner, 1982).
10. 'Straight from the horse's mouth', Andrew Merton archives.
11. Frank Harris, *Oscar Wilde: His Life and Confessions* (Wordsworth Editions, 2007).
12. Alphonse Daudet, *Lettres de Mon Moulin* (Nelson Éditeurs, 1900).
13. S. Baring-Gould, *A Book of the Riviera* (Methuen & Co., 1905).
14. Ibid.
15. 'The worst has happened', Andrew Merton archives.
16. Ibid.
17. John Baxter, *French Riviera and its Artists* (Museyon Guides, 2015).

Chapter 2 - La Mauresque

1. Somerset Maugham, *Cakes and Ale* (William Heinemann, 1930).
2. Ibid.
3. Garson Kanin, *Remembering Mr Maugham*. Forward by Noel Coward (Hamish Hamilton, 1966).
4. Bryan Connon, *Somerset Maugham and the Maugham Dynasty* (Sinclair-Stevenson, 1997).
5. Beverley Nichols, *A Case of Human Bondage* (Secker & Warburg, 1966).
6. Somerset Maugham, *Strictly Personal* (Doubleday, Doran & Co., 1941).
7. Barry Day (ed.), *The Letters* (Bloomsbury, 2008).
8. Papers of Sir Cecil Beaton, St John's College, Cambridge (Beaton/A2/14a, No 53).
9. Ibid.
10. Note on Sutherland painting of Somerset Maugham by National Portrait Gallery, London.
11. Elsie Gladman, *Uncertain Tomorrows* (Excaliber, 1993).
12. Ibid.

Chapter 3 - The Glamorous Years

1. Stéphane Liégeard, *La Côte d'Azur* (Maison Quantin, 1887).
2. Guy de Maupassant, *Sur L'Eau* (Éditions Ligaran, 2015).
3. Jean-Louis de Faucigny-Lucinge, *Un Gentilhomme Cosmopolite* (Perrin, 1990).
4. F. Scott Fitzgerald, 'Babylon Revisited', *Saturday Evening Post*, 21 February 1931.
5. Jean Chalon, *Florence et Louise les Magnifiques: Florence Jay-Gould et Louise de Vilmorin* (Éditions du Rocher, 1987).
6. Bevis Hillier, *Art Deco of the 20s and 30s* (Studio Vista/Dutton, 1968).
7. Le Corbusier, *The Decorative Art of Today* (MIT Press, 1980).
8. Le Corbusier, *Towards a New Architecture* (Martino Fine Books, 2014).
9. Herbert Hoover, speech accepting the Republican nomination at Palo Alto, Calfornia, 1928.
10. Harvey Levenstein, *We'll Always Have Paris: American Tourists in France since 1930* (University of Chicago Press, 2004).

Chapter 4 – The Casa Estella

1. Discussion with Andrew Merton.
2. Guest book of Villa Eilenroc, Cap d'Antibes. 1867.
3. Alexander Woollcott, 'The Owner of Ben Finney', in *The Big New Yorker Book of Dogs* (Random House, 2012).
4. Richard Chapman, *Dallas Pratt: A Patchwork Biography* (Mark Argent, 2004).
5. Ibid.
6. Ibid.
7. Ibid.
8. Ibid.
9. Ibid.
10. Ibid.
11. Ibid.
12. Ibid.

Chapter 5 – Le Château de l'Horizon

1. Tom Miller, *Seeking New York: The Stories Behind the Historic Architecture of Manhattan – One Building at a Time* (Universe Publishing, 2015).
2. 'King Edward Smiles on Maxine Elliot', *New York Times*, 22 August 1909.
3. Ibid.
4. Diana Cooper, *The Rainbow Comes and Goes* (Michael Russell, 1979).
5. MS181. Diana Forbes-Robinson Collection. Raymond H. Fogler Library. University of Maine.
6. Ibid.
7. Diana Forbes-Robertson, *My Aunt Maxine: The Story of Maxine Elliott* (Viking, 1964).
8. Ibid.
9. Ibid.
10. Ibid.
11. 'A White Palace Floating', *Punch*, No. 205, 1943.
12. Forbes-Robertson, *My Aunt Maxine*.
13. Letter from Maxine Elliott to Winston Churchill, 10 February 1939, Churchill Archives Centre, Churchill College, University of Cambridge (CHAR 1/343/33).

14. J. Bryan and Charles Murphy, *The Windsor Story* (William Morrow, 1979).
15. Ibid.
16. Maxine Elliott to Winston Churchill, 27 January 1939, Churchill Archives Centre, Churchill College, University of Cambridge (CHAR 1/343).
17. Vincent Sheean, *Between the Thunder and the Sun* (Macmillan, 1943).
18. Ibid.
19. Letter from Winston Churchill to Maxine Elliott, Churchill Archives Centre, Churchill College, University of Cambridge (CHAR 1/323).
20. Letter from Maxine Elliott to Winston Churchill, 20 June 1939, Churchill Archives Centre, Churchill College, University of Cambridge (CHAR 1/343/34-36).
21. Noel Coward, *Future Indefinite* (Methuen Drama, 2014).
22. Ibid.
23. Letter from Air Field Marshall Sir Arthur Harris to Winston Churchill, 22 March 1945, Churchill Archives Centre, Churchill College, University of Cambridge (CHAR 20/1978/171).
24. Ibid.
25. Ibid.

Chapter 6 – Villa La Reine Jeanne

1. Diana Cooper, *Trumpets from the Steep* (Michael Russell, 1979).
2. Ibid.
3. Philip Ziegler, *Diana Cooper: The Biography of Lady Diana Cooper* (Faber & Faber, 2011).
4. Frederick Treves, *The Riviera of the Corniche Road* (Cassell and Co., 1921).
5. Hugo Vickers. Obituary: Paul-Annik Weiller. The *Independent*, 11 November 1998; his official title was Commandant Paul-Louis Weiller, therefore he was often called 'The Commander'.

Chapter 7 – Villa Le Roc

1. *Sports Illustrated*, 13 September 1982.
2. Diana Cooper, *The Rainbow Comes and Goes* (Michael Russell, 1979).
3. Vincent Sheean, *Between the Thunder and the Sun* (Macmillan, 1943).
4. Peter Stansky, *Sassoon: The World of Philip and Sybil* (Yale University Press, 2003).
5. Michael Bloch (ed.), *Wallis and Edward: Letters 1931–1937 – The Intimate Correspondence of the Duke and Duchess of Windsor* (Summit Books, 1986).
6. Ibid.
7. Ibid.
8. Graham Payn and Sheridan Morley, *The Noel Coward Diaries* (Da Capo Press, 2000).
9. J. Bryan and Charles Murphy, *The Windsor Story* (William Morrow, 1979).
10. Ibid.

Chapter 8 – Le Moulin

1. All Eric Dunstan quotes are from his unpublished diaries.
2. Michael Bloch (ed.), *Wallis and Edward: Letters 1931–1937 – The Intimate Correspondence of the Duke and Duchess of Windsor* (Summit Books, 1986).
3. Ibid.
4. Joyce Grenfell, *The Time of My Life: Entertaining the Troops – Her Wartime Journals* (Hodder & Stoughton, 1989).
5. Ibid.
6. Winifred Fortescue, *Laughter in Provence* (William Blackwood & Sons, 1950).
7. Ibid.
8. Email exchange with John Halsey.

Chapter 9 – The Villa Aujourd'hui

1. Cass Warner Sperling and Cork Millner, *Hollywood Be They Name: The Warner Brothers Story* (Prima Publishing, 1994).
2. Ibid.

3. Bette Davis, *The Lonely Life: An Autobiography* (G.P. Putnam's Sons, 1962).
4. Elsa Maxwell, *How to Do It: Or the Lively Art of Entertaining* (Rizzoli International Publications, 2005).
5. Eric Dunstan, his unpublished diaries.

Chapter 10 – Méfiance

1. Beverley Nichols, *The Unforgiving Minute* (W.H. Allen, 1978).
2. Geoffrey Cox, *Countdown to War* (William Kimber, 1988).
3. Somerset Maugham, *Strictly Personal* (Doubleday, Doran & Co., 1941).
4. Peter Fleming, *Operation Sea Lion: The Projected Invasion of England in 1940* (Simon and Schuster, 1957).
5. Arthur Marder, *From the Dardanelles to Oran* (Seaforth Publishing, 2015).
6. Oxford English Dictionary definition.
7. Report from F.C. Stone, British Consulate employee at Monaco, to Anthony Eden; The National Archives, Kew (FO369/2789, K.8598).
8. Maugham, *Strictly Personal.*
9. Ibid.
10. Ibid.
11. Report from F.C. Stone.
12. Maugham, *Strictly Personal.*
13. Report from F.C. Stone.

Chapter 11 – The American Train

1. 'Man of the Year', *Time*, 4 January 1932.
2. Admiral William Leahy. US Ambassador to Vichy France. 1941–2.
3. Ian Ousby, *Occupation: The Ordeal of France 1940–1944* (Pimlico. 1997).
4. Jean-Louis de Faucigny-Lucinge, *Un Gentilhomme Cosmopolite* (Perrin, 1990).
5. Evelyn Waugh, *Officers and Gentlemen* (Chapman Hall, 1955).
6. Letter from Harold C. Stuart to Mrs Stuart, official American group in detention, 16 February 1943. Georgetown University Library, Special Collections, Julie Kernan.
7. Ibid.

8. Letter from Constance Ray Harvey to Betty, 3 September 1943. Box 1 Folder 1, Sophia Smith Collections of Women's History, Smith College Libraries, Smith College.
9. Ibid.
10. Letter from Harold C. Stuart to Mrs Stuart.
11. Letter from Robert A. Jakoubek to Bobi, official American group in detention, 7 June 1943. Ruth Cowan Papers (MC417, Folder 131–134), Schlesinger Library, Radcliffe Institute, Harvard University.
12. Letter from Barry Dierks to his mother, official American group in detention, 12 July 1943. Ruth Cowan Papers (MC417, Folder 131–134), Schlesinger Library, Radcliffe Institute, Harvard University.

Chapter 12 – Waiting for Melpomene

1. Donald Caskie, *The Tartan Pimpernel* (Oldbourne, 1957).
2. Ibid.
3. Marcus Binney, *The Women Who Lived for Danger* (Hodder & Stoughton, 2003).
4. 'Le Chant des Partisans', lyrics by Maurice Druon and Joseph Kessel, music by Anna Marly, 1943.
5. Letter from Eric Sawyer to Lord Selbourne, Head of SOE, 3 March 1943; The National Archives, Kew (HS 6/595).
6. Letter from D/R to S.O, 5 March 1943; The National Archives, Kew (HS 6/595).
7. Ibid.

Chapter 13 – La Domaine du Sault

1. Elsa Maxwell, *Elsa Maxwell's Café Society*, Vol. 1, No. 1, 1953.
2. Elsa Maxwell, *I Married the World* (William Heinemann, 1955).
3. Eve Pell, 'La Femme a la Mèche Blonde', *Ms*, Spring 2005.
4. Honor Moore, *The White Blackbird: A Life of the Painter Margarett Sargent by Her Granddaughter* (Viking, 1996).
5. Robert H. Adleman and Colonel George Walton, *The Champagne Campaign: The Spectator Airborne Division that Turned the Tide of Battle in Southern France in 1944* (Leslie Frewin, 1973).

6. Letter from Polly Cotton to Charles Anglesey, in Maureen Emerson, *Escape to Provence* (Chapter and Verse Books, 2009).
7. Victor Werny, Historien du L'association culturelle du Pays Pugétois.
8. Adleman and Walton, *The Champagne Campaign*.
9. Ibid.
10. Letter to Ruth Cowan from Isabel Pell, 1945, American Red Cross. Ruth Cowan Papers (MC417, Folder 464), Schlesinger Library, Radcliffe Institute, Harvard University.
11. Mercedes de Acosta, *Here Lies the Heart* (Ayer Company, 1975).
12. Ibid.

Chapter 14 – The Champagne Campaign

1. Robert H. Adleman and Colonel George Walton, *The Devil's Brigade* (Naval Institute Press, 1966).
2. G-5. Headquarters Southern Line of Communications, APO 39, Civil Affairs, Nice, 20 January 1945. WWII European Theatre Army Records.
3. *L'Espoir* – Nice Edition, 20 March 1945.
4. Archives Municipales de Menton, Livre d'Or Cote 306, 23 February 1946.
5. Letters from 1945. Ruth Cowan Papers (MC417), Schlesinger Library, Radcliffe Institute, Harvard University.
6. Letter to Ruth Cowan from Antoinette Hardisty, 10 September 1945, Insular and Foreign Operations, American Red Cross. Ruth Cowan Papers (MC417, Folder 464), Schlesinger Library, Radcliffe Institute, Harvard University.
7. Letter from Barry Dierks to Ruth Cowan, 5 July 1945, American Red Cross. Ruth Cowan Papers (MC417, Folder 464), Schlesinger Library, Radcliffe Institute, Harvard University.
8. Letter from Ruth Cowan to Baron Hubert Lejeune, 1945. Ruth Cowan Papers (MC417, Folder 464), Schlesinger Library, Radcliffe Institute, Harvard University.

Chapter 16 – All Change

1. John Baxter, *French Riviera and its Artists* (Museyon Guides, 2015).
2. Andrew Merton archives.
3. Michael Bloch (ed.), *Wallis and Edward: Letters 1931–1937 – The Intimate Correspondence of the Duke and Duchess of Windsor* (Summit Books, 1986).
4. Andrew Merton archives.
5. Hugo Vickers, *Behind Closed Doors. The Tragic Untold Story of the Duchess of Windsor* (Random House, 2011).

Bibliography

Archives

Alumni Relations, Thistle Yearbook, Carnegie Mellon University.
American Field Archives of the American Field Service and AFS Intercultural Programs.
Les Archives Départmentales des Alpes-Maritimes.
Les Archives Municipales de Cannes.
Les Archives Municipales de Menton.
Churchill Archives Centre, Churchill College, University of Cambridge.
DigitalCommons@UMaine, Special Collections, University of Maine.
Frederick Forsch collection on Winston Churchill, 1886–1974, Dartmouth College Library.
India Office Records and Private Papers, The British Library.
Inventaire Général du Patrimoine Culturel.
Library and Archives, Magdalen College, University of Oxford.
The Library, St John's College, University of Cambridge.
Liverpool Record Office, Central Library and Archive.
Manuscripts and Special Collections, University of Nottingham.
Musée de la Résistance Azuréenne.
The National Archives, Kew.
Office of the Historian, US Department of State.
Patrimoine Provence-Alpes-Côte d'Azur Base Merimée.
Raymond H. Fogler Library, University of Maine.
Schlesinger Library, Radcliffe Institute, Harvard University.
Smith College Libraries, Smith College.

Special Collections Research Center, Georgetown University Library, Georgetown University.

Publications

Abramovicci, Pierre. *Szkolnikoff*. Éditions du Seuil. 2001.

Acosta, Mercedes de. *Here Lies the Heart*. Ayer Company. 1975.

Adams, Peter. *Eileen Gray: Her Life and Work*. Harry N. Abrams. 2009.

Adleman, Robert H. and Walton, Colonel George. *The Champagne Campaign: The Spectator Airborne Division that Turned the Tide of Battle in Southern France in 1944*. Leslie Frewin. 1973.

—— *The Devil's Brigade*. Naval Institute Press. 2004.

Association des Amis des Archives de Cannes. *Les Années Folles*. 2014.

—— *Un Siècle de Vie Cannoise, 1850–1950*. 2014.

Astier de la Vigerie, Emmanuel d'. *Seven Times, Seven Days*. MacGibbon & Kee. 1958.

Augeard, Michel Roger. *Melpomène se Parfume à L'Heliotrope*. J.C. Lattés. 2012.

Azzouz, Ashraf and Massey, David. *Maisons de Hammamet*. Dar Ashraf Editions. 2006.

Baring-Gould, S. *A Book of the Riviera*. Methuen & Co. 1905.

Baussy, Alex. *Cannes d'Hier et Aujourd'hui*. Imprimerie de Noailes. 1966.

Baxter, John. *French Riviera and its Artists*. Museyon Guides. 2015.

Beaton, Cecil. *The Wandering Years: Diaries 1922–1939*. Weidenfeld & Nicolson. 1961.

—— *Self Portrait with Friends: Diaries 1926–1974*. Edited by Richard Buckle. Weidenfeld & Nicolson. 1979.

—— *The Unexpurgated Diaries*. Introduced by Hugo Vickers. Weidenfeld & Nicholson. 2002.

Bentheim, Annick de and Fray, François. *Barry Dierks architecte méditerranéen: La Côte d'Azur et la Modernité*. Catalogue d'expositions. Réunion des Musées Nationaux. 1997.

Bertram, Barbara. *The French Resistance in Sussex*. Barnworks Publishing. 1995.

Bertrand, Gustave. *Enigma*. Plon. 1973.

Bilas, Charles and Rosso, Lucien. *Côte d'Azur: Architecture des Années 20 et 30*. Les Éditions de L'Amateur. 2007.

Binney, Marcus. *The Women Who Lived for Danger*. Hodder & Stoughton. 2003.

Binyon, Laurence. *For Dauntless France: An Account of Britain's Aid to the French Wounded and Victims of the War*. Hodder & Stoughton. 1918.

Bloch, Michael (ed.). *Wallis and Edward. Letters 1931–1937 – The Intimate Correspondence of the Duke and Duchess of Windsor*. Summit Books. 1986.

Blume, Mary. *Côte d'Azur: Inventing the French Riviera*. Thames & Hudson. 1994.

Bradbury, Ray. *We'll Always Have Paris*. William Morrow Paperback. 2010.

Bresson, Jean. *La Fabuleuse Histoire de Cannes*. Éditions du Rocher. 1981.

Brome, Vincent. *The Way Back*. The Companion Book Club. 1958.

Bryan, J. and Murphy, Charles. *The Windsor Story*. William Morrow. 1979.

Buckmaster, Maurice. *Specially Employed*. Batchworth. 1952.

Calder, Robert. *Willie: The Life of W. Somerset Maugham*. Heinemann. 1989.

Cameron, Roderick. *The Golden Riviera*. Weidenfeld & Nicolson. 1975.

Caskie, Donald. *The Tartan Pimpernel*. Oldbourne. 1957.

Chalon, Jean. *Florence et Louise les Magnifiques: Florence Jay-Gould et Louise de Vilmorin*. Éditions du Rocher. 1987.

Chapman, Richard. *Dallas Pratt: A Patchwork Biography*. Mark Argent. 2004.

Charbonnières, Girard de. *Mon Chemin Vers De Gaulle*. Éditions de Papyrus. 1989.

Churchill, Peter. *Of Their Own Choice*. Hodder & Stoughton. 1952.

—— *Dual of Wits*. Hodder & Stoughton. 1953.

—— *All About the French Riviera*. Vista Books. 1960.

Clarke, Jeffrey J. and Smith, Robert Ross. *Riviera to the Rhine*. Centre of Military History, U.S. Army. 1993.

Cole, Lesley. *Noel Coward*. Penguin. 1978.

Colville, John. *The Fringes of Power*. Sceptre. 1986.

Connell, Brian. *Knight Errant: A Biography of Douglas Fairbanks Jnr*. Hodder & Stoughton. 1955.

Connon, Bryan. *Beverley Nichols: A Life*. Constable. 1991.

—— *Somerset Maugham and the Maugham Dynasty*. Sinclair-Stevenson. 1997.

Constant, Caroline. *Eileen Gray*. Phaidon. 2000.

Cooper, Lady Diana. *The Rainbow Comes and Goes*. Michael Russell. 1979.

—— *Trumpets From the Steep*. Michael Russell. 1979.

Cordell, Richard A. *Somerset Maugham: A Writer for all Seasons*. Indiana University Press. 1969.

Coward, Noel. *Semi-Monde*. Methuen. 1999.

—— *The Noel Coward Diaries*. Edited by Graham Payn and Sheridan Morley. Da Capo Press. 2000.

—— *Future Indefinite*. Methuen Drama. 2014.

Cox, Geoffrey. *Countdown to War*. William Kimber. 1988.

Crisell, Andrew. *An Introductory History of British Broadcasting*. Routledge. 1997.

Daix, Pierre et al. *1918–1958: La Côte d'Azur et la Modernité*. Reunion des Musées Nationaux. 1997.

Daudet, Alphonse. *Lettres de Mon Moulin*. Nelson Éditeurs. 1900.

Davis, Bette. *The Lonely Life: An Autobiograaphy*. G.P. Putnam's Sons. 1962.

Day, Barry (ed.). *Noel Coward: The Letters*. Bloomsbury. 2008.

Decaux, Alain. *Les Heures Brillantes de la Côte d'Azur*. Librarie Perrin. 1964.

Decèze, Dominique. *La Lune Est Pleine D'Elèphants Verts*. J. Lanzmann & Seghers. 1979.

Dewarin, André (Colonel Passy). *Souvenirs 1: 2e Bureau Londres*. Raoul Solar. 1947.

Digiuni, Didier. *Cannes 1939–1945*. Alandis Editions. 2002.

Dixon, Wheeler Winston. *Death of the Moguls: The End of Classical Hollywood*. Rutgers University Press. 1950.

Dufeu, Philippe Keun. *Cahiers Histoire de la Guerre*. Issue 14. 1997.

Dupouy, Raphael and Lartigue, Dany. *La Riviera de Jacques Henri Lartigue*. Reseau Lalan. 2007.

Ellman, Richard. *Oscar Wilde*. Hamish Hamilton. 1987.

Emerson, Barbara. *Leopold II of the Belgians*. Weidenfeld & Nicolson. London. 1979.

Emerson, Maureen. *Escape to Provence*. Chapter and Verse Books. 2009.

Erlanger, Philippe. *La France Sans Etoile*. Plon. 1974.

Faucigny-Lucinge, Prince Jean-Louis. *Un Gentilhomme Cosmopolite*. Perrin. 1990.

Fitzgerald, F. Scott. 'Babylon Revisited'. *Saturday Evening Post*. 21 February. 1931.

Fleming, Peter. *Operation Sea Lion: The Projected Invasion of England in 1940* (Simon and Schuster, 1957).

Foligot, Roger and Kauffer, Rémi. *Eminences Grises*. Fayard. 1992.

Foot, M.R.D. and Langley, J.M. *M19: Escape and Evasion 1939–1945*. Biteback Publishing. 2011.

Forbes-Robertson, Diana. *My Aunt Maxine: The Story of Maxine Elliott*. Viking Press. 1964.

Fortescue, Winifred. *Laughter in Provence*. William Blackwood & Sons. 1950.

Franck, Peggy Miller. *Pride's Crossing*. Commonwealth Editions. 2009.

Funk, Arthur Layton. *Les Alliés et la Réstance*. Edisud. 2001.

Gabler, Neal. *An Empire of Their Own: How the Jews Invented Hollywood*. W.H. Allen. 1989.

Galante, Pierre. *Les Années Chanel*. Mercure de France. 1972.

Garner, Philippe. *Eileen Gray: Design and Architecture*. Benedikt Taschen. 1994.

Gaussot, Philippe. *Melpomene se Parfume au Camphre*. Editions Marco. 1946.

Gillois, André. *Histoire Secrète des Français à Londres de 1940 à 1944*. Hachette-Littérature. 1973.

Gladman, Elsie. *Uncertain Tomorrows*. Excaliber. 1993.

Goissard, Antony. *La Construction Moderne*. No. 47. August 1930.

Graves, Charles. *Royal Riviera*. Heinemann. 1957.

Grenfell, Joyce. *The Time of My Life: Entertaining the Troops – Her Wartime Journals*. Hodder & Stoughton. 1989.

Guiringaud, François de. *Melpomene, la Panthère et le Chimpanze*. Éditions La Brochure. April 2017.

Gupta, Partha Sarathi. *Power, Politics and the People*. Anthem Press. 2002.

Harris, Frank. *Oscar Wilde, His Life and Confessions*. Wordsworth Editions. 2007.

Higham, Charles. *The Duchess of Windsor: The Secret Life*. John Wiley & Sons. 2004.

Hillier, Bevis. *Art Deco of the 20s and 30s*. Studio Vista/Dutton. 1968.

Hoare, Philip. *Noel Coward: A Biography*. Simon & Schuster. 1995.

Honeycombe, Gordon. *Selfridges: Seventy-five Years – The Story of the Store*. 1984.

Howarth, Patrick. *When the Riviera Was Ours*. Routledge & Kegan Paul. 1977.

Johnston, Shirley and Schezen, Roberto. *Great Villas of the Riviera*. Thames & Hudson. 1998.

Jones, Ted. *The French Riviera: A Literary Guide for Travellers*. I.B.Tauris. 2004.

Kanigel, Robert. *High Season in Nice*. Little, Brown. 2002.

Kanin, Garson. *Remembering Mr Maugham*. Hamish Hamilton. 1966.

Kernan, Thomas. *Report on France*. Bodley Head. 1942.

—— *Now With the Morning Star*. John Lane. 1944.

Langley, J.M. *Fight Another Day*. Collins Ltd. 1974.

Lasalle, Mike. *Complicated Women: Sex and Power in Pre-Code Hollywood*. St Martin's Griffin. 2001.

Le Corbusier. *The Decorative Art of Today*. MIT Press. 1980.

—— *Towards a New Architecture*. Martino Fine Books. 2014.

Leishman, Marista. *Reith of the BBC: My Father*. St. Andrew Press. 2006.

Lenthéric, Charles. *The Riviera: Ancient and Modern*. T. Fisher Unwin. 1895.

Levenstein, Harvey. *We'll Always Have Paris: American Tourists in France Since 1930*. University of Chicago Press. 2004.

Lewis, Alfred Allan. *Ladies and Not-So-Gentle Women*. Viking. 2000.

Liégeard, Stéphan. *La Côte d'Azur*. Maison Quantin. 1887.

Long, Helen. *Safe Houses are Dangerous*. William Kimber & Co. 1985.

Lytton, Neville. *Life in Unoccupied France*. MacMillan. 1942.

Manceau, Henri and Guizol, Jean-Paul. *Auribeau: Village Provençal*. Éditions Municipales d'Auribeau. 1985.

Marder, Arthur. *From the Dardanelles to Oran*. Seaforth Publishing. 2015.

Marwick, Arthur and Simpson, Wendy (eds). *War, Peace and Social Change: Europe 1925–1959*. Open University Press. 1989.

Masheck, Joseph. *Adolf Loos: The Art of Architecture*. I.B.Tauris. 2013.

Massigli, René. *Une Comédie des Erreurs*. Plon. 1978.

Masurel, Antoine. *Les Reseaux de Renseignment Pendant la Resistance dans les Alpes Maritime*. Musée de la Resistance Français, Nice.

Maugham, Robin. *Somerset and All the Maughams*. Longmans Heinemann. 1966.

Maugham, Somerset. *Cakes and Ale*. William Heinemann. 1930.

—— *Strictly Personal*. Doubleday, Doran & Co. 1941.

Maupassant, Guy de. *Sur L'Eau*. Éditions Ligaran. 2015.

Maxwell, Elsa. *R.S.V.P.* Little, Brown. 1954.

—— *I Married the World*. William Heinemann. 1955.

—— *The Celebrity Circus*. W.H. Allen. 1964.

—— *How To Do It: Or the Lively Art of Entertaining*. Rizzoli International Publications. 2005.

McIntyre, Ian. *The Expense of Glory: A Life of John Reith*. HarperCollins. 1993.

McNulty, Thomas. *Errol Flynn: The Life and Career*. MacFarland & Co. 2004.

Miller, Tom. *Seeking New York: The Stories Behind the Historic Architecture of Manhattan – One Building at a Time*. Universe Publishing. 2015.

Moore, Honor. *The White Blackbird: A Life of the Painter Margarett Sargent by Her Granddaughter*. Viking. 1996.

Mousseau, Jacques. *Le Siecle de Paul-Louis Weiller*. Éditions Stock. 1998.

Neave, Airey. *Saturday at M.1.9: History of Underground Escape Lines in N.W. Europe in 1940–45*. Coronet Books. 1985.

Nichols, Beverley. *All I Could Never Be*. Jonathan Cape. 1949.

—— *The Sweet and Twenties*. Weidenfeld & Nicolson. 1958.

—— *A Case of Human Bondage*. Secker & Warburg. 1966.

—— *The Unforgiving Minute*. W.H. Allen. 1978.

—— *Twilight: First and Probably Last Poems*. Bachman & Turner. 1982.

Nouveau, Louis. *Des Capitaines par Milliers*. Imperial War Museum Collection. 1957.

Ophüls, Marcel and Harris, André. *The Sorrow and the Pity* (*Le Chagrin et la Pitié*) screenplay, West Germany and Switzerland, 1969.

Ousby, Ian. *Occupation: The Ordeal of France 1940–1944*. Pimlico. 1997.

Panicacci, Jean-Louis. *Les Alpes-Maritimes de 1939 à 1945: Un Départment dans la Tourmente*. Éditions Serre. 1989.

Paulu, Burton. *Television and Radio in the United Kingdom*. Palgrave Macmillan. 1981.

Payne, Graham and Morley, Sheridan (eds). *The Noel Coward Diaries*. Little, Brown. 1982

Pell, Eve. *We Used to Own the Bronx: Memoirs of a Former Debutante*. Excelsior Editions. 2009.

Perrier, Guy. *Le Colonel Passy et les Services Secrets de la France Libre*. Hachette. 1999.

Poirier, Jacques R.E. *The Giraffe Has a Long Neck*. Leo Cooper. 1995.

Pound, Reginald. *Selfridge*. Heinemann. 1960.

Renoir, Jean and Koch, Carl. *The Rules of the Game* (*La Regle du Jeu*). Nouvelle Edition Francaise, screenplay. Paris, 1939.

Richards, Brooks. *Secret Flotillas: Clandestine Sea Operations in the Western Mediterranean, North African & the Adriatic 1940–1944*. Routledge. 2004.

Richards, Grant. *The Coast of Pleasure.* Jonathan Cape. 1928.

Richardson, Derek. *Detachment W. Allied Soldiers and Airmen Detained in Vichy France 1940 and 1942.* Paul Mould Publishing. 2004.

Ring, Jim. *Riviera: The Rise and Rise of the Cote d'Azur.* John Murray. 2004.

Sandys, Celia. *Chasing Churchill: Travels with Winston Churchill.* HarperCollins. 2003.

Scharparelli, Elsa. *Shocking Life.* J.M. Dent & Sons. 1954.

Sheean, Vincent. *Between the Thunder and the Sun.* Macmillan. 1943.

Silver, Kenneth E. *Making Paradise: Art, Modernity and the Myth of the French Riviera.* MIT Press. 2001.

Smith, Jane S. *Elsie de Wolfe: A Life in the High Style.* Atheneum. 1982.

Sperling, Cass Warner and Millner, Cork. *Hollywood Be Thy Name: The Warner Brothers Story.* Prima Publishing. 1994.

Staggs, Sam. *Inventing Elsa Maxwell: How an Irrepressible Nobody Conquered High Society, Hollywood, the Press, and the World.* St. Martin's Press. 2012.

Stansky, Peter. *Sassoon: The Worlds of Philip and Sybil.* Yale University Press. 2003.

The Story of the Star 1888–1938: Fifty years [of] Progress and Achievement. 'The Star' Publications Department. 1938.

Thomas, Bob. *Clown Prince of Hollywood: The Antic Life and Times of Jack L. Warner.* McGraw Hill. 1990.

Treves, Frederick. *The Riviera of the Corniche Road.* Cassell & Co. 1921.

Trez de, Michel. *First Airborne Task Force.* Cassell & Co. 1921.

Ulrich-Pier, Raphaele. *René Massigli (1888–1988). Une Vie de Diplomate.* Tome I. P.I.E.-Peter Lang. 2006.

Vago, Pierre. *Une Vie Intense.* AAM Éditions. 1999.

Vickers, Hugo. *Loving Garbo: The Story of Greta Garbo, Cecil Beaton and Mercedes de Acosta.* Jonathan Cape. 1994.

—— *Behind Closed Doors: The Tragic Untold Story of the Duchess of Windsor.* Random House. 2011.

Warner, Jack L. and Dean Jennings. *My First Hundred Years in Hollywood: An Autobiography.* Random House. 1965.

Waugh, Evelyn. *Officers and Gentlemen.* Chapman Hall. 1955.

Welcome to the Riviera. United States Riviera Recreational Area. 1942.

Weller, Charles E. *The Early History of the Typewriter.* Forgotten Books. 2012.

Williams, Alfred. *No Name on the Door: A Memoir of Gordon Selfridge.* W.H. Allen. 1956.

Wilt, Alan F. *The French Riviera Campaign of August 1944*. Southern Illinois University Press. 1981.

Windsor, HRH Edward, Duke of. *A King's Story: The Memoirs of the Duke of Windsor*. G.P. Putnam's Sons. 1951.

Windsor, Wallis. *The Heart Has Its Reasons: The Memoirs of the Duchess of Windsor*. Michael Joseph. 1956.

Woodhead, Lindy. *Shopping, Seduction & Mr Selfridge*. Profile Books. 2007.

Woollcott, Alexander. 'The Owner of Ben Finney'. *The Big New Yorker Book of Dogs*. New Yorker Magazine. 12 May 1928.

Ziegler, Philip. *King Edward VIII: The Official Biography*. Knopf. 1991.

—— *Diana Cooper: The Biography of Lady Diana Cooper*. Faber & Faber. 2011.

Zorbaugh, Harvey Warren. *The Gold Coast and the Slum: A Sociological Study of Chicago's Near North Side*. University of Chicago. 1929.

Index

Places are in France unless stated. Numbers in italic refer to the plate section.